Best Wishes
Pixie Farthing   Aug 2008.

FROM WHEN I CAN

REMEMBER

OVERLEAF: *Cross Farm.*

FROM WHEN I CAN REMEMBER

Pixie Farthing

Jimmer Publishing

First published in Great Britain in 2007 by Jimmer Publishing

A CIP Catalogue of this book is available from the British Library

ISBN 978-0-9556404-0-7

First edition

Reprinted 2008

Illustrations by James Weaver

Designed and typeset in Sabon by Will Weaver

Printed and bound in Great Britain by Biddles Ltd, King's Lynn, Norfolk

With love to

My husband Alan

Our children
James, Sophie, Kim, Vicky & Will

Our grandchildren
Jenny, Holly, Charlotte, Chloe, Jack, Georgina and Dudley

And our great grandson
Harry

CONTENTS

ACKNOWLEDGMENTS

To my son Will Weaver for the design of the book,
to my son James Weaver for the illustrations,
to Stephen Rice for typing my manuscripts.

All photographs are supplied by the author with the exception of:

CHAPTER 2: *Evelyn Saye (Tod), youngest sister of Ada*
from the Glen Jacob collection
CHAPTER 4: *Lily and Stan Johnson*
from the Valerie Baveystock collection; *Mary Hayward the toenail clipper* from the Glen Jacob collection
CHAPTER 8: *Ken Hayward* from the Glen Jacobs collection
CHAPTER 9: *Edna Dallas at Peldon Hostel*, also *land girls*
from the Edna Smy collection
CHAPTER 11: *West Mersea School and Belisha Beacon*
from the Brian Jay collection
CHAPTER 14: *Peter French teaches the children*
from the Peter French collection
CHAPTER 16: *Holiday Gang*
from the David Matthews collection
CHAPTER 17: *Michael Matthews*
from the David Matthews collection
CHAPTER 18: *Mrs Lane the Fortune Teller*,
also *Rev. Derby, Brian Woods Colchester United, Lucy Lane*
from the Sylvia Thompson collection

FOREWORD

I was prompted to write this book after my grandchildren started asking about our family history and what Mersea was like when I was a child. Their questions made me realise that I should write it all down, not only for them, but also for future generations.

When I started writing I didn't realise how difficult it would be to revisit the past. It has been an emotional but rewarding experience.

Many of the people mentioned here have long since passed away, their stories untold. In telling my story, part of their stories will also be told, ensuring our past is not lost or forgotten. Written through my own memories and with careful research and the co-operation of friends and family, I wish to pay tribute to all those involved in shaping my early life.

This is my story of my Mersea.

The Mersea I remember was home to a different breed of people who commonly used words not always found elsewhere – my family always referred to chickens as 'coopies'.

This book contains many examples of old, local expressions. If you can't readily understand what I'm trying to say, the glossary of terms at the back of the book should be helpful.

CHAPTER 1

Oil lamps, coopies and the wind-up gramophone

OVERLEAF: *Peter Farthing and little Pixie Farthing.*
ABOVE: *Work on the farm. Pictured from left:*
Jim Farthing, Sidney Russel, unknown, Pud, Peter Farthing.

My story begins at Cross Farm, a fifteenth century farmhouse situated on the small island of Mersea, ten miles south of Colchester – Britain's oldest recorded town. In 1939, Mersea Island was home to two thousand five hundred people and the two main sources of income were farming and fishing.

Cross Farm was jointly owned by Jim and Oliver Farthing. The fields closest to the house were used for free range chicken farming, fattening up a few pigs and pasture to provide summer grazing and winter hay for the two horses. Further east, exactly one mile away on the East Mersea Road, was a five acre field called Hubbards Croft. This was used for seed growing and was planted under contract to Suttons, the national seed company. The short journey there would be made either on bike or by horse and cart.

Work on the thirty acres on and around the farm started at dawn and finished at dusk. Two thousand chickens had to be fed, watered and mucked out. After the eggs had been collected and sorted onto trays, any soiled ones would be cleaned by hand with a damp cloth as hard earned money would be deducted by Powlings Egg Packers for any that were dirty or undersized. Chicken and pig meal deliveries from Marriage's mills in Colchester were unloaded and stored in the large feed sheds which, unfortunately, attracted rats and mice. The outdoor cats that slept in the barns helped to keep the numbers down but Dad still needed to use an air gun on the rat population.

With no machinery other than horse-drawn ploughs and

harrows, this really was labour intensive farming. My mother told me later that she frequently worked in the fields, starting at four o'clock in the morning before the seeds shaled in the heat of the sun. And before going to the field she would pack a basket with bread, wine and cheese, ready for their morning break.

My early memories of Cross Farm – or simply 'The Cross' as the family knew it – are quite vivid. The lane leading to the beautiful old farmhouse was a rough track made by centuries of wear by horse-drawn carts, people on foot and later by bicycles and motor vehicles. Primroses blossomed each spring under the hedges on both sides of the lane. As a child I loved to pick bunches of the pretty yellow flowers for my mother who always carefully arranged them in a lovely little cut glass vase. The water came from a bucket which stood by a stone sink in the kitchen. There was no running water at Cross Farm – just a well at the bottom of the garden where water was pumped by hand. This well provided very cold but very clear, fresh water. Occasionally the pump refused to work and a bucket was lowered into the well on a rope. There was then often a green sheen on the water but in those days nobody seemed too worried about it.

The Cross originally provided a home for William and Sophia Farthing and their thirteen children but over the years the rambling old house with its nine bedrooms and ten ground floor rooms had been sub-divided to accommodate three separate Farthing families in self-contained homes. Anyone stepping over the threshold of any of the three homes would immediately sense a feeling of real warmth and atmosphere. Those walls had many a tale to tell.

My parents, Jim and Ada Farthing, lived in the far end of the farmhouse, away from the lane. Oliver and Maude lived in the middle and Pud Farthing lived in the end which ran by the side of the lane. No one quite knew why he was called Pud – except that he was a rather thick-set chap. Clarence

Cudmore (who was related to the Farthings) and his wife Dorothy (Dolly), moved to The Cross from Mill Road so that Dolly could become Pud's housekeeper. They had two young girls, Cynthia and Jane, who loved the busy way of life on the farm. When Pud died, aged 63, Clarence and his young family continued to live on at The Cross but sadly Clarence died tragically five years later, leaving Dolly to bring up the two girls on her own.

Our home at the far end is, of course, the most memorable to me and the easiest to describe. The back door opened into a typically large, old fashioned farmhouse kitchen with a stone floor covered in coco matting. This helped to take the chill off the feet, especially during the cold winter months. Onions and herbs harvested from our garden hung from the beams. Cured hams added to the welcoming aroma. Old oil lamps cast all sorts of shadows around the room and were responsible for wonderfully romantic, often eerie sensations when the shadows moved due to gentle breezes shifting the curtains.

Ada, my mother, had a natural flair for interior design and soft furnishings. Before marrying, she worked for some very wealthy people and probably acquired some of their tastes. Our sitting room, with its highly decorative oil lamps, featured a beautifully polished dining table which converted into a full size billiard table. The piano was also highly polished. It was a wonderful instrument, made to order by Mann's music shop in Colchester around the 1920s. Its tone was quite unusual and to this day it remains in my family. It is now enjoyed by my grandchildren and anyone else who chooses to play it.

A solid mahogany sideboard stood proudly against the wall. When the doors were opened, a celerette revealed a vast range of alcoholic beverages including home made wines which had been decanted into glass containers. There were two sections in the sideboard and the left hand cupboard was kept full of glasses to ensure that the correct glass for each drink selected could be used. Mum would never dream of putting whisky in a wine glass or wine in a sherry glass. It simply was not done.

The open fireplace was a comforting feature during the winter months. The hearth was stacked with logs that gave off a lovely smoky smell when they were burning. I can remember lying on the large drop-end settee when I was tired, often drifting off to sleep. I'd wake up and see my Mum sitting in one of the huge armchairs. But Mum rarely sat down for very long. She was a very busy lady.

The staircase to the bedrooms was very narrow and on reaching the main double bedroom, the floor sloped down towards one end which gave you a feeling of being slightly off balance. Being just a little girl, the old mahogany inlaid bed always looked enormous. It was certainly very high because a sprung horsehair mattress was laid on the bed springs, then on top of the mattress was a lovely soft feather bed. Then came a blanket which over the years had become rather worn and consequently itchy. Over this was the crisply starched bottom sheet. The long bolster pillow that lay along the head of the bed was also stuffed with feathers as were the two further single pillows which were covered with white lace trimmed pillow cases. The top sheet on the bed was always starched and snow white. The blankets were pure wool and on top of these were the silk bedspread and a silk eiderdown to match the bedspread. This was Mum and Dad's bed. I loved to get in; it always felt so luxurious. Sometimes I would pretend to be cold or if I couldn't sleep I would get in this very special bed just for a cuddle.

Gazing at the long mirror on the wardrobe I would see weird reflections from the candles. Especially odd shapes would form from the washstand jug and basins. There was a matching pair on the washstand, one for Mum and one for Dad. The toothbrush holder also cast strange shadows - with the toothbrushes standing upright they looked like funny little old men.

The cupboard underneath opened to reveal two chamber pots standing side by side. I hated using these pots because I was too little to lodge on the rim and had to bob precariously over the top. I much preferred my own little pot.

The garden too is a place full of fond memories. Before the war there were wonderful parties where children, mums, dads, grannies and granddads gathered on the lawn to play croquet. Later they would listen to the latest records played on a wind-up gramophone. The parties went on long after dark. Candles and oil lamps were lit and brought into the garden as the only other light would be from the moon and stars. Home-made wine was available in abundance and after a fair amount had been consumed the dancing would start to the music on the gramophone. Sometimes the person responsible for the gramophone would forget to wind it up and the music would gradually get slower and slower, and the voice singing would get deeper and deeper. Suddenly the handle would get turned again and the deep voice would quicken to the right tone, much to the amusement of the partygoers who would then carry on dancing.

My Dad, Jim, was the youngest of thirteen children which explained why there were so many relatives. Sophia, his mother, was forty-five years old when he was born – one of seven girls and six boys. I think they all got married, except Pud. Although Pud was a bachelor he didn't go short of women - or wine. He was notorious for being irresponsible. Any money he earned was 'invested' in the pub.

One day, when one of his brothers suggested that he should perhaps pay some money into an insurance scheme in case something happened to him, Pud wasn't inclined to do this. His reply was,

"If they don't bury me for love, they will for stink."

Pud's mother, Sophia, always worried about him and when

she died she left an old purse containing gold sovereigns so that Pud could have a decent funeral. His carefree and generous nature meant he was certainly very popular and his personality got him out of all manner of scrapes and predicaments. Many tales have been remembered and retold by family and friends. Here are just three of them.

One evening, long after dark, Mum and Auntie Maude were on their way home with only the light of the moon shining down on the hard, uneven tracks in Cross Lane. Periodically the light was cut out as the evening breeze blew clouds across the moonbeams. Suddenly, Auntie Maude caught her breath, grabbed Mum's arm and whispered,

"Ada, look by the ditch - there's something in there. It looks like a body."

"It is Maude. I reckon it's Pud. He's probably drunk - go and shake him," said Mum.

"Not likely. You go and shake him, he might be dead," said Maude, who was a very nervous person.

Mum - being of a more adventurous nature - bent down to shake the body. Suddenly, Pud bellowed out in a loud voice, making Mum recoil in fright.

"Frightened of me, are ya? Thought I was dead, did ya? Well I'm glad you two gals came along when ya did 'cos I got time to go back for another drink."

Off he went back to the Fox where he avoided a fight by using his sharp wit.

When he arrived at the pub one of the local lads, having had too much to drink, was being abusive and became aggressive to Pud. Pud simply said,

"Look 'ere mate, your mother ain't roight, yer father ain't roight, now how the hell can you be roight? Now, why don't ya jest piss off and shut up?"

A burst of laughter rang out through the crowded pub and the young drinker sat down quietly looking dejected.

Another famous tale about Pud was the time he took a job

as a Night Watchman for a firm carrying out road works along East Road. Pud's job was to light the red oil lamps which gave warning that there was danger of either uneven ground or holes that could be a hazard to the public.

It was mid week. Billy Farthing, Pud's nephew, was out with some of his friends walking along East Road when Bill, seeing the Night Watchman's hut at the side of the road, realised that 'Uncle Pud' was working and would be sheltering inside the hut. He beckoned to his mates to stop and on peering inside saw Uncle Pud sitting on the narrow bench, fast asleep. The boys, whispering to themselves, guessed that he had been to The Fox for a drink before starting his night shift. They started to giggle.

"Let's give him a ride, shall we?" said Bill, who was well known for his jokes and pranks. The boys agreed readily.

"I reckon he must have had the best part of a tidy few drinks before starting work," said Bill, who was familiar with the way Pud like to indulge.

"C'mon then, you lot. Let's shove it, shall we?"

The boys pushed the little wooden cabin, which was mounted on four wheels, right down to the bottom of Seaview Avenue, which was about half a mile long. As they reached the bottom of the road loud abuse could be heard coming from the Night Watchman's cabin.

"It's that bloody boy, Bill. I'll kill 'im that I will, when I get me hands on 'im."

The boys ran off as fast as they could...

And finally, Pud's funeral service was held on the lawn at The Cross. During the proceedings, one of the farm's pet magpies repeatedly flew around the garden squawking 'Hello Ada'.

Although Jim and Oliver employed men to work for them (including Pud when he was sober) there were many times when more hands were needed on the farm and there were always family members ready to help. Extended family, particularly younger members of both my mother and father's side, looked forward to staying at The Cross during the whole of the summer period. Helping on the farm wasn't really considered a chore as they enjoyed every moment of their stay. They would ride on Poppy the horse, take a turn in the horse and cart, help with the hay making, feed the pigs and help to collect the hundreds of eggs which also had to be cleaned ready for sale.

Market day at Sheepen Road in Colchester was also an important part of the farming community. It was the centre for socialising and catching up on gossip. And a quick bevvy in the pub to quench the thirst would be an added incentive to linger a little longer.

Sadly, everything changed after Oliver's death in 1937. Jim continued on his own, trying to manage for a couple of years, but it was a real struggle. With the onset of the war, the difficulties continued.

CHAPTER 2

Major Moncrieff, long goodbyes and Peter's pranks

OVERLEAF: *'Lady Ada Saye' c.1896. 18 years old before getting married to Jim Farthing.*
ABOVE: *Evelyn Saye (Tod) on Mersea beach. Before getting married to Fred Hayward.*

At precisely eleven a.m. on 3rd September 1939 the news came over the wireless that we were at war with Germany. Everyone was in deep shock and the news had a devastating effect on both young and old, particularly in families where loved ones would soon be leaving home to fight for their country.

Jim and Ada's only son, Peter, was twenty years old and they knew that every able bodied male over eighteen years of age would soon be conscripted into the armed forces. The young men who volunteered were able to choose the regiment they would serve with so Peter decided to volunteer for the army and was then able to join The Essex Yeomanry.

World War Two brought yet more problems for Jim. His farm workers had been called up to serve in the armed forces and it was increasingly difficult to get labour. The war soon created acute shortages of essential animal feeds. Without labour and without reliable deliveries of animal feeds, running Cross Farm became a real problem.

It wasn't until 1941/42 that I became aware of the real happenings of the war. The whole household would be alerted to the dangers of enemy aircraft overhead by the noise of the wailing sirens. I knew all the hustle and bustle was serious and although just a little tot I sensed the daunting atmosphere of the unknown.

An air raid shelter had been put up in Auntie Maude's back

room. Although it was designed to be put up outdoors, it was agreed that it would be easier and safer to access - and more convenient than having to go outside in bad weather and on cold, dark nights. It was large enough to shelter everyone living at Cross Farm and became part of our daily lives.

One night, after the warning sound of the siren, I heard Mum shout to Joan,

"Quick, get Pixie to the shelter and I'll get the candles, matches and torch."

Joan was one of the relations on my mother's side and was always full of fun.

Everyone was rushing about at the same time. I had got used to being woken up from a deep sleep, wrapped in a warm blanket and carried to my cot in the shelter. Although I was really too big for the cot, it didn't take up too much room and it was my place of safety when an air raid was going on. There was a feeling of being safe in the shelter and everyone would joke and giggle. Looking back now, perhaps it was a way of hiding their true feelings and fears.

We hadn't been in the shelter too long before Mrs Ardley from Brierly Hall, the farm next to us, turned up. Every time an air raid was on she ran across the fields to be with us. She said she always felt safe when she was with Ada – my Mum did have a rather special way of being able to give out comfort when it was needed.

It was a sight to behold when Mrs Ardley ran across the field in fright, tripped at the ditch and fell in the muddy water. Being a rather heavy lady, she had a problem getting on her feet again. She was absolutely covered in mud and in a state of fright – very shaky and breathless. Everyone looked at her. It was a funny sight but we were able to contain our chuckles. Finally she succumbed to a nip of whisky.

On this particular night it wasn't long before we heard the sound of the 'all clear' siren which meant we could get back to bed and Mrs Ardley could go back home across the field.

But before she left, I got my usual kiss,

"Goodbye me little 'ol darlin', see yer in the morning'."

I waved goodbye and wiped my cheek where I had got the wet kiss. I don't know where the rest of Mrs Ardley's family went when the sirens wailed but she was always safe with us.

My morning visit would be across the field with Mum or another adult to collect our daily milk. I would often be given a little pot of cream all to myself. Mrs Ardley always greeted us with,

"Hello me darlins, however are yer?"

Without waiting for a reply she would say,

"Come and see Ardley."

I liked Mr Ardley but his thick glasses used to frighten me as they magnified his eyes. I can remember him picking me up and I would say,

"Take your garses off Ardley."

He was such a kind man and he would reach up and remove his glasses just to please me and make me feel better. Once he'd taken his glasses off, I would give him a cuddle.

It's quite strange how people's lives, without warning, suddenly veer off in another direction - and that is exactly what happened to us. I was playing in the garden one day when an old gentleman came to the door. He was very well dressed, in a tweed suit, and was carrying a walking stick hooked over his arm. When he knocked at the door he was invited in by my mother.

Dad was busy in the garden but I heard Mum's voice call,

"Jim... Jim can you come in for a moment."

Dad went indoors after cleaning his dirty boots at the door. I, like most children of my age, was of a nosey disposition and decided I must go and see who this old man was. On entering the room the old gentleman turned to me and smiled.

"Hello, little girl. And what is your name?"

I was never known to be a shy child so I replied,
"I am Pixie Farthing."

"Well that is a pretty name."

"Yes," I replied, "they call me Pixie because of the pixie bonnets I wear."

"I have been talking to your Mummy and Daddy about your pretty coloured clothes."

I just looked at this old gentleman thinking he was a bit strange and wondering what was the matter with my clothes. I hadn't been indoors at the onset of the conversation about the colour of my clothes and what I was wearing. But even if I had been, I really wouldn't have understood the implication of it all anyway.

Apparently, the colours of my clothes - red and gold - were the colours that had made Marks and Spencer famous. Because I was wearing these colours and because he thought I was cute, he wanted permission to have my portrait painted by a famous artist. My mother was very flattered and would probably have agreed there and then but Dad wasn't at all sure and said he really wanted time to think about it. The old gentleman, called Major Moncrief, agreed that they should both have time to think it over and said that he would like to visit again in a week's time. He made his way to the door and Mum let him out.

"Well Jim. What do you think of that?" Mum asked my Dad.

"I don't know mate," he said thoughtfully. Then rather more firmly, "but I ain't gonna have her picture used for advertising. No! T'ain't so likely!"

My Dad was a very thoughtful man with a true Mersea accent, and was proud of it. He was a very honest man and had principles. I loved my Mum dearly. She had the same strong principles as Dad but she was also a bit of a snob. Before she married Dad she was known locally as 'Lady Ada Saye.' Dad was Jimma. Mersea was notorious for nicknames.

Dad was very well read and had a lovely handwriting style. He was also a good musician and played the cornet in the local brass band. He played the piano well and could play virtually anything on request. It was especially nice when everyone gathered round for a family sing song. His talents also extended to drawing and painting and I have been told that he once illustrated a nursery rhyme book for one of his family. To retain the special humour of this wonderful man I will try to write exactly the way he would have spoken.

A week passed and Major Moncrief duly returned, carrying his walking stick. This time he wore a sort of tweedy trilby hat.

"Good afternoon Major, do come in," my mother greeted him.

"Good afternoon, Mrs Farthing," he replied, taking off his hat.

Mum showed him through to the sitting room. I was quite excited at seeing the old gentleman again and decided to sit on his lap. I noticed as he laughed that he had some gold teeth. I don't know what made me keep quiet but I did - I didn't even mention them. I don't know if it was my sixth sense or the good manners that my mother had taught me. A few minutes later Mum appeared at the door with a tea tray.

While they were drinking tea Mum had to explain that Dad was working in the fields and was unable to leave his work. It was left to Mum to tell the Major that my parents had decided against having my portrait painted. I think he was both surprised and disappointed at their decision. He carried on talking for a while and then decided it was time to go home. He said he would come and visit again someday though.

People were coming and going all the time these days - lots of uncles and cousins in uniforms. They all looked extremely smart but there was a subdued atmosphere. After they'd visited us there would be the long goodbyes. I hated saying goodbye. I could feel the sadness that went with these farewells and it made me feel tearful. However, there was always a party first with plenty of food and wine. I can remember being stood on the enormous kitchen table at one of these parties and singing:

"I've got sixpence
A jolly, jolly sixpence
I've got sixpence
To last me all my life.
I've got tuppence to spend
And tuppence to lend
And tuppence to take home to my wife."

I was rewarded with a round of applause and followed the applause with a curtsey, after which I got some pennies for my moneybox.

I knew it could be a long time before we saw our uniformed relations and friends again. Maybe that's what inspired me to put on my entertaining performance. I could make people laugh and be happy, if only for a little while.

I was playing with my doll near the back door one day when I heard a motor car coming down Cross Lane. It was unusual to hear a car in the lane and I ran out just in time to see Major Moncrief getting out of the car. He went round to the passenger side and helped a well-dressed lady out of the car. Mum must have seen them coming and was waiting at the door on their arrival.

"Good morning Mrs Farthing, I have brought my housekeeper, Mrs McGary to meet you and your family. I do hope it's not inconvenient for you."

My mother replied that it was quite alright and shook hands with Mrs McGary.

Mrs McGary had an urgent need to go to Scotland and Major Moncrief was looking for a replacement housekeeper for just two weeks. He was asking my mother if she would kindly consider working for him for the two weeks that Mrs McGary would be away. Mum was talking with them for some while. I could understand most of what was going on but I wasn't at all sure if I liked the idea of staying in another house. It sounded as if we had got to sleep somewhere else for a time. I really didn't want to do that. I thought that my Dad wouldn't want to either. Mum agreed to discuss it with Dad when he came in at one o'clock for his dinner.

We always had dinner at one o'clock. Tea was at five thirty and supper at nine thirty. After supper was cleared away, breakfast was laid ready for the next morning. Supper was usually a cold meal - ham and pickles or cheese, cold chicken with perhaps cold vegetables left over from dinner. And always accompanied by a glass of wine, just to help with a good night's sleep.

When Dad came in for dinner Mum told him all about the Major's visit. She related from beginning to end the conversation which had taken place regarding Mrs McGary going to Scotland and the Major wanting Mum to be his housekeeper for a fortnight.

"Well Jim, do you think I should go and discuss it with them over afternoon tea tomorrow? That's what they have suggested."

"Ada mate, the only way y'ull find out is to goan see."

She did go and see. Afternoon tea was more than interesting. The Major promised a very good rate of pay for the fortnight that Mum would be working there but she was expected to live in the cottage - with Dad and me of course - for the whole fortnight. Before leaving, Mum was shown over the Major's home - Waldegrave House - and also Waldegrave

Cottage where we would be living for the fortnight. Mum was impressed with the house and liked the cottage. The gardens were quite large but we were used to lovely gardens.

Mum had precious little time to decide whether or not she would be prepared to work for the Major. He wanted her to commence duties as a housekeeper the following Monday, and he wanted her decision the very next day.

Financially they had really been struggling at The Cross since the outbreak of war and the money Mum would be earning for this fortnight would be very useful. Neither Mum or Dad liked being short of money. It was something they had never been used to.

Mum decided she would like to work for Major Moncrieff and Dad was agreeable to the arrangement. He would be able to cycle back to the farm each morning and sleep with us at Waldegrave Cottage at night. The Major was delighted when he heard the decision on Monday morning. Mum was feeling a bit apprehensive but kept reassuring to herself that it was only for two weeks.

Every week Mum and Dad sent money to Peter. They wanted to be sure that he wasn't short of cash while he was in the forces. A soldier's pay wasn't very much and was nice to be able to socialise when off duty. I expect most parents were striving to do the same for their loved ones, not knowing when they would see them again. From the time that Peter joined the army, our door was never locked. Mum said she couldn't lock the door at night in case he came home and couldn't get in. I think that Mum had made up her mind that as long as the door was left open he would definitely be returning home again. Consequently our door was left unlocked all through the war years. What a lovely place to live where your door can be left open day and night and no harm comes to your home.

Peter had gone to a private school as a child then to the Art School and finally, before going into the Army, he had served his apprenticeship as a carpenter and gained all his qualifications. He then went to work for Clifford White, Barfield Road, West Mersea - a relatively large family run builders' merchant, carpenter, and undertaker. Their business activities also included an insurance company and an estate agency.

Peter was a prankster. One day he went into the boss's office where there was a large pine chest containing tools owned by Mr White. Peter made a turban from material that lined the coffins and put it on his head. After removing all the tools, he clambered into the box and instructed his young apprentice, Claude Cudmore, to get some of the men to come into the office. Claude was then to tap the box so Peter could open the lid and pop up like a genie, playing a makeshift flute that he had fashioned from a piece of scrap copper piping.

When Peter joined the Army he was allowed to take his motor car, an MG sports car. He was Batman to the Adjutant and was able to use his car to carry out various errands and to deliver important messages. Dad had bought him the car while he was still at art school. The noise of the engine could be heard at Cross Farm as the car was driven over The Strood on his journey home from Colchester – over a mile away.

We had been at Waldegraves for ten days out of the fourteen when the postman arrived early one morning. He hadn't been gone long when there was a knock on the cottage door. Mum opened the door to see the Major standing there.

"Good morning Mrs Farthing. I would like you to come to work early this morning as I have received a letter from my housekeeper and I need to discuss the contents with you urgently."

" I can be across in about ten minutes," Mum said,

obviously surprised and curious.

"Good day, I will see you soon then," he replied looking as perplexed as my mother as he walked away.

Mum began to surmise many different scenarios so it wasn't long before she walked across the drive to Waldegraves House. She let herself in and made her way to the study where she knocked gently on the door.

"Come in, Mrs Farthing, do sit down." Mum took a seat and the Major began to explain.

"I am afraid I've had some rather bad news this morning. Mrs McGary, my housekeeper is unable to return to work due to personal circumstances. I was rather hoping that you can stay on for a while longer until I can get a replacement."

"Well, Major, I will have to talk to my husband first, but I shouldn't think there will be a problem."

"Very well, Mrs Farthing. Perhaps you could let me know your decision this evening."

Mum told Dad all about the Major wanting her to stay on until he could get a replacement for his housekeeper. Dad agreed that it would be alright. He said the ten days they had been at the cottage so far had been quite enjoyable so another couple of weeks wouldn't be too much to manage.

Those two extra weeks turned into a few years. Our old home at Cross Farm was, sadly, eventually sold.

CHAPTER 3

Auntie Dot, an aggressive gander and the plane crash

OVERLEAF: *Susan (left) and Pixie whilst living at Waldegraves Cottage.*
ABOVE: *Dorothy Farthing, 'Auntie Dot'.*

The gardens were especially nice. The gravel drive leading to Waldegrave House was edged with flowers which seemed to follow all the seasons - primroses, polyanthus, bluebells, violets and various wild flowers. The main house faced onto lawns and a sunken garden surrounded by rose trees with a sundial in the centre. Beyond the gardens a pathway led to a wooded glade meandering down to The Decoy. Just before the wooded area there was a very large tree where Dad made me a swing with thick rope and a wooden seat. My swing hung from a stout branch of the tree and was strong enough to be enjoyed by adults as well as children. Sometimes I would bounce on the swing and the vibration of my bouncing would disturb the birds. They would fly off, annoyed, with a fluttering of wings.

While Peter was stationed in Norfolk he met and fell in love with Dorothy Simms. Dorothy was a Sergeant in the Women's Auxiliary Air Force, known as the WAAF. She played an important role as a plotter on early radar equipment. Most of the time she was working on highly classified projects which naturally had to be kept secret.

Peter and Dorothy were married in 1941 in North Walsham, Norfolk and in 1942 Dorothy Farthing came to live with Mum and Dad at Waldegraves Cottage. I called her Auntie Dot and grew to love her nearly as much as my Mum and Dad.

Dot came from Solihull in Birmingham - far removed from the rural setting in which she was now living. Dot helped Mum with the usual household chores and adapted very well to a coal-fired oven, oil stoves and Tilly lamps - not forgetting the tiny little oil lamps which were taken up to bed every night.

But there was something I had noticed lately about Auntie Dot. She seemed to be getting rather large.

"You're getting fat," I said quite bluntly one day.

"Yes, my darling, I wondered how long it would be before you noticed. In a few weeks time I am going to have a baby and I'm keeping it safe and warm in my tummy until it's ready to be born."

I stood there summing up the situation. There hadn't been a baby in the family since I was born. I knew about the cows and sheep having calves and lambs as I had seen them at Lord's Farm next door just after they had been born. But a baby inside Auntie Dot's tummy - well that was amazing!

"Do Mum and Dad know?" I asked her.

"Yes darling, they both know and they are pleased that you will have someone to play with."

About a week had passed since we had the conversation about the expected arrival of the new baby. I was playing happily in the garden and was walking by the stable when the two geese waddled past followed by the gander with his long neck stretched high and his yellow beak clicking. Suddenly, without warning, he pushed his neck forward and began hissing at Auntie Dot. The gander, which was enormous, was getting closer and closer. She began to back up to the stable doors. By this time he had started to flack his wings and his webbed feet were off the ground. Auntie Dot screamed. I was absolutely petrified. I ran screaming for my Dad to come quickly. Mum was rushing from the house, having heard the commotion, shouting,

"Jim, Jim, come quickly."

Dad came running round the corner, brandishing a spade which he used to hit the gander and to divert it away from Auntie Dot. She was shaking all over and Mum led her indoors.

"Bleedin' nasty rotten sod," Dad said, loud enough for me to hear. I ran off indoors to see how Auntie Dot was feeling. Mum was making a cup of tea and it appeared that Auntie Dot was feeling much better but Dad insisted that Doctor Grant should be called in to make sure all was well with the baby. Mum went over to the Major who had a telephone in the main house and asked permission to use his phone. He was more than helpful and telephoned the doctor himself. Mum returned home across the yard and by this time the colour was returning to Auntie Dot's face. It wasn't long before the doctor arrived and after a consultation and examination he confirmed that all was well with Auntie Dot and the unborn baby.

During the day of 14th July, 1942 a strong healthy baby girl was born at Waldegrave Cottage. She was named Susan May Farthing.

I can still remember hearing her first cries as they echoed through the upstairs window, and everyone's relief that all was well. I would now have a young companion to play with.

I can also recall a very scary evening. It was 26th November, 1942.

Mum had prepared the Major's evening dinner and was about to carry it on the tray across the drive to Waldegrave House. The Major had his dinner at precisely the same time every evening because he was diabetic and it was essential for him to have his meals on time. Susan and I had both been in the tin bath in front of the roaring hot fire. Susan had managed to perform her usual trick of weeing in the bath as she was lifted out. I can still remember complaining.

"Why can't I have my bath first? She always wees in the water."

"It won't hurt you," said Auntie Dot, "Just spit in the water before you get in and you'll be lucky."

I didn't really believe her but I thought I might as well spit in it as there was already wee in the water and I could possibly be 'lucky'. The reason Susan always had the first lot of water was because it needed to be cooler, then it was topped up with more hot water from the copper for me. There wasn't enough water to have two separate baths. Anyway, that load of spit I rolled round in my mouth before spitting it out into the bath did actually bring me luck that night.

My hot bath had made me feel tired and I was laying on the settee directly under the window when first the siren went off. Then there was a really strange noise. Not a doodlebug but still a weird, horrible drone.

"Sounds like a plane in trouble," said Dad, running out into the garden. Auntie Dot followed behind.

"Get back indoors Dot, it's coming down. It's clipped the trees!"

She ran back indoors, shoved Susan under the table, and shouted to me.

"Pixie, get under the table!"

I jumped from the settee but didn't have time to get under the table. Auntie Dot bent her body over mine, cuddling me for protection. The horrible chugging sound continued for only a matter of seconds then suddenly the blast of the impact of the plane crash caused the window to be blown into the room. Large splinters of glass shredded the soft upholstery cloth on the settee and the wind was causing the curtains to blow eerily across the jagged gap where the window had been. If I hadn't ran to Auntie Dot when I did, I would have been cut very badly.

At the same time, Mum was walking across the drive with the Major's dinner. She always covered the tray with a large table napkin but the force of the explosion blew the napkin off the dinner. Soot from the chimney fell all over Mum and the Major's dinner.

"Whatever shall I do Jim? It's ruined his dinner and I haven't time to do anything fresh."

"Well mate, he's lucky to get anything at all. Yu'll just hev ter blow on it."

I think that's exactly what she did do. Dad wasn't overly keen on the Major anyway so I suppose he didn't care whether he had soot on his dinner or not. The Major called Dad 'Farthing', never 'Mister Farthing' or 'Jim', and Dad thought it was rude and uncalled for. In fact, one day Dad answered him back. I think he said something like,

"I have a handle to my name."

Not long after, he was called to the Major's private study for a discussion. Mum begged him not to be rude. Dad said,

"I won't be rude mate but I won't call him 'Sir' either."

Dad had been used to employing men. He treated everyone equally and with respect. I think he would have been quite happy to be called Jim or Mister Farthing but not just 'Farthing.'

Sadly, the plane that eventually crashed in East Road after clipping the tops of the trees by the side of the cottage had a crew of three Canadians on board. They all lost their lives. One of the engines from the plane actually crashed into a bungalow near the Fox Inn. We heard the news from some of the uniformed men who called at our house to talk to Dad about what had happened and what we saw on this terrible night.

The entire neighbourhood realised how lucky we were that there weren't more fatalities. Our postman, who arrived early every morning, was imparting a further tale of the horrendous plane crash while drinking a cup of tea. I listened with interest to what he was telling my Dad.

Several of the local boys aged about thirteen or fourteen

had ignored the barriers which had been put up to close off East Road because of the plane crash. Peter Green's name was one that was mentioned. They ran down Cross Lane, which backed onto the field where the crash had occurred. The boys hid in a ditch for a while, then moved slowly and stealthily across the field to get a better view of what was going on. Suddenly, one of the boys saw something shining in the grass. He bent down to retrieve the small object and to his horror saw a human finger with a ring still intact. It must have been the ring which, glimmering in the dull November light, attracted the attention of the young lad. Apparently, the person who had been wearing it was identified and traced to his family as a result of the ring being found by the local youngster.

Major Moncrief was always very kind to me. Mum would do the cleaning every morning while he was in his study dealing with correspondence. When he'd finished he would call for me to go into his study. I'd sit on his lap and be allowed to use the stamp which would emboss his address on the top of the writing paper when I pushed very hard on the handle. I would then stick the postage stamps on the envelopes. He would also allow me to write with his fountain pen. I thought that was marvellous. Ever since I first met this old gentleman I was fascinated by his gold teeth and I still couldn't help looking at the glimmer of gold when he smiled.

But it wasn't all fun and games at Waldegraves. Our sitting room had a door which opened directly on to the stairs. There was just enough room after stepping off the last step downstairs to stand and open the door. There was also a lock which was operated by slotting either your thumb or first finger into a small dent and sliding it across. The lock was never used and I had been told never to play with or touch this lock. Curiosity, however, got the better of me. I remember wondering what would happen if I tried the lock. I put my thumb in the lock and slid it across - it was easy. I had to do it one more time because I needed to convince myself that I wouldn't get locked in. This time it went across easily but when I tried to unlock it again it was stuck fast. I began to feel a bit panicky. I tried to unlock it again and again but it just wouldn't move. I screamed,

"I can't get out. I can't get out!"

Several grown-ups were talking at once, all telling me what to do. I knew just what to do but I couldn't do it. I was crying and screaming at the same time. Then I remembered there was another stairway, leading down to the stables outside. I ran upstairs to the bedroom that led to the room over the stables but standing across the door was a huge Victorian chest of drawers. I knew the chest was there and I had seen Dad slide it across when he went to the storage room. I tried so hard to move the large chest but couldn't shift it. I ran, screaming, all the way downstairs, hopeful that someone would have been able to open the door. I was still locked in. I tried so hard to move the latch across. My hands were bleeding where I had tried to unlock it. I could hear Mum saying,

"Jim, hurry, hurry, do something. She'll go mad if she's left in there much longer."

"The door has got to come off its hinges. That's the only way we'll get her out," my Dad said.

Everyone was in a panic except Auntie Dot, and she was now telling me that it wouldn't be very long before Dad would have me out and that it would be a good idea to just sit on the bottom of the stairs and wait. I felt a little better when I could hear the tools being used.

"It's nearly done now," said Auntie Dot.

Then Dad said, "It's off now."

At last I was out. The blood was still dripping off my fingers. Auntie Dot got a bowl of warm water and poured in some Dettol that made it turn white like milk. After my hands had been bathed, plasters were stuck over the small cuts and the drama was over. Dad put the door back on its hinges again - but without the lock. He made sure of removing it.

Foxes, Doodlebugs and Nanna Saye

OVERLEAF: *Lily and Stan Johnson.*
ABOVE: *(Top) Mary Hayward, the toenail cutter;*
Dorothy and Pixie at Nanna Saye's.

At a very young age I was able to identify and name various species of birds. I spent so much time with Dad who taught me so much about nature. He showed me the beautiful as well as the cruel side of mother nature. I so much enjoyed collecting the chicken's eggs. Sometimes I'd feel underneath the hens to retrieve the eggs which had just been laid - they were lovely and warm. Occasionally, if a hen was broody, she would get annoyed and try to peck me. A broody hen made a clucking noise, not the usual cackle. If this happened, Dad would remove her from the chicken house because her only aim would be to sit on the eggs to keep them warm ready for hatching. This was bad for the fresh eggs laid by the other hens. I was well informed on broody hens because it delighted me to see the end product. I would often plead with Dad,

"There's a broody hen Dad, please let her sit on some eggs."

And he would always answer, "I don't know about that, dear. I'll hev to think about it."

My pleading nearly always worked. The breeding box would be made ready with plenty of hay or straw for the mother hen to make a nest and she would then patiently sit on the eggs until it was time for them to hatch. She would shuffle gently and turn the eggs regularly for a few weeks. Finally cracks would appear as the chicks pecked their way out of the shell. During this period of waiting I was allowed to feed and water the hen every day. It was important to make her get off the nest for food and water as some hens were so keen to sit and hatch their eggs that they wouldn't bother to eat or drink. It was such a wonderful sight to see the chicks hatching. At first they would appear looking wet and bedraggled but very quickly they became gorgeous, fluffy and yellow. I'd watch them grow up, first protected by a small wire netting run on the grass before finally being moved to the larger chicken run with the other hens.

The hens were guarded as much as possible from natural predators but foxes were more than capable of outwitting Dad and the protection he was able to give the chickens. I can remember one morning after he'd been down to let the hens out we all sat down to have breakfast while listening to the news on the wireless. Dad had his usual 'squint' at the newspaper before going back out into the garden. He returned within minutes looking both sad and angry.

"Whatever's the matter Jim?" Mum asked.

"It's those bleedin' rotten nasty foxes. They've got the chickens."

Auntie Dot, Mum and myself went outside to see the devastation. The chicken wire fence had lifted at the bottom which enabled the fox to force his way in and kill the chickens. There were chickens without heads, chicken wings and feathers laying around everywhere - probably the work of more than one fox. It had all happened in broad daylight and we hadn't heard a sound. Dad went and got his twelve bore, double-barrelled shotgun from the cupboard under the stairs and filled his pocket with cartridges ready for action. I knew exactly what he had in mind and what he was going to do.

"Please can I come with you, Dad."

"Not today."

"Please, Dad."

He gave in again, as usual. I loved being with him. I was used to going with him when he went shooting. His gun would be open at the breech, resting comfortably and safely over his arm. As we moved stealthily through the grove at the end of the garden we saw further evidence of the fox's killings but no sign of the fox. Suddenly as we came into the open space, Dad said,

"Get down."

I knew immediately I must lay down in the grass, totally still and be quiet. The gun went 'clunk' as it was shut, ready to be fired, then 'bang'! Quietly and gently I raised myself from the grass, expecting to see a dead fox - but it was just a rabbit. Tomorrow we would have rabbit stew for dinner. Because of rationing and a widespread shortage of meat, rabbit stew and dumplings had become a tasty and desirable dinner.

As we made our way back home there was an ominous sound overhead - an intermittent cough-like drone like an aeroplane that was about to break down. I knew the sound only too well. It was a doodlebug - a pilotless, jet-propelled aircraft which flew at a low altitude carrying a ton of high explosives. The doodlebug was designed to explode on impact when it ran out of fuel. I was quite frightened as I always was when I heard this sound. We watched as it moved overhead, heading towards the River Blackwater. The mark of the German swastika could be seen quite clearly. For us, the immediate danger was over. The air raid siren was going off. If the doodlebug continued up the river it would almost certainly be brought down by the guns placed along both sides of the River Blackwater - both on Mersea and Bradwell. Bradwell rarely missed their target.

We hurriedly made our way home, passing Fellar our dog who was sitting outside his large kennel, trembling. Usually he came with us when we went shooting. He was a good gun dog and well trained. Fellar was a Collie cross Labrador, had a soft jaw and was excellent at retrieving. When we at last arrived indoors the 'all clear' siren could be heard. And there was a kettle boiling on top of the kitchen range.

"Would you like a cup of tea Dad?" asked Auntie Dot.

"Don't mind if I do, mate," replied Dad in his usual way.

* * *

Our main dinner was served at one o'clock in the afternoon, every day. And almost every day after dinner we walked the two miles to the village to see Nanna Saye.

Our journey to Nanna's was always on foot and began on the rough track which ran beside a field of cows. Their big brown eyes would gaze enquiringly at us as we walked along the twin tracks that had been carved through years of cart traffic. On a hot day the cow's tails would continually swish to ward off flies and they'd give us a friendly moo as we walked past. At the end of the track was a five-barred gate which had to be opened and shut again when the cows were in the field. After closing the gate we could proceed up Waldegraves Lane which was bordered on both sides by hedges and ditches.

Auntie Dot pushed Susan in her pram and I'd hold Mum's hand, letting go occasionally to hop and skip along or even pick some wild flowers from the hedgerows. As we approached the top of the lane there was a wooden cottage on the left-hand side where Stan and Lilly Johnson lived. Stan used to be employed by Dad at Cross Farm. Mum would stop and have a chat with Mrs Johnson. I really liked her - sometimes she would give me a sweet. One day as Mum was talking at the gate I was very fidgety and kept grabbing at my dress round the waist.

"Whatever's the matter with the little darlin', she don't seem to be able to keep still!" exclaimed Mrs Johnson.

"My knickers keep slipping down," I replied.

"Well we can't have that can we? You come along with me and I'll see what I can do."

I followed on down the path and went indoors. Mrs Johnson went to her workbox and found a length of elastic.

"Jest you lift your dress up darlin' and I'll soon fix them there drawers for yer."

And fix them she did. The elastic was tied around my knickers firmly at the waist with a bow, and we were able to proceed on our journey to Nanna Saye's.

Our journey to the village was always a social occasion, chatting and exchanging gossip with all the locals as we passed their homes. Just around the corner from the Johnsons' was a pair of white wooden cottages. The first one, The Willows, belonged to the Whitings and next door was the Jones's. I hoped that Mum and Auntie Dot wouldn't stop and talk again as I was getting fed up with all the adult conversations. Besides, I wanted to get to Nanna's.

Nanna Saye was my Mum's mother. She was bed-ridden and looked after by Auntie Tod, Mum's youngest sister. As far as anyone knows she gained this mysterious nickname from calling her little trolley a 'Tody' when she was small. Thereafter she became 'Tod'. Auntie Tod was married to Fred Hayward - Uncle Fred as we called him. Their four children were Mary, Ken, Dorothy and Rodney. They all lived in Rainbow Road.

Dorothy, two years older than me, was my favourite cousin. We were more like sisters than cousins. My eagerness to get to Nanna's wasn't to see Nanna but to play with Dorothy. Nanna was a very big lady and I found her daunting. She shouted her orders to everyone, and expected immediate results.

One day she ordered Mary to cut her toe nails. Mary wasn't very keen to oblige on this occasion but Auntie Tod used her authority and persuaded her 'to be kind to the ol' girl.' Mary reluctantly agreed but not only did she cut Nanna's toe nails, she cut her toe as well. I'd never heard such a commotion. Dorothy and I kept well out the way but we did get the giggles. We thought that maybe Mary had snipped her toe for purpose. As we stood outside the door in the hallway we heard Nanna calling Mary a 'wicked, wicked girl'. Suddenly, the door flew open and Mary flounced out with an angry look on her face.

"Miserable ol' sod," she murmured.

Nanna was always having bad turns. I'm not sure of the exact cause but during the course of these bad turns she would shout,

"I am dying, I am dying."

I would always think to myself, "I hope she doesn't die today."

It also worried me what she would look like if she did die. During these bad turns everyone would rush about, plumping up her pillows, opening the window for fresh air and finally getting her bottle of smelling salts. The smelling salts were absolutely disgusting, making your eyes water if a really big sniff was taken. I knew all about them because I'd tried them once.

Another of Nanna's medicinal remedies were her Mitcham mints. They were tiny little hot peppermints which she kept in a jar in the sideboard cupboard. I wasn't sure exactly what these mints did for her but they did seem to make her feel better. I was allowed to have one occasionally but all it did to me was to burn my tongue. Some years went by before she eventually made her way to heaven.

When Nanna was at her best, she would sit up in bed and knit. She made beautiful jumpers, cardigans, shirts, baby romper suits, and even lovely little smocked baby dresses. In fact she would make anything the family required.

Dorothy and I came in very useful, as we would wind the wool into balls from the skeins of wool. We took it in turns. I would hold the skeins over my wrists while Dorothy wound the ball of wool. When it was my turn to wind the ball it always ended up looking much smaller because I somehow managed to wind it too tight.

Nanna's bedsitting room was situated downstairs with the window facing Rainbow Road. Anyone passing by was able to see her sitting up in bed and they could wave to her. The small table that stood by the window, with a chair either side, was used on occasions by Dorothy and myself to have dinner or tea with Nanna. Neither of us would dare to even consider leaving the table until she had said grace, and then we had to ask permission to leave the table. Our little thanksgiving prayer was,

Thank you for the food we eat
Thank you for the flowers so sweet
Thank you for the birds that sing
Thank you God for everything. Amen.

After we had been given permission to leave the table, we would go out into the garden or even to play in the road which was quite safe as there was little or no traffic. It was ideal for the large tricycle we played on - I think it probably belonged to Nanna in her healthier days before she was confined to bed. One of us would ride on the saddle, one on the handlebars and one on a ledge at the back. We also used a standard size child's tricycle which gave us a great deal of pleasure, especially when we linked it up to the large trike with a tow-rope. This was very exciting, with the most dangerous part of the game being the fast journey down the hill at the bottom of Rainbow Road.

The journey home was more hurried, with just a quick hello to Oiley Green, who lived in Grange Cottage next to the Fox Inn. I didn't know what his real name was but he had a wooden leg and rode a big tricycle. I often wondered if he was called 'Oiley' because his leg squeaked - but I never found out.

CHAPTER 5

Lead toys, War Bonds and a windfall Sunday joint

OVERLEAF: *Auntie Violet ('Nee' Farthing) and Will Hewes (probably their wedding day).*
ABOVE: *Dudley Sargent (the butcher).*

Dad had announced that we would go and visit Auntie Violet and Uncle Will who lived in Victory Road. I was quite excited as I enjoyed going to see Auntie Violet. She baked the most wonderful cakes, her speciality being chocolate walnut sponge. The nuts came from the walnut tree that grew in their back garden but with the rationing of basic foods it was now more and more difficult for Auntie Violet to keep up her usual supply of home made cakes. Butter was rationed at four ounces (113g) per person per week and sugar at eight ounces (226g) per week.

Auntie Violet would ask Dad,

"Well boy, hev yer got me any grease terday?"

"Yes, mate, I got a bit for yer. Ada's saved yer some, and there's some dripping as well."

Dripping was the fat which came out of meat while cooking and Mum would put it into a basin to go hard. Dripping was very tasty, either on hot toast or sliced bread, but Auntie Violet also used it in her cooking. I particularly liked the jelly that gathered under the hard block of dripping. Mixed with the solid fat it was delicious when spread over fresh bread.

Auntie 'Violie', as Dad called her, was always pleased to see us. I think Dad was probably her favourite brother. Sometimes Mum would cycle down with us but today it was just me and Dad. I rode on the crossbar of his bike, sat with my legs straddled either side of the crossbar on a soft feather cushion which made a very comfortable seat. My feet rested on the ledge just above the mudguard as I held on to the centre of the handlebars, pretending that I was the one responsible for propelling the bike along the road and that it was me doing the steering.

I played with toys that were kept in a big square biscuit tin in Auntie Violet's sitting room. The contents of the tin were all toys of war. There were uniformed lead soldiers - some in action with guns, tin trucks, Red Cross lorries and tanks. My favourite was a gun, which shot matchsticks. The toys belonged to Paul Jasper. Paul was a lot older than me and lived with Auntie Violet and Uncle Will. He was really like a son to them. Occasionally Paul's two younger brothers, Peter and Jeremy, would also stay with Auntie Violet and Uncle Will.

I hadn't been playing with the toys for very long when Dad said,

"Come on dear. We're just popping down the road for a while."

I quickly packed the toys back into the biscuit tin and tucked the tin down by the side of the armchair. I then followed Dad to the gate and clambered on to the cushioned crossbar of his bike. We were going to the bottom of the road to the Victory Hotel where there was a War Bond auction sale. When we arrived there were various items being offered for sale. Everything was on display on trestle tables and all the various goodies were there to encourage buyers to invest more money in War Bonds. My attention was immediately drawn to a home-made rag doll. She was huge - bigger than me.

"Look at that doll, Dad. Please will you buy her for me?"

"I don't know dear. We'll hev ter see how much it goes for."

There were toys, iced cakes, glass bowls and such like. Lady Joanna Crane was among the people helping to organise the event and raise money for the war effort. She lived in 'Besom House' opposite the Victory Hotel and her husband was Major Crane. Dad bid for a number of items before the doll was held up.

"We now have lot number twenty," the auctioneer announced. "This beautiful handmade doll has attracted a lot of interest. Now what am I bid for this very desirable toy? Shall we start with five pounds?"

A lady put up her hand then a man put his hand up. Then Dad started bidding too and other people were bidding. Then it was just between my Dad and a lady. It seemed to go on for a long time before I heard the auctioneer say:

"Any advance on fifty pounds? Going once, going twice." The hammer banged on the table.

"Sold to Mr Farthing for fifty pounds."

I was over the moon. Dad went and collected the doll and handed it to me.

"There y'are me little mate. Is that what yer wanted?"

I knew he could see the delight in my eyes and I also knew that he was just as pleased as I was. Dad purchased various items including War Bonds. Although the doll was sold for fifty pounds it also meant that fifty pounds was invested in War Bonds. The same applied to all the other items - money was invested in Bonds to the value of the item purchased.

It was such a lovely afternoon it was very hard to believe that there was actually a war going on. But suddenly there was a sharp reminder when we heard the sound of the heavy engines and the rattle of amphibian tanks as they passed the Victory Hotel, making their way up Hove Hill. Their journey had started at Point Clear, then up the River Blackwater to West Mersea. Their first arrival on Mersea had astonished the local fishermen as the extraordinary amphibian tanks chugged up the creeks and clambered over the mud to where the ideal practice grounds were - the marshes of the Blackwater Estuary, mainly Feldy and Sunken Island in Salcott Creek. Their main landing ground on Mersea was in front of Wyatt's Boat Yard. The tanks - or alligators as they were known - continued up the hill. My moment of apprehension passed as the soldiers and tanks rumbled away. They looked awful, with their guns poking out. The men would often have nets over them which made them look even more sinister.

My mind returned to my rag doll and the sale that was taking place on this splendid day. When the sale had finished and the raffles had been drawn we cycled back up Victory Road to High View where Auntie Violet had a lovely sponge cake and tea waiting for us. When it was time to go, my rag doll accompanied us as the third passenger on the bicycle, her legs dangling over the crossbar of the bike and her long arms tucked firmly under my hands on the handlebars. I took my usual position on the cushioned crossbar and Dad peddled all three of us home.

This dolly was my pretend companion for most of the war, often becoming my dance partner, dancing in time to music on the wireless. I would watch us both dancing round and round in the reflection of the front of the polished piano. Sometimes there would be a doll's tea party and the miniature tea set would be set out. At other times I would put her under the table and shelter her from the dangers of war.

My day today started with waking up and listening to the sound of the wood pigeons murmuring and the gentle rustling of the leaves in the trees. The curtains were blowing from side to side as the breeze swept through the open window. Then the smell of breakfast cooking came wafting upstairs. It was the smell of bacon and eggs that induced me to get out of bed and get dressed.

A large kettle of hot water stood on the stove ready for my morning wash. Mum poured the hot water into a white enamel bowl then stood the bowl in the large kitchen sink ready for me to use. I was unable to reach the cold water tap so Mum ran the cold water into the bowl until it reached the right temperature. I had to stand on tip-toes to reach the green soap on the wooden draining board and the tin that contained a hard pink block of Gibb's tooth cleaner. My glass of cold water and toothbrush were there ready for me. After dipping my brush in the cold water I rubbed the toothbrush vigorously over the pink block, gathering as much cleaner onto the toothbrush as was necessary to clean and shine my teeth. After rinsing my mouth out I watched the pink spit go slowly down the plughole. By the time I had finished with my toiletry, my breakfast was on the table - egg, bacon and fried bread. It wasn't long before Auntie Dot and Susan came downstairs. Then I heard the back door open and Dad came in from the garden.

"Mornin' everyone," he said, "I've just seen the Major and he's going to the village in his car this morning. He's asked if I want to go. And little Pixie too."

Dad looked at me and smiled.

"Do you want to go as well?" he asked.

"Oh yes please!" I answered, my face beaming.

"Well then, he's goin' in about an hour so make sure yer ready and don't keep him waiting."

"I am ready now." I replied eagerly.

It was precisely one hour later when the major's car appeared. I ran outside, knowing that my seat would have already been put in place by opening a rear hatch on the car - a very smart upholstered seat would then spring into place. The seat was open to all weathers and on a cold day there was a tartan rug to tuck around my knees. The two front passengers were enclosed and protected from the elements. With the Major driving, Dad in the passenger seat and me in the sporty bit at the back, we motored down to the village. There were not many cars on the road during the war and the villagers turned their heads and waved as we drove past. I felt proud to be in this grand car - rather like a princess.

After going to the Post Office, then Cock's the butchers and Barclays bank, we made our return journey which was both enjoyable and uneventful. Dad went to help the Major put the car in the garage and I ran off through the garden, intending to have a go on the swing. Suddenly there was an explosion which seemed to rock the ground where I was running. I stopped in my tracks. I was absolutely petrified. For a few seconds it felt as though my legs were never going to move. Then they instinctively went into action, carrying my body to the place I most wanted to be, which was safe indoors. I had just got in when yet another explosion occurred, this time rattling every door and window in the house. It was terrifying. Then another explosion, and another. The whole house was shuddering with each blast. At last my Dad was at the door.

"Don't be scared," he tried to reassure me. "I bet the cattle have strayed into the minefield. Come on now, give us a cuddle, and y'll be alright."

I think both Mum and Auntie Dot were relieved to hear Dad's explanation for the big bangs. He was, of course, right, and I imagine they were probably Jack Lord's heifers that had strayed.

At the time of this gruesome happening, my uncle, Dudley Sargeant, was visiting us. He married Auntie Joan and by a strange quirk of fate he was a butcher. After investigating this horrendous accident, Dad and Uncle Dudley came home and told Mum and Auntie Dot of their findings.

"Ada, mate, you've never seen anything like it. There's meat blown all over the show. Me and Dudley are goin' off again for a while, jest ter have another look."

"Can I come?" I asked.

"No. You stay there and behave yourself," said Dad.

I knew by the tone of his voice that he wouldn't change his mind. He then went down to the garden shed, returning with a number of hessian sacks, which he and Uncle Dudley took with them.

When the men returned, they took the bulging hessian sacks to Dad's garden shed. Eavesdropping their conversation regarding the contents of the sacks it appears that Uncle Dudley did a grand job with the meat. He was an excellent butcher. I think the old saying 'God helps those who help themselves' probably applied to this occasion. All the extended family and friends were able to enjoy a good old Sunday roast, a real rarity in the war years.

Our garden was full of fresh vegetables, neat rows of cabbages, lettuce, carrots, swedes, spinach, runner beans, onions, and so on. The potatoes were dug up and stored under clamps made of straw with earth piled on top to keep the potatoes fresh until next years' crop came into season. The same happened with the apples and pears but they were stored on wooden trays and wrapped in newspaper to protect them from the frost and bright light. Some of the apples didn't keep quite so well as others but I remember Darcy Spice kept really well, although the skin would wrinkle up slightly by the end of the winter.

We were virtually self-sufficient. Mum and Auntie Dot made jams and chutneys from the fruit in the garden. There were red, black and white currants, strawberries, gooseberries, raspberries and tomatoes - which I hated. In the cold frame Dad grew huge melons, marrows and cucumbers. I don't think there was one patch of ground that wasn't put to good use. Dad gave vegetables to other members of the family who were less able at gardening than he was. From the time we had Cross Farm the family looked to Dad for help and he was always there to give it.

CHAPTER 6

A chance encounter, gifts from the sky and a win at the Legion

OVERLEAF: *Nanna Saye in her later years.*
ABOVE: *Grandad Tom and Nanna Saye.*

Most days followed a familiar pattern. Mum looked after Major Moncrief's house in the morning and then after dinner we walked the two miles to visit Nanna Saye.

On one of these days we were walking along East Road and as we approached The Fountain Hotel we passed a lady pushing a smart cream pram with a young child playfully bouncing up and down. The lady was very pretty and gave me a lovely smile. I can remember thinking that I liked her. Auntie Dot took hold of my hand and said,

"Come on Pixie. Hold on to the pram as this corner is dangerous."

I turned my head and the lady with the posh pram raised her hand and waved. I wasn't to know what a major part this small gesture was going to have in my later life.

It wasn't far to go now before we would be at Nanna's. We turned the corner into Kingsland Road and approached the cycle shop which was owned by Mr Cornelius, a kindly man who my Dad always called 'Snuffy'. Just opposite was a shoe shop owned by Mr French. This was where we purchased our new shoes and also had our repairs done. I loved looking at the new shoes in the window. I really wanted some black patent shoes with ankle straps.

We were now about to turn into Rainbow Road but Auntie Dot carried straight on down to the village with Susan to get her National dried milk at the Food Office and also some of our special orange juice. Mum and I carried on down Rainbow Road to Nanna's. When we got there I was quite disappointed to learn that Dorothy wasn't allowed to play as she had done something really terrible.

Auntie Tod had been to the Post Office to collect Nanna's pension. Before she went she had said to Dorothy,

"Now mind you be a good girl and sit with Nanna and don't dare get off the bed until I get back."

Dorothy sat on the bed playing with her doll for a time but then decided to brush and comb Nanna's hair. The gentle brushing and combing soon made Nanna fall asleep. Slowly and gently Dorothy slid off the bed, her feet touching the ground with barely a sound. She bent down and picked up the curling tongs that were laying on the hearth. Quietly she shifted the fireguard away from the fire but realised it wasn't necessary for it to be moved as the tongs would fit quite easily through the wire with the guard still in place. She proceeded to place the tongs in the fire to heat up ready for a curly hairdo - not for herself but for poor unsuspecting Nanna who was now sleeping soundly.

Carefully, Dorothy removed the tongs from the fire. She climbed quietly back onto the bed and without further ado started curling Nanna's hair. Whether it was the smell of singeing hair, or an unpleasant dream, the old girl suddenly moved her head and at the same time gave out a loud moan. Dorothy jumped with fright and accidentally touched and burned Nanna's ear with the hot tongs. It also turned her white hair an odd gingery yellow colour. Nanna Saye now had straight white hair on one side and curly coloured hair on the other side. Fortunately Auntie Tod arrived home just in time to help repair the damage and to quieten Nanna's temper.

It wasn't long before Auntie Dot and Susan arrived back from the village and as it looked like rain Mum said we should make an early start home. I was quite ready to go home as Dorothy was miserable and subdued after her escapade. Part of her punishment was a smack across the hands with a willow stick which was kept in one of a pair of china boot ornaments. The boots stood on either side of the wooden mantelpiece over the kitchen range. The twiggy sticks were selected from the willow tree in the garden. I felt so sorry for Dorothy as I had never been punished with smacks. The journey back home today seemed endless, my mind filled with sadness for Dorothy.

Unlike Cross Farm, there was no air raid shelter at Waldegrave Cottage and I have to admit it was something I didn't really miss. I hated the damp smell and the hemmed in feeling of the shelter with no windows. When the sirens went off Dad always went outside to watch the skies. If he felt there was any impending danger I was told to sit under the table, then cushions were placed on the floor ready for me to curl up in comfort. On occasions, I was allowed to go out in the garden with Dad. The sky would be lit up by searchlights as they attempted to pick out the enemy aircraft. My little hands would clutch firmly on to Dad's big hand - I knew I would always be safe with him.

In the morning, after a busy night in the sky, I could run in the surrounding fields and find strips of silver paper lying on the grass. To me it was like a treasure hunt. In reality, the silver strips were dropped from planes as a strategy used by enemy aircraft to confuse the radar equipment. The Americans' name for the silver strips was 'chaff' and the British name was 'windows'. My collection of silver strips had various uses - my dolls had belts of silver round their waists, various pictures were created in scrapbooks and at Christmas time our tree would be adorned with silver. Silver wasn't the only thing that fell from the sky. One morning Dad came into the sitting room excitedly calling,

"Dot! Dot, come with me for a minute."

Auntie Dot looked at Mum who gave an agreeable nod which suggested that she should go and see what Dad wanted.

She followed Dad outside. A few minutes later they both returned carrying what to me appeared to be white material and thick string.

"What have you got there?" I asked.

"Nothing you need to be concerned about young lady," said my Mum.

"You go and play with your doll," Dad said.

Even at my tender age I was intelligent enough to realise that there was something interesting going on and it was something they didn't want me to know about. Although I appeared to be playing with my doll, I was really taking in quite a lot of the conversation. The material was a parachute which had been found in the field adjoining our garden and now this important and mysterious bundle was being stuffed in the cupboard under the stairs.

"Well Dot mate, we shall hev to report this little lot later on," Dad said.

"I know Dad. I wonder what happened to the pilot? Where could he have gone?"

They didn't have to wait too long to find out the answer to the disappearance of the person who had been on the end of the parachute which was now hidden under our stairs. All was revealed when the postman arrived. He told Dad that a man had been arrested in the night. Supposedly he had baled out of a plane that went down over the River Blackwater. No mention was made about what we had got in our cupboard - it wasn't too important anymore.

A few months later it was decided that the material under the stairs could now be put to good use. The old treadle sewing machine was put to quite a few hours of work making up nightdresses, blouses and petticoats for Susan and me. It was a lovely, light cream silk - clothes to be proud of!

It was Friday, 6th August, 1943 and we'd all been getting

excited about the charity concert which was being held in the British Legion Hall. The proceeds were in aid of the British Red Cross Society and the British Legion Distress Fund. Everyone young and old got caught up with the excitement and the enthusiasm of being able to contribute to helping with the war effort. It was indeed an honour to be able to perform in the concert and help in this way.

My cousin Mary had been rehearsing for the great day for some time now and her excitement and anticipation was so contagious that we all got caught up with it. Dorothy and I had been watching Mary practise her tap dancing. We'd even been trying to copy some of her routines. Now the day was upon us and we couldn't wait to see the performance. Mary had to leave much earlier than the rest of us because of all the preparations before the concert started. The title of the concert was 'The Jolly Family' and it certainly lived up to its name. The 'Family' included Gwen Kilsby, Mary Hayward, Mary Larke, Pansy Cook, Betty Green, Doreen Mole, Peter Green, Ron Carr and Marie Carter. Mr Norman Carter was the pianist and producer of the well arranged show which included choruses, dialogues, short sketches, tap dancing and community singing. The highlight of my day was the announcement which came just after the half time interval. Mr Carter, the producer, came to the centre of the stage and announced that there was to be a talent competition.

"Come on now, boys and girls, ladies and gentlemen, I am sure we must have plenty of hidden talent in the audience."

I looked at Dorothy and said "Let's go and sing, shall we?"

"No, I'm not going up there," said Dorothy, "you go if you want to, but I'm not."

I couldn't wait to get on that stage. I looked at Mum and said,

"I'll go."

"Are you sure you want to get up there in front of all these people?" she asked.

"Yes, I can do it," I replied confidently.

As I walked up the Legion hall I was aware of people on either side of me sitting comfortably on their chairs. There was a ripple of conversation and I could hear Mr Carter saying,

"Here comes a very young contestant. Come along now, there will be a prize for the winner."

There were two small queues of contestants lined up on either side of the stage just behind the curtains. The first contestant was a singer. She sounded alright and after she had finished her song there was a round of applause. Next came a boy who looked quite a bit older than me. As his name was announced he started to sing - if you could call it singing! I stood there dumbstruck by his performance. He just marched across the stage shouting at the top of his voice,

"Shoot them doodlebugs down boys... shoot them doodlebugs down boys... shoot them doodlebugs down boys."

The audience laughed and applauded. I knew I could at least compete with the doodlebug boy. It was my turn next and the excitement was making my tummy feel quite fluttery. I could hear my name being announced.

"We now have little Pixie Farthing who is going to tap dance for us."

I had already given my name and what I was going to do. The music started playing as I looked out into the audience. There were such a lot of people and they were all watching and waiting. This was a dream come true! My feet began tapping and dancing in time with the music. I put so much effort and movement into my dance. It was so far removed from my usual kitchen table entertaining. The dance was about to end and as I slowed down the audience began to clap and cheer. I ended with a curtsey.

"Well done Pixie. Do you know any more dances?" asked Mr Carter.

"Yes," I replied. " I can do a hula-hula dance."

There was no stopping me now - the magic of an

appreciative audience and the sound of Hawaiian music brought out the best in me. I did everything that Mary had taught me. I wiggled my hips round and round, thrusting my tummy out at the front and bottom out at the back, both hands rotating first at my left hip, then to the right hip. I kept my rhythmic performance up until the music stopped and again I ended with a curtsey. The audience clapped and clapped, and cheered at the same time.

"Thank you once again little Pixie Farthing," said the announcer.

I made my way down the steps at the side of the stage and walked quietly back to my seat and Mum. I was feeling quite proud of myself. There were a few more entries for the talent contest and then the entire cast of 'The Jolly Family' came on stage to sing.

Saving, saving, helping to win the war,
Whenever you think you have saved enough,
Go on and save some more!

The audience joined in and the community singing went on for a while longer while the cast were changing for the grand finale. Lastly, Mr Norman Carter announced the winner of the talent contest.

"Well ladies and gentlemen, we have now come to the end of our show and I would like to announce the winner of the talent competition. The decision of the judges was unanimous and the winner is Pixie Farthing."

The audience was clapping as I walked up to the stage to collect my prize. I had won a National Savings Card with a 2/6d National Savings stamp stuck on it. I was delighted. I had only to save six stamps and then I could get a fifteen shillings (75p) National Savings Certificate from the Post Office.

I still have the newspaper cutting.

CHAPTER 7

Dad's Army, weekend leave and more nappies

OVERLEAF: *Picnic at Waldegraves. Pictured from left: Peter Farthing, Ada Farthing, Pixie Farthing, Nanna Simms, Susan Farthing and Dorothy Farthing.*
ABOVE: *Susan with her doll and doll's pram.*

I was much too young to fully understand what the war was all about but Dad would look at The Daily Express every day and comment on what was going on in our country and in the large cities. London was being heavily bombed with huge loss of life and thousands of people were being made homeless. There were horrendous pictures of devastation all over the country. Colchester, our nearest garrison town, ten miles away, was also subjected to heavy bombing by the Germans.

Mersea Island, strategically, could have been an ideal landing place for the enemy and the defences against possible invasion were evident everywhere. Beach huts had been removed, the beach and fields bordering the coast were heavily mined and rolls of coiled barbed wire were in place, surrounding the whole Island. Victoria Esplanade – known by locals as 'the concrete road' - was closed to the public and looked very bleak and unfriendly, particularly with pillboxes bristling with machine guns and anti tank weapons. Searchlights were also positioned in various places around the Island to search out marauders in the night sky.

Uncle Jack Saye was in the Home Guard and he helped to operate the searchlight positioned along Victoria Esplanade. It took two men to get the large Lister diesel engine working to produce a thirteen-million candle power light. One night Uncle Jack arrived on duty and found to his dismay that he was the only man there to get the searchlight operational.

He knew that he was quite capable of starting the diesel engine on his own because he was a bus driver and had plenty of practice with diesel engines on the buses. He was suddenly faced with the dilemma of whether to start the engine single handed, although strictly speaking it was against the rules, or should he wait for the backup of the other Home Guards, who would arrive any minute. There was very little choice left for him as he heard the warning sound of the air raid sirens. He got the diesel engine turning over, ready to operate the searchlight. Within minutes other personnel turned up, including a very well-spoken Army Officer.

"Who, may I ask, started that engine?" asked the officer.

"I did, Sir." replied Uncle Jack.

"On your own, man?"

"Yes, Sir."

"You had absolutely no right whatsoever to start that engine on your own."

"Oh bollocks," replied Uncle Jack, knowing full well what the rules were.

"If you were in the regular army, I would put you on a charge of insubordination," shouted the officer."

Uncle Jack decided at that point that retreat was the best part of valour and walked off to the magazine, an underground room where arms, ammunition and explosives were kept. This room was sited under Victoria Esplanade and was, I believe, accessed through an underground tunnel.

There were many men and women like Uncle Jack who were unable to join the regular armed forces for various reasons including age, physical ability and health but this didn't deter them from being committed to helping save the country. There was the Home Guard - known as 'Dad's Army' because they were mainly men who were too old for the forces. There were also youngsters with a minimum age of fifteen or sixteen - too young for the services. Even if these men lacked expertise, they certainly didn't lack enthusiasm.

One evening they were all summoned together for some extra training. The chairs were already set out in neat rows across the hall. The men, young and old, were all arriving on time. They sat down noisily on their seats, shuffling about and chatting loudly to each other.

"Quiet!" called out the uniformed sergeant who had just arrived.

There was immediate silence and the man commenced with his very useful advice on what should and shouldn't be done by the voluntary services during various circumstances during war.

"What steps would you take if we were being invaded by the enemy?" asked the sergeant.

"Long 'uns and quick 'uns" shouted one of the more humorous and older locals.

These men did a grand job working countless hours voluntarily, as did the ARP (Air Raid Precautions). One of their many jobs was to rescue people trapped in buildings or buried under rubble. They would also act as messengers for the local police and fire brigade and undertake fire watching. There was the Observer Corps too, which was mainly engaged in spotting enemy aircraft. All the voluntary services did whatever was asked of them.

Last night was another restless night, with us having to get up out of our nice warm beds. I awoke suddenly to the warning sound of the wailing siren, the two-minute signal, rising and falling in pitch. Susan started to cry and Auntie Dot was talking to her in comforting tones. I just wanted the noise to stop. Sometimes it would make me shiver. It was making me shiver and tremble tonight. Perhaps it was the bleak sound of the wind and the rain coupled with the noise of the overhead planes that made it all the more sinister. Susan had settled down on the cushions under the table and was covered over with a blanket.

"Put the kettle on Ada mate and make us a cuppa tea," said Dad as he made his way to the back door.

Mum poked the fire, encouraging the coals to burn red and hot, ready for the kettle which was placed on the hob. Dad had left the back door open as he went outside and I could see the searchlights reaching far up into the sky. We now had a searchlight about two hundred and fifty yards from the house, just at the end of the rough track by the white gate that led directly into Waldegrave Lane. The sound of the guns could be heard and there was no let up with the wind and rain. Dad was still outside watching the sky. Suddenly there was a shout from Dad.

"Dot! They've shot it down over the water!"

Dot had served with the Womens' Royal Air Force and kept characteristically cool on this occasion.

"Jim! The kettle's boiled. Come and have your cup of tea," said Mum.

"Ok, mate, I'm jist cummin'."

Mum, Dad and Auntie Dot had tea but I had my cup of cocoa while listening to Dad describing how the enemy aircraft had been brought down over the river. It was with great relief that we heard the constant pitch of the all clear siren. We could now go upstairs to bed, including Susan who was still fast asleep under the table.

By the following morning the wind and rain had stopped and the sun was shining brightly. The birds were singing and it was as if the war had gone away. But it hadn't really and the noise of the scary sirens would without doubt be giving out their frightening warning sound yet again - it could be tonight, tomorrow, or even a week's time. Breakfast was over and Dad was reading the Daily Express.

"Please will you read Rupert to me, Dad," I asked. "Come on then, dear," said Dad.

I climbed onto his lap ready for my story. Every day there

was a small illustrated picture story about Rupert Bear in the newspaper and each day Dad read me the serialised caption. When the story was finished I got off his lap and ran out into the garden. I glanced up the drive and could see a uniformed figure walking down towards the house. I knew that walk. My tummy jumped with excitement. It was Daddy Peter. He was home.

I don't really know why I called him Daddy Peter – probably it was just easier to say than Susan's Daddy.

"It's Daddy Peter! Come quickly, it's Daddy Peter!" I shouted.

My shouting brought everyone outside. Mum came from the Major's house, Auntie Dot came running out of the door with Susan in her arms and Dad was following at the rear with a spade in his hand. What a wonderful surprise! Susan was now standing on the ground and Auntie Dot was being cuddled tightly and kissed by her husband. We all got his attention in turn.

"I tried to let you know I was coming but the phone lines were all down. I've got forty eight hours off,"" said Daddy Peter as he cuddled me and Susan, his little daughter.

"Dad-dy," said Susan.

The time passed very quickly and it was soon time for Daddy Peter to return to Norfolk where his regiment was stationed. The goodbyes were very sad and anxious, nobody knew exactly when we would see him again. It was always secretly kept in everyone's mind and never spoken about. I knew the tension and felt like crying.

"Come on Pixie, give me a big hug. It won't be long before I am home again," said Daddy Peter, bending down for my kiss and cuddle.

It was a round of kisses and cuddles and then he was away again.

* * *

Auntie Dot had started to wear her baggy floral smocks and today the linen line was full of nappies which hadn't been used for some time. Curiosity got the better of me.

"What are those nappies doing on the line?" I asked.

"Well it won't be too long now before Susan has either a new brother or sister. Isn't it exciting?" said Auntie Dot.

I didn't answer. I couldn't feel at all excited. Susan was a bit of a nuisance, especially when she mucked up my games and took my toys. In fact she was very bossy and with another baby on the way, it could be a nightmare. I went off into the garden but it wasn't long before I heard Mum calling me.

"Pixie! Pixie!"

"Yes, I'm coming Mum!"

I was so pleased to see Ann Lord, my best friend from the next door farm standing there.

"Do you want to go and play with Ann?" asked Mum.

"Yes please." I said, as we both ran up the driveway together.

The large, white gate at the end of the drive was closed. Although there was a small tradesman's gate at the side, it was still more fun for us to climb over the big gate, dropping onto the stony ground the other side. I guess that's why the adjoining field was known as Stone Field. To the right of us was the stile which we climbed next and then we were on our way across the field to Waldegraves Farm House where Ann and her brother David lived. As we entered the yard we had to move to one side as Molly, the land army girl, was leading a herd of cows into the field. The cows were lowing contentedly. Soon they would be grazing on the lovely rich grass. Molly was wearing her snood - a thick net which covered her hair. I remember thinking that I would love to wear a snood when I was old enough. Ann was calling me.

"Come on then, hurry up. Let's go and play on the haystack!"

I ran after Ann who was climbing the wooden ladder that stood against the haystack. By the time I reached the ladder Ann was already sliding down the other side. After a few more jumps and slides by the pair of us the stack began to look very untidy. Our screams and laughter had drawn the attention of Alba Green, the cowman - his real name was Albert - and he had come to see what we were getting up to.

"Get off that stack roight now! Yer makin' a roight mess a things," he said.

We obeyed and ran off giggling to ourselves, leaving Alba to rake up all the hay that had been scattered about by our playful antics. Wondering what to do next, we decided to make a play den. Both of us worked extremely hard fetching and carrying suitable material from the outbuildings to make our playhouse. During our search we found large pieces of wood, rolled-up felt, an old hessian sack, bricks, old buckets with holes in the bottom and various other bits and pieces.

"Let's fill the sack with hay. It will make a nice cushion," suggested Ann.

"Alright. You hold the sack open while I put the hay in," I replied.

Ann held the sack open. I was gathering the hay together when suddenly there was movement. I froze. I just knew it would be either a rat or mouse. Luckily it was just a tiny mouse which scurried away quickly into the safety of the hay. As I hated both rats and mice, the thought of this tiny creature crawling up my arm made me shudder.

"It's your turn to put hay in the sack," I said quickly.

"You're just scared," taunted Ann.

"No I am not," I replied.

"Oh well you hold the sack open then," said Ann impatiently.

When the sack was full of hay we tied it up with string, making a comfortable cushion for the floor of our den. By the time our den had been completed it was dinner time but I decided to ask to go to the toilet before going home. I was very impressed with the lavatory at the farm. It was upstairs and was in the same room as the bath. The fascination of pulling the chain and watching the poo swirling down, then disappearing and leaving clear water in the pan, fascinated me. As I sat there swinging my legs backwards and forwards I began wondering where it all went.

Our lavatory at home was a small building a few yards from the back door. After lifting the latch and opening the wooden door, there was just enough room to accommodate one person sitting comfortably. At the back of the tiny building was a small hatch where the lavatory bucket was positioned ready for use. Every day it was sprinkled with disinfectant and when it was full, Dad emptied it into a large hole which he had dug at the bottom of the garden.

"Hurry up Pixie!" Ann shouted. "It's time you went home for dinner."

My Dad stood at the door waiting for me. I took hold of his big hand, which was rough from constant outdoor work, and we made our way home across the field. I stopped from time to time to pick a bunch of assorted buttercups and daisies, ready to make a daisy chain after we'd had dinner.

CHAPTER 8

Ferrets, *a new arrival and the German doll*

OVERLEAF: *Fellar, our dog.*
ABOVE: *(Top) Paul Jasper; Ken Hayward, aged 19.*

The end of a sultry summer was fast approaching. Late afternoon had an autumnal feel with little power left in the sun. Trees at the side of the house were beginning to shed their leaves which fluttered to the ground, chased by the wind into untidy heaps. The little hard-tyre bike I was riding wobbled into the heaps of leaves, scattering them further up the drive. This little miracle machine of mine was purchased by Dad only a few days ago from the rag and bone man when he called to buy rabbit pelts. The bike was lodged on the carrier of his trade bike. I watched as Dad asked the man, who was dressed in tatty old clothes,

"Is the bike for sale?"

"Yes, mate, " he replied.

The pelts, plus money, were exchanged and the bike was mine.

Dad had tried a couple of times to teach me to ride, but I couldn't quite get the balance right. When my cousin Ken and his mate, Hubert Pamment turned up, I excitedly showed them my bike.

"Christ, gal, that's a right little corker," said Ken.

"But I can't ride it yet," I said.

"C'mon, mate, let's show her how to ride it," said Hubert.

Ken held the bike steady, while I sat on the saddle. Hubert went a few yards up the drive and waited for Ken to give me a push.

"Now shove her back again," said Ken.

This went on for a while, with either one or the other

grabbing me if I was about to fall off. And it wasn't long before I was able to balance and pedal the bike unaided.

"I can do it all by myself," I shouted excitedly.

The noise and laughter brought Mum and Dad out to see me riding my bike. After praising my efforts, everyone disappeared indoors, leaving me to enjoy my late afternoon cycling. It wasn't long before I decided to follow them indoors. The smell of Mum's cakes cooking in the oven was too much to miss. The first batch out of the oven sat on the cooling rack waiting to be eaten. Mum then transferred them onto a large plate and asked me to hand the cakes round. Dad was telling the boys that he planned to go ferreting in the morning. One of his mates was coming round. He told the boys they could join in if they wished. However, it was unfortunate that they had already planned their day.

"Am I allowed to go?" I asked.

"Depends on the weather and if you behave yourself between now and the morning," said Dad. I knew that this was almost a positive, 'Yes'.

"We'd better be off now," said the boys, gathering up their jackets and cycle clips ready to cycle home.

"Cheerio, mate," said Dad, and off they went.

After a fairly quiet night, the next day dawned with a frost in the air. I could feel the cold chill on my face as I lay in bed with the covers and eiderdown nearly over my head. Suddenly, I remembered we were going ferreting and this thought was enough to make me want to get up out of my warm bed. I took my neatly folded pile of clothes and carried them downstairs so that I could get dressed in front of the warm fire. A large saucepan of porridge was simmering gently on the stove while Mum was toasting bread on the hot coals of the open grate on the end of a long-handled toasting fork. The rest of the toast was being kept warm on a plate placed on the hearth.

I had just about finished my breakfast when I heard the

sound of a bike coming down the drive - it must be Bert arriving. After getting permission to leave the table, I went to the sink and rubbed the flannel quickly over my face, put my wellies and coat on and ran straight into the garden where Dad was already taking the ferrets out of their hutches and placing them in their carrying boxes, ready for our hunting. As I stood there watching I realised how much I really disliked these creatures with their elongated bodies and rat-like appearance. Beneath their soft furry exterior was a sinister and vicious nature.

Dad had got quite fond of these little animals. There was an understanding between them. The ferrets knew their job. Dad - with a certain amount of affection - had skilfully trained them to be good hunters. Two ferrets had been selected for today's work - one white and one cream, male and female. The male is called a 'Hob' and female a 'Gill'. When fully grown, it's easy to see that the female is smaller in size. When I asked Dad how he could tell the difference when they were younger, he said that I wasn't old enough to know. I wondered how old I had to be.

Bert was busy getting the nets out of the shed. I thought it would be helpful to let Fellar off his chain. He was barking excitedly, his animal instincts and the scent of the ferrets were already making him sense the pleasure of hunting rabbits. The three of us, plus dog, ferrets and equipment made our way through the garden and into the private woods opening up on land rich with rabbit warrens. The surrounding area was protected by blackberry bushes, trees and hedges. I glanced about me, wondering if there were any foxes in the vicinity.

The animal world is a strange place, with many unexplained mysteries and rules. Normally, a fox would hunt and kill rabbits, but there seems to be an exception to this rule, especially when the fox lives amongst the rabbits. He will not hunt or kill the neighbours he lives with - they will be safe and left alone. The fox will go and hunt for rabbits further afield. Or is there an even greater sense of reasoning within the mind of the 'Sly, Cunning Fox'? Has he a pantry on his doorstep should there be a very hard winter? Would he then kill his neighbours?

I watched the purse nets being spread over the holes in the warren. A purse net has a ring at either end of the net with a draw cord threaded. The draw cord has a peg attached which is then pushed into the ground. When all the nets were securely fixed, Dad slipped the gill ferret into the warren which made the rabbit bolt into one of the nets. Dad and Bert with their expertise, constantly listened and watching out for a rabbit in a net. The holes in the nets were large enough for the ferret to skim through, leaving the rabbit to be killed humanely with a single hit at the base of the neck.

The hob (male) ferret wasn't used today. He was only used if the gill (female) didn't surface. He would be entered into the warren on a length of cord tied to his collar, the measurement of the cord going down the hole being noted so that the gill could be found, then dug out, should it be necessary. When the ferret doesn't surface, it could mean that it has killed and eaten a rabbit and with a full belly, has fallen asleep. It may then be necessary to return the next day to find and collect the, 'Bleedin' thing,' as Dad used to say.

One of the worst - and thankfully rare - things that can happen when ferreting is for a buck rabbit to kick a ferret to death with his back feet. Fortunately, today was a straightforward and successful morning with a catch of five rabbits. Both the ferrets had been installed safely in the carrying boxes. The rabbits that had been caught today had each been slit through one of the back legs at the first elbow with a penknife. The other leg was slotted through the slit so that the rabbits could be hung on a length of wood and carried home. As we went back through he woods, the five dead rabbits dangled sadly from the length of wood, heads jogging limply in time to the pace of the walkers, who would

soon be skinning and getting them ready for the stew pot.
I'd had enough of hunting and decided to go home.

"I'm going home now Dad," I said running through the
long grass.

"Alright, mate. Tell yer mother I won't be long"

"Bye, Bert," I called.

"Bye, little gal," said Bert.

As I walked in the back door, I could hear the familiar
sounds of 'Workers' Playtime' on the wireless. The delicious
smell of steak and kidney suet pudding was carried into the
room by the puffs of steam rising from the large, black
enamel saucepan bubbling away on the stove. The lid rose
every now and again under the pressure of the steam to reveal
the linen cloth that covered the tasty pud. Dad arrived back
indoors just in time for the, ' pip, pip, pip' sound on the
wireless, followed by,

"This is the BBC one o'clock news…"

The news was pretty dismal, with accounts of the war, both
home and away. While the news was on I knew it would be
foolish to even think about talking as I would be put in my
place immediately by Dad, who would tell me to,

"Be quiet while the news is on."

Although most of the news was bad, everyone had an
urgent need to know what was going on.

Auntie Dot had been away for a few days now, and we
were all missing her. She was staying with Auntie Violet and
Uncle Will at High View and would remain there until the
baby was born. Waldegraves Lane was virtually impassable,
with deep puddles and ruts reaching all the way to our house.
Victory Road would be much easier for the doctor and nurse
to access, especially with the blackout restrictions of no street
lights. Cars, vans, lorries and even bicycles had to have special
headlight covers.

It was Thursday 22nd March, 1944 and Dorothy knew
that the birth of her baby was getting close. The pains were

now coming at regular intervals and happening more frequently. Auntie Violet was aware that it was time to send Paul down the road to the phone box at the bottom of Victory Road to call for the doctor. He struggled to get his bike out of the shed, the blackness of the night making it very difficult. There wasn't even a crack of light coming from the indoor windows, as the blackout curtains were very efficient. The torch on Paul's bike wasn't much help as it was protected by a special shield allowing the minimal amount of light to shine through. The upper half of the glass had to be completely obscured and the lower half of any reflector had to be treated with black paint.

It was a short, quick journey in the black of the night to the bottom of the road. Paul hurriedly dropped his bike to the ground. He wasn't quite sure just how urgently the doctor was needed but he was treating it as though it was very urgent. After phoning, he made his way back up the hill, knowing that Doctor Grant and Nurse Menzies were on their way. They both arrived about the same time, the nurse on her bike and the doctor in his car. The baby arrived in the early hours of the twenty-third. He was a very good size, with a strong pair of lungs. A red-faced baby brother for Susan, with hardly any hair.

After Uncle Will and Auntie Violet had seen the baby, Paul then had a look at him and said,

"He looks just like Mussolini," which is what he told Mum when he telephoned after breakfast to let us all know the good news.

Mum was overjoyed to hear that the new-born baby was a boy. She adored boys and looked forward to spoiling him. His Daddy came home on forty-eight hour compassionate leave to see his new son, who was soon to be named Terry James Farthing.

Terry was indeed idolised by Mum, and she soon became a very important person in his life. In fact, I think it could be assumed that the baby wasn't sure who his mother really was because of the attention she gave him. Auntie Dot didn't mind, as she was grateful to be able to share the responsibility of caring for her baby. Susan was only twenty months old and still needed a lot of attention. It was an arrangement that was appreciated mutually by Auntie Dot and Mum and carried on into the years.

A few weeks prior to the end of the war, the postman arrived with a large brown paper parcel addressed to Auntie Dot. It had been opened and resealed with the usual wartime tape bearing the words:

'OPENED BY THE CENSOR'.

Anyone on active service writing home would be subject to having their letters scrutinised and any offending words which may have been considered a threat to security - perhaps their locations - would be crossed out using a blue-pencil. I watched Auntie Dot as she tore away the brown paper, keeping the string on one side to be re-used, then, lifting the lid of the cardboard box to reveal the contents, which was a large, unbreakable baby doll. I was hoping so much it was for me, but within seconds I was feeling the disappointment of knowing that the doll wasn't for me, but for Susan. Auntie Dot was reading the enclosed short letter out loud, which said,
'I will be sending another doll as soon as possible for Pixie.'
I watched Susan grab hold of the doll, at the same time wishing that it wouldn't be too long before my parcel arrived. I moved towards Susan, hoping to have at least a small share of her doll but she ran off with it, tucking it behind the cushion on the armchair and sitting at the front of the chair to prevent me from sharing or even having a look at her

new doll.

But it was only a matter of a few days before the second parcel arrived. The postman delivered the same type of package to the door, but this time as the parcel was handed over the slight tilt of the package caused the sound of, 'Mumma' to come from inside the parcel.

"I wonder what this could be?" said Auntie Dot with laughter in her eyes.

"My doll!" I replied excitedly.

I watched in anticipation as the parcel was undone, stretching up on tiptoes to peer inside the box. There inside was the most beautiful china doll with real dark brown hair cut into a fringe just above matching dark brown eyes that opened and closed. I had never seen such a beautiful doll. This time it was my doll!

It wasn't brand new, but very special. Surely it was a miracle to have travelled all through the wartime post without getting damaged or broken. My doll had an inscription on the back of its neck which said, 'Made in Germany'. The dark brown eyes gazed at me as though it wasn't a doll but a real person. If my doll could talk it would probably have told me that the previous owner was a little German girl who'd fled with her family from their home for fear of their lives, leaving possessions scattered everywhere. Part of the house had been bombed, leaving some rooms intact. Amongst rubble and debris was a doll that was rescued by a British soldier and posted off to England to be loved and cared for - by me.

One of the weapons used in the First World War was poison gas, so in World War Two the Government built up a stock of gas masks ready to be issued free to everyone - including babies and children. There was special design for very young children, similar to the adult mask but produced in bright red and blue colours, making them far more attractive and fun to use and called the 'Mickey Mouse' mask. Luckily, the feared poison gas raids from the Germans didn't materialise and people gradually began to feel more confident about leaving their gas masks at home. My gas mask was only ever used as a toy, playing imaginary games with my dolls. It was indeed a strange turn of circumstances that now led me to be playing with a German doll.

Peter's War (i)
Apprehension, broom handles
and petrol shortages

OVERLEAF: *Peter, behind the steering wheel of his car.*
ABOVE: *(Top) Edna Dallas standing in front of The Hostel at Peldon, 1942; Landgirls working near The Peldon Rose, 1942. From left: Edna Dallas, Rose Doree, Emmy Curd, 'Bunny' Webb the foreman.*

On 3rd May, 1939, Peter left his home at Cross Farm, West Mersea in his red MG sports car to enlist at The Drill Hall, Stanwell Street, Colchester. Feeling excited about this new adventure, he put his foot down hard on the accelerator, getting maximum speed from his car as he roared across the Strood to the mainland.

The ten-mile journey from Mersea Island to Colchester gave him time to reflect on the lifestyle he had become used to. His mind stretched right back to the time when he first started private school, going on to win a scholarship to the Art School on North Hill, Colchester. After attending both night school and serving a three-year apprenticeship with Clifford White he was now a qualified carpenter. War was inevitable and he was just twenty years old - would he ever get the chance to use his skills? A wave of apprehension swept over him as he drove into Stanwell Street, parking his car as close as he could to The Drill Hall. On entering the hall there were many other young men on the same mission as himself, including Ron Copeman, George Cole ('Boots') and Ken Markland, all of whom remained comrades during most of the war years. Today he had been declared 'fit for service' in the Royal Regiment of Artillery, The Essex Yeomanry and would now be known as:

'Gnr [Gunner] 918090, 147th Regiment 413 (Colchester) Battery'

The actual medical received was rudimentary but considered adequate. The volunteers were ordered to return home and await notification and instructions by post when their services would next be required.

Peter made his way to the car knowing that his carefree, decadent way of life was seriously going to change. His fashionable clothes were soon to be replaced by army uniform. Sitting back in the car he helped himself to a cigarette, lighting it with the lighter that he kept in his top pocket of his jacket. He relaxed back into the seat, puffing away at his cigarette, taking stock of what was now inescapable - 'The Bloody War'.

His first evening of army training began at the Drill Hall. It proved to be far less exciting than anticipated both by him and the other new recruits. They were told that there would be a variation of training during the two evenings attended every week consisting of 'square-bashing' (marching), saluting practice, lectures on artillery tactics and gun drill.

Major C.A.C. Turner had been given the task of raising a battery of around two hundred men and after giving some very convincing talks about the needs of the army to local businesses he was indeed lucky to enlist men from the Borough Treasurer's Department; Electricity Department; staff from the banks; insurance companies; estate agents and other young men from all walks of life. Over a period of a month these men had been signing up for service in the army. Tonight was their first night. Many new friendships were formed. They were all of the same mind and would fight for their country.

It wasn't long before the authorities commandeered an old warehouse at Parry's Oil Mill at Hythe Quay, only a mile from Colchester Town Centre, for training the troops. The Drill Hall days came to an end.

Unfortunately, the equipment necessary to train fighting soldiers was in short supply and half of the men were using broom handles as substitutes for rifles. Peter had to use a broom handle and found it difficult to contain his humour. Glancing at his mate standing next to him he whispered,

"Christ almighty, Boots, the only way to kill the enemy is to poke him up the arse. We've got more guns than this at home on the farm."

Many of the men were still waiting for uniforms and having to make do with brown drill overalls (fatigues) which were the next best thing until another batch of uniforms arrived. Eventually, everyone was issued with brand new khaki battledress, followed by new boots, which were very heavy and uncomfortable, and in many cases a bad fit. The new uniforms lifted the morale of the men but the shortage of equipment encountered by the new recruits was almost unbelievable. Four-wheeled trucks were requisitioned from commercial enterprises like farms and haulage businesses. The vehicles were vital in transporting guns and the men for their specialist training as gunners. Guns operating from the Quay had huge wooden wheels measuring about four feet in diameter and were restricted to a speed of eight miles per hour. The clunking sound of these guns moving slowly along the road would break the silence of the day, and could be heard all over the vast area of the Quay.

All the soldiers were billeted nearby. Those already living in Colchester were allowed to be billeted at home. Peter travelled home each day in his car, often accompanied by mates who enjoyed staying at Cross Farm. A particular attraction was the large billiard table in the lounge. A relaxed game of billiards and free-flowing home made wine were rare luxuries.

At the end of four months full-time Army Training, the men had some idea of what life in the army was really like. On 1st September, 1939 Peter was 'Called to Colours'. It was also on this day that the blackout proper began. All the street lights were switched off to avoid helping enemy bombers. The *journey back to Mersea Island was hazardous and seemed unending with the headlights on Peter's car and those on other vehicles extinguished. White lines had already been painted on kerbs and lamp posts to help guide pedestrians and motorists, but it was of little help along the road to Mersea, as there was nothing but hedgerows and grass verges running along the edges of the road. It was an eerie sensation driving along not knowing what was round the next corner. As he approached The Peldon Rose he reminded himself to the danger of an unseen high tide, which may be covering the road to Mersea. Normally, the headlights of the car would pick out the shimmer of the water on the road. He slowed right down until he was sure the road was clear.*

He made just one more return journey to the mainland before the Prime Minister, Neville Chamberlain announced that Britain was at war with Germany. It was the morning of 3rd September at 11:15 that he spoke on the BBC. His voice was tired and strained. Britain had called for an undertaking from Hitler to withdraw his troops from Poland:

"I have to tell you now, that no such undertaking has been received and consequently this country is at war with Germany."

Peter's daily journey to The Hythe finished on 9th September, 1939, when he was posted to Chelmsford Regimental Headquarters at 167 Broomfield Road. Chelmsford was only thirty miles away from home but it was still a sad and emotional day for his Mum and Dad, seeing him load up his car with all his gear. At last he was nearly ready to leave and was realising just how much his home and family meant to him. His heart was sad, but he managed to put on a brave face for the benefit of his parents.

"It won't be long before I am home on leave, Mum," he said, giving her a big hug. His Dad gave him an affectionate handshake as Peter kissed him goodbye.

"Cheerio, mate. See yer soon."

"Don't forget to write," called his Mum.

"I won't, Mum."

His car moved off up Cross Lane, leaving an emptiness that only parents know. The wind was blowing in the right direction for the sound of his car to be heard as it crossed the Strood and left the Island – for how long?

The posting at R.H.Q. Chelmsford lasted only until early March 1940. The next move was to Newmarket in Suffolk. It was here that Peter became 'batman' to a Captain Illingworth, who was at that time attached to the regiment.

Peter had always had it in him to be able to entertain and make people happy. When off duty he made the most of his many talents; stand up comedian, deft with cards and sleight of hand tricks. He could also play the trumpet. One of his party pieces was to accompany 'Boots' Cole on the piano with his carpenter's saw, getting a pretty accurate tune out of the saw. His audience would be amazed and amused as the notes vibrated from the saw. Tonight, the pub was full of people, men and women from the armed forces mingling with the locals. Everyone was trying to forget the war for at least a few hours. Peter was up at the bar buying the first round of drinks for his colleagues, anticipating that it would prepare their mood for the moment when he would perform his 'chase the lady' trick. He put down his glass of beer on the side of the table, allowing enough room to be able to play cards. Taking out his pack of cards he shuffled them in a way that suggested he was an expert. He then selected three cards from the pack - Queen of Hearts (the lady) plus two other cards. Turning to his mates he said,

"Come on, you lot. Let's see who can find the lady."

The three cards, which were face up, were placed face down.

"Now. Keep your eyes on the lady and tell me where she is."

It appeared quite simple to everyone as he swapped the cards around. It was easy! His audience were selecting the moves correctly.

"Come on, now. Who wants to put money on it?"

As soon as the money was placed, The Lady would have disappeared. It became a challenge too good to resist with everyone thinking that they would be a winner. The money he won with his sleight of hand trick bought more rounds of drinks for all. He was described by his mates as, 'A Loveable Rogue'; 'Converter of Virgins', 'Seeker of Peace'.

Many of the men had forty-eight hours leave at the weekend and Peter had promised to drive two of them back, dropping them off at Colchester. However, with petrol rationing he was a bit worried about having enough coupons for the return journey back to the camp. If Uncle Harry was in Mersea at the weekend he would be able to buy some off him. Uncle Harry knew a man who knew somebody that was able to get coupons on the Black Market - at a price, of course. If Uncle Harry wasn't at Mersea at the weekend, he would have a problem. He couldn't let his mates down. Tomorrow night he would be on guard duty. A plan was already hatching his mind. He knew he shouldn't be thinking these thoughts but...

A jerry can of petrol siphoned from one of the parked army tanks could be the answer.

During the course of the day he made sure he looked a busy man, pencil behind his ear, bag of tools in one hand and notepad in the other. It was during the time he was looking busy that he had the opportunity to acquire a piece of rubber hose, ready for tonight's plan. He was feeling more than guilty at the task he had set for himself. The only way he began to feel better was the thought that he wouldn't be letting his mates down. He would be able to give them a lift back to Colchester as he knew neither of them had enough money for their train fare home. As his thoughts moved forward he remembered something that his Auntie Tod often said - 'God helps them that help themselves'. Chuckling to himself he reckoned that the interpretation of this statement was highly debatable.

The time had arrived for him to start his night shift on guard duty. He was in luck. It was a perfect night for 'the job' - very dark with no moon. The only sounds were from night birds and small creatures rustling in the grass. In the far distance, searchlights scoured the skies for enemy aircraft. The night was quiet. He moved to the place where he had concealed the jerry can and rubber tubing. The rest was easy apart from the foul taste in his mouth. It was after he completed his shift on guard duty he met up with some of his colleagues. They had been laughing and joking together when someone commented about his breath smelling of petrol. With one of his tell-tale grins he said,

"Oh, it's probably lighter fuel. I spilt some when filling up my lighter."

Retreating to a safe distance, he was able to pop a sweet in his mouth to conceal the incriminating odour.

The weekend went quickly for Peter. Trying to visit close family, he also managed to make time to visit the new WLA (Women's Land Army) Hostel situated in a very rural setting on the outskirts of Peldon Village. As it was only four miles away from home, he decided to use his bike in order to save some of his precious petrol. It was hard to resist a bit of socialising with some attractive females. The Hostel building had an unimposing appearance from the outside, but the girls said the atmosphere inside was homely and comfortable with all modern conveniences.

Peter got chatting to a very attractive girl. Her name was Edna Dallas, and she said when she first joined the WLA her

*dreams were to be posted on a farm with a sunny bedroom,
which would catch the sun peeping in at dawn. However,
reality set in and her dreams were shattered with her first
billet being at the Hostel in Peldon. Her bedroom was part of
a long dormitory of cubicles that held two double bunks
apiece. Each of the four girls had their own wooden lockers
for their personal possessions. Every morning they were called
at six-thirty. Only twelve hand basins in the wash room and
three bathrooms between forty girls meant a real free for all.
The worst was having only four toilets between the lot of
them, which, on occasions led to a discreet visit to the bushes
outside. There was a spacious recreation and dining room but
unfortunately none of the local men visiting the girls could get
a foot over the threshold. The supervisor in charge of the girls
was a stickler for rules. Her office window had to be passed
before being able to enter the building and she kept a diligent
watch for any male admirers.*

*Peter had a lot of respect and admiration for the WLA
girls. He knew only too well what life on the farms and land
entailed - driving tractors, weeding, pruning, milking cows,
planting, harvesting, as well as mucking out pig sties and cow
sheds. They had undertaken what was regarded as exclusively
male jobs and it wasn't unusual for them to work fourteen
hours a day. Many of the girls were warmly welcomed and
well looked after, but some were unfortunately the object of
derision. However, they were doing a brilliant job helping the
war effort, but as they worked hard, they knew how to play
hard, too. After all, no-one knew what tomorrow would bring.*

*Abberton Village Hall became one of the venues where
people in the armed forces got together with many civilians to
dance the evening away to one of the popular military bands.
The Land Army girls were often seen cycling to Abberton.
Other local venues to host such bands were The Fountain
Hotel and The British Legion Hall, both in West Mersea -
well within cycling distance for the girls. These were*

wonderful evenings of romance and fun organised to relieve the tensions of war. Peter was taking down the dates of the next dances and promised to meet some of the girls when he got another weekend off. Suddenly there was a loud clanging of a bell coming from the Hostel.

"What the hell is that!" he exclaimed.

The girls laughed.

"It's time for us to go indoors!"

As he gazed around he was amazed - but not altogether surprised - to see various couples emerging from the seclusion of the surrounding bushes.

"Well, bugger me. If it don't look like half the Island's here! Yo, boui," he said, moving into the Mersea dialect.

"Yo, boui," was the reply from the other man, grinning from ear to ear.

Regaining his attention, the girls went on to say there was soon to be another dance at East Mersea Golf Club. The club had been requisitioned by the army and taken over by the Royal Artillery. The last dance they organised was a resounding success. It was by invitation only and the girls at the Hostel were their guests. It was well organised with army trucks calling at the Hostel to collect the girls, who all looked very attractive in their uniforms - a fawn cotton shirt, corduroy breeches, green woollen jumper, and lace-up shoes over knee-length woollen socks. Not exactly a ball gown, but just as smart and very safe. Their uniforms were issued without underwear, so they had to use their clothing coupons for attractive underwear, 'just in case.'

Peter reckoned if he managed to get home on the weekend when the dance was on, it was possible he could get an invitation, in which case he would see them there. It was time for the girls to go indoors. He grabbed his bike and rode hurriedly home. He was looking forward to his supper and he wanted to spend a bit more time with Mum and Dad before returning to camp.

CHAPTER 10

Peter's War (ii)
Intensive training, the invasion and VE Day

OVERLEAF: *Physical training. Top left,* GNR FARTHING.
ABOVE: *Peter Farthing, 10th September 1940.*

The surrender of Belgium and dissolution of France made invasion imminent. Mersea Island was closely guarded by The Somerset Light Infantry, who were fully armed and positioned in army huts either end of The Strood to check everyone's identity. Explosives had been secretly laid under The Strood and, in the event of an invasion, an electronic device would be activated to blow up the only road access to the mainland. There were telltale grids on the roadway, similar to drains, where the explosives had been planted. Peter drove up to the sentry box and showed his identity card. A feeling of gloom loomed over him as his car passed noisily over the grids in the road. He knew only too well what lurked beneath the road surface. How long would it be before he returned home again, and would everything be the same?

Rumours that when they returned to camp, 147 Field Regiment would be on the move for extra training were soon proved to be correct. One of the moves was to a tented camp at Wetheringsett, Suffolk. Another station was at Holt in Norfolk. This had been a happy and memorable time, especially as it was there he met the poised, attractive and intelligent Sergeant Dorothy Simms A.C.W. WAAF.

By the early part of January 1942 there was a big Divisional exercise at Thirsk in Yorkshire. The whole Division moved overnight on snow bound roads in temperatures well below zero. The seventy-mile journey to Welbeck for the imaginatively-named, 'Exercise Welbeck' seemed unending. The Regiment continued to move around various training grounds, working hard on course firing, anti-tank firing and other exercises in readiness for war.

The chaps in the camp were in a state of disbelief when Gunner Farthing was granted fourteen days agricultural leave from the twenty-fourth of August to the sixth of September 1942.

"How the bloody hell did you wangle that one, Farthing, you crafty bugger?" said one of his mates.

"Well, it's like this, mate. There's an urgent need for my services at home with the harvesting and a terrible shortage of labour," was his cheerful reply.

Frome was to be the next base for more training exercises, with the Regimental Headquarters billeted in a very nice country house and grounds just outside the Somerset town. Their next move to Lynton in Devon was to give the men a well-earned rest and some relaxation by the sea. The Regiment had been training continually for months, working to a very high standard and sleeping out in all weathers, often for nights at a time. It was no wonder they were becoming exhausted. On the first of November, Regimental Headquarters moved to Cambuslang, south of Glasgow, where more specialised training took place with 105mm self-propelled (SP) guns. These were of American origin and inexplicably known as, 'Priests'. Although Regimental Headquarters was generally responsible for providing the soldiers with knowledge and experience, which to most was sufficiently satisfying, the real action was to be with the batteries and guns.

There was no break in the intensive training, and early in January 1944 a move was made to Rothsay on The Isle of Bute in bleak weather conditions. This was a combined operation with the Royal Navy, where the SP's were loaded onto a Landing Craft Tank (LCT) - an open-ended flat-

bottomed vessel that carried tanks to practice a 'run in' shoot.

Towards the end of the month, yet another move was made to further their skills at the Muir of Ord and the weather was worsening as they continued practice operations on The Moray Firth. By early March the Regiment was thankfully back in England, making a slow convoy down to Weeting Hall, Brandon, Suffolk. The men's moods varied, depending on the task in hand. For the time being, they were happy to be on their way home. It was a long journey, but they made it seem to go quicker by breaking into dubious songs, composed for the Army by the troops. It was as though everyone's life had been put on hold, with no one having any control over what was happening to them. Everyone was waiting for orders that had to be obeyed without dissent or question. Every night saw the fury of enemy bombers trying unsuccessfully to gain supremacy in the skies. The whole nation - as well as the Germans - suspected an allied invasion of Europe. No one knew exactly when, but it would be soon.

A two-week pause for rest, maintenance of vehicles, exchange of SP's that were now twenty-five pounders, instead of the American 105mm, meant that serious war tactics were in place. Anyone getting any leave at this stage would be extremely lucky. But most were hoping desperately to see their families and loved ones before leaving the shores of England.

At the end of March the whole Regiment was moved south to Bournemouth. Regimental Headquarters had been allocated the comforts of The East Cliff Hotel, which had been requisitioned by the War Office, along with other smaller hotels along the East Cliff. Three very big exercises were carried out in quick succession, ' Smash 1, 2 and 3'.

It was a harrowing time for everyone, involving beach landings in Studland Bay. At the end of these exercises, the troops were considered to be ready for actual invasion. Secrecy was of the utmost importance as this extreme game of bluff was being played against the enemy. The whole of

Southern England was sealed off, with security checks on all outgoing and incoming traffic. Families were to be left in ignorance as to where their loved ones were as they moved from the comforts of Bournemouth to a campsite on the edge of the New Forest near Beaulieu in Hampshire.

The weather was good and the fresh green leaves of the ancient countryside offered a welcome seclusion to those living under canvas. It wasn't long before the whole area was filled with troops and weaponry. The job of waterproofing the vehicles had been tackled and completed in extremely good weather and the open-air life seemed to be suiting the men. Peter was on form, using his entertaining talents that included saucy songs, naughty jokes and a few impressions. Camp was completely sealed now and all letters were censored with any inadvertent information being blue-pencilled out. The envelopes were then re-sealed carefully to avoid covering up the affectionate and sometimes risqué abbreviated messages on the outside such as; S.W.A.L.K. "Sealed With A Loving Kiss"; H.O.L.L.A.N.D. "Hope Our Love Lasts And Never Dies" and N.O.R.W.I.C.H. "[K]nickers Off Ready When I Come Home".

The Germans were stepping up the night bombing of Southampton Docks but remained oblivious to the vast concentration of troops camouflaged and hidden close to other major docks all around England. By the end of May, all were fit and ready for battle. On the second of June the vehicles were loaded with fuel, ammunition, food, water and personal kit. No expense was spared and at the last minute, newly designed rimless helmets were issued, replacing the old pre-war tin hats, which had rims that tended to get in the way, especially when working in the close confines of a tank. The new helmets were far superior and offered more protection.

Midnight on the second of June saw the Regiment sitting down for their last meal in the camp. Afterwards, unit by unit *departed on a slow journey through dark country lanes toward the embarkation point at Hope Beach, arriving at sunrise. The guns and vehicles were loaded onto the waiting LCT's, covered with camouflage netting then moved slowly off to sit in Southampton Water. The organisation of the Regiment embarking on an armada of over two hundred ships, all at the right time, was a strategic masterpiece.*

Only Gunner Farthing was to know the reason for him being delayed from participating in the early D-Day landings. He didn't embark until the twelfth of June (D + 6). One advantage was that by this time the strong winds and high seas had eased. It was now calm, fine and sunny. No amount of training could have prepared them for the magnitude of the horror they encountered in battle after leaving the home waters of England. These were all young men, who had never been in action before. They were fighting for real, rapidly gaining experience that no training could re-create. Peter found himself amongst many heavy battles. One in particular always stayed in his memory.

They were under heavy gunfire. Peter ran to take cover, jumping into a trench with other soldiers. As he raised his head, he witnessed the fatal shooting of his mate. Peter began shouting - blaming himself. He should have grabbed him; warned him of the danger. His instinct was to get to him and pull him to safety, but he couldn't. He was being restrained by the other men. He could do nothing but cry. He knew the only way to survive was to pull himself together. He reached into his left-hand pocket, where he kept a small hip flask containing whiskey. With badly shaking hands he managed to unscrew the top and get the flask to his trembling lips. By now his whole body was shaking. Some of the liquid ran down his chin, but the whiskey he managed to swallow had the instant calming effect he had craved.

* * *

The first day of August saw another day of very hard fighting with the enemy well entrenched and using for the first time a Jagd Panther, a type of self-propelled gun with armour that proved virtually impenetrable. And it wasn't only soldiers who were suffering in this terrible war. As each successive village was razed to the ground, the surrounding green fields were littered with the bodies of cattle that had been in the line of fire from artillery barrages. It was a sad sight for anyone to see. The battles raged on. It was during the night in August that the Regimental Headquarters was shelled, but they were fortunate not to have any serious casualties. On this night, Peter could have been a victim of German gunfire if it hadn't been for his 'lucky' hip flask, still being carried in his top left-hand pocket. He really thought he had 'copped it' as he felt the thud against his chest. Later he would say it wasn't just luck. It was, he insisted, 'a bloody miracle'.

Fierce fighting continued everywhere. Battles raged on land, sea and in the air with large loss of life and appalling casualties. The Americans and Canadians were also suffering heavy losses, battling by our side for world peace.

November 1944 saw so much rain that the tanks were getting bogged down, and by the thirtieth they had to come out of action, with the Regimental Headquarters moving back to Geverick. At least the bad weather forced a short but well needed and deserved rest.

Christmas was extremely cold with temperatures well below zero. Everyone was determined to enjoy the Christmas festivities, including dinner in the traditional English manner, but their thoughts were back home with their families. The early part of January produced weather conditions with twenty-nine degrees of frost and the tanks were all camouflaged with whitewash ready for another operation in snowbound conditions.

As the weeks went by The Allies steadily gained ground, with the Air Force preparing the way. There were times when the Germans offered little or no resistance, often giving themselves up as prisoners of war. At last we were winning.

For the past two weeks it was evident that the 'Bloody War' in Germany was nearly over. Troops could now begin to believe that they had a chance of surviving and that they would soon be seeing their families and dear old England again. On the evening of 4th May, at nine o'clock, a message came through from Brigade Headquarters to say that Germany had surrendered unconditionally and hostilities would cease at eight a.m. on the 5th May. The news was received with an explosion of flares and Verey lights to start celebrations that lasted most of the night. The weariness of war had been replaced with the excitement of V.E. Day.

Before 413 Regiment moved on to Hanover, they spent several days digging vehicles out of the mud - where they had become bogged down during the final advances - and more victory celebrations.

Hanover was a very sorry sight, with seventy five percent of the city reduced to rubble. But there were still about three hundred thousand inhabitants left, in addition to forty-five thousand displaced people of twenty-one different nationalities. These people, who were all homeless, were a major problem to control as their main interests were focused on food and loot.

The building occupied by Regimental Headquarters contained a cellar, which served as a lock-up for curfew breakers or other undesirables to cool off. Peter found himself gazing at the ruins all around him, wondering about London and home. Would it be as bad as this lot? He could recall the horror of one night's bombing at the beginning of the Blitz in September 1940, when four hundred and thirty East Enders had been killed during a German raid. It was hard to imagine what the losses totalled nearly five years later.

It was strange that he could actually feel sorry for these people now suffering around him, particularly the prisoners working in the cookhouse, serving up tasty, wholesome food to our servicemen. The poor men would watch expectantly, hoping that food would be left on the plates, so that they could take it home later to their starving families. Knowing how much the prisoners needed the food, our soldiers always left some on the plates.

The strict rules prohibiting anyone serving in the Armed Forces from fraternising with the Germans stopped any sort of socialising - particularly with female company. And with a curfew imposed, Hanover turned into a ghost town at night.

The 11th June took the Regiment north again to Kiel. When they arrived, it was no surprise to see the same sort of devastation that they had witnessed in Hanover. Buildings were reduced to rubble with many just holding on under crumbling walls. The harbour was littered with half-submerged boats, including a battleship. It was altogether a sad and sorry sight, but these were the throes of war. It was in Kiel that Peter caught up again with his mate, Bombardier Ken Markland. Ken had seven days leave and was about to return to England.

"Ken, mate - I've just got one more picture to take on this film in me camera. If you stand in front of that tank over there, I'll take a photo of you as a souvenir of the war."

"All right," said Ken as he posed for his picture. The camera clicked as the picture was taken. Peter wound off the film, handed it to Ken and said,

"Here, mate, do you mind getting it developed in England for me?"

He handed Ken the film, together with some money to pay for it to be processed.

"See you in a week's time," said Peter with his cheerful grin.

After Ken had left, he began to wonder about 'that grin' of Peter's. He had seen it many times before, especially when he was getting up to something, or about to do a card trick. Instinctively, he felt in his pocket where he had put the film and money. He had been well and truly had. The money was in German Marks. Why hadn't he been more observant! Peter was known for his tricks. Ken got Peter's film developed and printed and found that his photograph wasn't on the film. Was the thing a complete set-up, or had the film run out without Peter realising it? Ken never knew, and Peter never said.

"He was just such a likeable rogue," said Bombardier Markland forgivingly some years later.

Gunner Farthing returned to England on 19th August 1945. He was one of the lucky ones. Soon he would be re-united with his family with no visible scars. He would, however, carry in his mind the horrors of what he had seen and endured during the war for the rest of his life.

He suffered occasional nightmares of the war until the day he died.

CHAPTER 11

School milk, semolina and 'Blakeys'

OVERLEAF: *On the left is the school, pictured looking west.*
ABOVE: *To the right of the picture, a Belisha beacon stands on the opposite side of the road, facing the school.*

For some time the grown ups at home had been talking about me starting school. I listened with interest, not too sure when it was all going to happen. Cousin Dorothy attended the West Mersea County Primary School in the village but a private school had been discussed as I would get more attention and Mum believed that I would be taught to speak nicely.

"Mum, please let me go to school with Dorothy – I'll know more people there."

"You will do as you are told, young lady," was the reply.

Looking at Dad I appealed to him,

"Please Dad, let me go to the same school as Dorothy."

He looked over at Mum,

"Well dear, we shall have to weigh up all the pros and cons before we make a final decision."

The decision finally went in my favour. I started at West Mersea County Primary School on Monday, 9th April, 1945 - and it was a day I will never forget.

I was apprehensive and the journey to school by bike was both hazardous and memorable as I rode beside Mum along Waldegraves Lane. Her bike was big and tall and there seemed to be far more bumps and ruts in the lane than I remembered. And my little bike seemed to be continuously drawn into Mum's bike, with me wobbling dangerously close to her front wheel.

"Pixie, for goodness sake watch what you are doing or you will have us both off."

Mum spoke in a rather cross voice. I was close to tears. As

we approached the main road my fierce concentration just about kept the tears away. Then suddenly I did it again. I wobbled so much that Mum had to jump off her bike to avoid a collision.

"Any more of this nonsense young lady and you will walk to school!" said Mum.

I eventually managed to steer a straight course until we reached the school, despite the butterflies in my tummy. We leaned our bikes against the brick wall and went to the infants' classroom where we were greeted by the teacher, Miss Aldridge. She had a kind face, wore no make-up and her forehead was so shiny it might have been polished. Her cheeks had a fresh, rosy shine as well, and her plaited hair was wound all round her head.

"Come along dear and sit at the desk next to Joan while I write your name and address in the register," said the teacher.

I did as I was told, glancing sideways at Joan who I thought I had seen before. Suddenly I noticed Mum making her way to the door - without me.

"She can't leave me here," I thought to myself in a mad panic so I jumped up from my seat and grabbed Mum's arm.

"Don't go! Please don't leave me!" I yelled, but she ignored my pleading. She pulled her arm away. I could not believe that my Mum was leaving me in this awful room full of children I didn't know. And worse still, they were all staring at me.

Mum lifted the latch of the heavy wooden door as my screams got louder and louder. Miss Aldridge grabbed my arm and pulled me back but I still managed to grip the door. I had to get to Mum. I couldn't stay in this room, I just couldn't. But the door closed with a bang as Mum disappeared. I was now imprisoned. My fear turned to anger. As I kicked out at the teacher, my new school shoes came into contact with her shins. I felt ashamed at my actions - and now my finger was hurting.

"Look what you've done to my finger," I said, holding up

my grazed hand for her to see.

"It's only a small graze, I expect it got caught on the door. Now come and sit down at your desk. It won't be long before playtime."

I had lost the battle. I sat down trembling and feeling slightly sick. I glanced at Joan, the girl I was sitting next to, and remembered where I had seen her before. It was Joan Cornelius from the cycle shop in Kingsland Road. Dad called it "Snuffy's". She sat next to me sobbing silently. I began to feel sorry for Joan as tears rolled down her cheeks. My own problems seemed to fade away as I tried whispering to her.

"Are you staying for dinner?"

"No, Joan whispered back," shaking her head vigorously at the same time.

"Quiet please!" said the teacher raising her voice and looking in our direction.

I was pleased that Mum had arranged for Dorothy to accompany me back to Nanna's for dinner today. I had already made up my mind that I didn't like school. I was looking forward to the dinner break and hadn't really been paying attention to what the teacher was saying. Suddenly there was the sound of chairs scraping the floor and everyone seemed to be on their feet except me and Joan. They were all making for the door. I turned to a boy and asked him,

"What's happening now?"

"It's playtime silly," he replied.

Joan and I jumped up, pushing our little chairs under the table. Dorothy was waiting outside our classroom door and she explained that we had fifteen minutes playtime each morning and afternoon. I was overwhelmed by the range of games and the varied age groups. Most of the younger children remained in the small playground, which was allocated for the use of the infants.

But under Dorothy's wing I ventured into the large playground. The scene I witnessed there was awesome. I had never seen so many young people shouting, laughing and playing games together. I was mesmerised and excited about being able to participate. My attention was drawn to two older girls turning a long skipping rope. There was one girl skipping in the middle and a number of girls were gathered round singing,

There's somebody under the bed
Whoever can it be?
It makes me so frightened
That JENNY comes in with me.

Whoever's name was called would run in and start skipping. The song would then be repeated and another girl would swap places. As I gazed with interest at the skipping Dorothy grabbed hold of my hand.

"Come on Pixie, I'll show you where the lavatories are before the whistle goes."

I followed her across the playground to the long brick building where there were six lavatories. A couple of them were very small and low, especially for the infants. The others were larger but there was one at the end which was rather posh with a wooden seat that lifted up. This was for teachers only. They were all flush toilets, activated by pulling the long chain with a handle dangling on the end. The seats were horrible. The wooden seats didn't continue all round the toilet pan. There was a space in the middle at the front that left the white porcelain pan showing.

"What are the seats like that for?" I asked Dorothy.

"So's you don't wee on it," said Dorothy.

"Oh I see," I replied, wondering why anyone would wee on the seat.

Suddenly a whistle was blown. Then silence. All the noise and shouting had mysteriously stopped. The second blast of the whistle brought back the sound of children's feet running to their classroom doors where they waited in pairs for the teacher to open the door to let them in. I now felt more comfortable about going into the classroom than I did when Mum left me first thing that morning.

I cast my eyes around the entrance lobby which led directly into our classroom. Our hats and coats hung on the pegs. I could see my own hat and coat hanging there and it made me feel good to see something familiar. I went straight to my seat and sat down. Joan followed me, still looking rather sad. I gave her a cheerful grin but she just looked at me soulfully. Sitting at my desk, I noticed a crate of tiny milk bottles which stood by the teacher's desk. On top of the desk was a large box of drinking straws. I watched as Miss Aldridge bent down and lifted the crate of milk onto her desk, then pushed the perforated cardboard tops of the bottles with her thumb, allowing a nice round hole to appear for the drinking straws to be put into the bottles of milk. The class was beginning to get noisy.

"Quiet please, children," said the teacher, "I want you to quietly walk to the front of the class and get your bottle of milk, then return to your desk and drink your milk without making a noise." The class began to shuffle toward the teacher's desk.

"After you have finished drinking please put the empty bottles back in the crate."

There was one young boy right at the front of the class who kept putting his hand up. Miss Aldridge didn't seem to be taking much notice of him so he stood up letting his chair drag along the floor. As he stood there I could see that the seat of his trousers had worn rather thin, showing signs of greying underwear underneath. I really felt quite sorry for him. Our teacher bent down to listen to him and I heard her say in a rather loud voice,

"No you may not have the leftovers."

However there was an unopened bottle left in the crate,

which Miss Aldridge said he was allowed to have at dinner-time provided he behaved himself for the rest of the lesson.

After my first day at school, I started catching the school bus which stopped at the corner of Chapmans Lane, just half a mile from where I was living. It had already picked up the children whose homes were in East Mersea. Mr. Hucklesby, one of the schoolteachers, also travelled on the bus so the boys and girls were generally fairly well behaved.

There weren't many to get on at my stop, just the Parkins who lived in what was once The Workhouse, now called The Workhouse Cottages, and Brian Whiting who only had to walk a few yards to the bus stop. His Mum and little brother Colin would wave goodbye at the front gate.

Among the people already on the bus would be the Bibbys, the Dooleys, the Davis children, Rodney Hucklesby, the Riches, the Potters, Roma Fulcher from The Dog and Pheasant pub and Eddie and Ruby Diggins. Eddie always wore heavy black leather ankle boots which were very much like army boots. When he walked along the centre of the bus, the clomping sound of the metal 'Blakeys' on his boot soles could be heard all around the bus and even after arriving at school the sound could still be heard across the playground. He was also good at running and then sliding on the hard surface, sending sparks up from his feet.

If he ever felt threatened by anyone he would say: "I'll put a boot up your arse." That was usually more than enough to keep him from harm.

I settled down to school life remarkably well, even consenting to school dinners which were served up in the back room at the British Legion. The food was cooked on the premises, supervised by the cook, Elsie Whiting, who did an excellent job with the limited food that was available due to rationing.

There was always an expectant queue of hungry pupils wondering what they would be getting today. Mondays was never a surprise as every Monday was stew. Today being Tuesday, our imagination could be stretched - would it be real potatoes or would it be 'pom'? Food was now being served - it was pom (powdered potato) covered with a ladle of mince and carrots, a square of crusty pastry and chopped cabbage.

"What's for afters?" asked one of the boys.

"Semolina," replied Jean Lark, one of the dinner ladies.

I was pleased to hear about the semolina, as it was one of my favourites, especially with a dollop of red jam in the middle. Another favourite was Mrs Whiting's chocolate pudding with white sauce. The dessert I least liked was prunes and watery custard.

After dinner we walked back along the Barfield Road pathway to school, passing the school gardens and crossing the road at the familiar landmark of two rows of metal studs secured in the road. The metal orange balls of the Belisha beacons stood proudly on top of tall poles striped with black and white at intervals of about a foot. They were a source of attraction to some of the boys who on occasions would have a moment of devilment and jump up and try to hit them with their hands. The old metal beacons and the studs in the road were later removed and never replaced.

CHAPTER 12

A harsh lesson, Peter demobbed and a new house

OVERLEAF: *Our new house 'Craigmore' in Seaview Avenue.*
ABOVE: *The way 'Lynton' was when first built in 1907.*

After the mid-afternoon break we were all settling down waiting for the teacher to start the next lesson. As soon as I saw the oblong wooden boards being brought from the cupboard I knew that we would be making plasticine models. The teacher gave the boards to one of the boys sitting in the front of the class and asked him to hand one round to each pupil. Next came the large biscuit tin which contained enough round balls of plasticine for everyone in the class. Miss Aldridge was in charge of handing these out. When everyone had their balls of modelling dough she then gave out instructions for the lesson.

"Now children, I want you all to use your imagination, and make something to do with a birthday party."
Everyone started to chatter at once.

"Quiet now," said the teacher.

I wondered what to model my dough ball into. Then it came to me - I would make a cat. Carefully, I modelled the cat by rolling up a large ball of dough for its body, then a small round ball for its head. The ears and tail were more difficult. The whiskers were made by marking lines with the end of a pencil. It seemed to take quite a while to perfect my cat but it was obvious what it was. When I looked round to see what the rest of the class had done, I wasn't too impressed. I thought my cat was the best piece of work there. One girl had done a birthday cake with candles on it, which also looked very good, though.

"Please put your work on your boards and I will be round

to see what you have all done," said the teacher.

While she was looking at all the work, I began to wish that I had got some plasticine at home. Mum wouldn't let me have any as she said it was too messy and would get into the thick pile of our carpet. The teacher was now standing at my desk.

"Why have you decided to model a cat?" she asked.

"Because I would like to have a kitten when it's my birthday," I replied.

"Well it's a very nice cat. Well done," said the teacher.

After Miss Aldridge had seen everyone's work and commented on what they had done, she told us all to roll the plasticine back into balls so that it could be put away into the large tin. As I rolled my dough into a ball I again began to wish that I had got some plasticine at home. I wanted it so badly that I decided to halve my ball, making it into two balls. Looking quickly at Joan who was pre-occupied with rolling up her ball, I quickly put half of my ball in the pocket of my navy knickers - it was a tight squeeze as I already had my small white hanky in the pocket. I knew how wrong this was. I had never done anything like it before and it was making me feel very anxious but there was no turning back now. Miss Aldridge was moving from desk to desk, collecting up the plasticine balls. Soon she would be at my desk to collect my half size ball - what if she says something? What shall I do? My mind was in turmoil. Joan's ball was just going in the tin. Mine was next.

"That's rather small," said the teacher.

"Yes, I know. It was small when you gave it to me," I lied, feeling very hot and uncomfortable.

Nothing more was said, I had got away with it, and now I had some plasticine to play with at home. That evening I was playing quietly on the floor rolling out my plasticine on the hard cover of one of my books when Mum said to me,

"Is that plasticine you are playing with, Pixie?"

"Yes, Mum, it is," I answered sheepishly.

"Where did you get it from?" she asked.

"Nowhere," was my stupid reply.

"What do you mean, 'nowhere'? Did it come from school?" she asked.

I nodded without speaking.

"Did you take it?" she asked

Very guiltily, I again nodded.

"You know better than to do a thing like that," she said.

"I am sorry," I replied.

"You can give that plasticine to me right now."

I handed over my guilty secret, feeling quite relieved that it was all now in the open. Little did I know what was going to happen to me the next day.

It was time for me to leave to catch the bus for school. Usually, Dad would give me a ride on his crossbar to the bus stop, however, this morning Mum was getting her coat on and said she would be going to the bus with me. We both walked up to Waldegraves Lane and waited for the bus at the corner of Chapmans Lane. Few words were exchanged and when the bus arrived I expected Mum to return home. But instead she followed me on to the bus and sat down.

I found this all very puzzling but common sense prevailed and I kept quiet. I couldn't quite fathom out what was going on - I knew Mum wasn't happy. I didn't have to wait too long to find out. The bus arrived at the school where all the school children got off. Mum got off too. I went into the school premises with the rest of the pupils, leaving Mum at the gate. It wasn't too long before the whistle went and everyone lined up to go into the classrooms. I hung my coat up on the peg in the lobby and made my way to my desk.

As everyone sat down waiting for the register to be called, the door to the classroom opened and in walked Mum. I began to feel both nervous and embarrassed. What was she doing here? She walked straight up to the teacher's desk and spoke quietly to the teacher. The whole of the class was watching, wondering what would happen next. Then, I watched her put her hand in her right-hand pocket, and pull out a small, round ball of plasticine.

I wished the floor would open and swallow me up. The worst part was still to come. Miss Aldridge called me to her desk, Mum handed me the ball of plasticine and told me to apologise for what I'd done. Everyone's eyes were on me, waiting for me to say something. I handed over the incriminating object, saying how sorry I was, and returned to my seat. My Mum walked proudly along the length of the classroom, lifted the latch of the heavy oak door, which closed behind her with a loud bang. I knew in my heart that I would never again take anything that didn't belong to me. I had been well and truly punished - and so had Mum, who was a very proud and honourable lady.

I soon realised that life in our household was much easier than it was for many of the other children at school who seemed to have quite a hard home life. Sadly, many were poorly dressed and at times were badly behaved.

I very much wanted to be friends with everyone - both boys and girls - but it didn't always happen that way. There were occasions when I felt that they were laughing at me. I had always called Mum, 'Mummy,' and my Dad, 'Daddy'. Today in the playground, I shouted to Dorothy,

"Mummy's meeting me after school."

I soon realised that some of the children were laughing at me but I couldn't quite understand why. Then, I was mimicked by one of the boys, saying,

"Mummy's meeting me after school", at the same time giggling.

Still puzzled, I asked Dorothy, "Why are they laughing

at me?"

"It's because you call your Mum and Dad, Mummy and Daddy," said Dorothy.

"Oh, what have I got to call them, then?" I said.

"Well, Mum and Dad would be better," she replied.

I felt really humiliated by their taunting and decided there and then that my parents would have to be called Mum and Dad from now on. I wasn't quite sure how to approach them. It would be strange to say Mum and Dad but I was a proper schoolgirl now and I needed respect from the other kids in the playground. It wasn't too hard to get them to agree to the change, especially when I explained that all the other children called their parents Mum and Dad and I wanted to be the same.

I soon developed the social skill of being able to befriend, play and socialise with all the kids at school. It didn't matter whether they were 'Posh' or 'Poor' I just wanted to enjoy the experience of their company and join in with their games.

After Daddy Peter was demobbed, he spent a few weeks adjusting to home life again, enjoying the peaceful surroundings of Waldegraves House and the comfort of Waldegraves Cottage where we had been living for a large part of the war years.

It was now time for a change as the cottage wasn't really big enough for all of us to live together comfortably. Daddy Peter was becoming restless and wanted to start work. He was talking to Dad about various options he was considering when Dad replied,

"Well boy, I don't see no reason why you shouldn't set up on your own. You know what ya doin, you've got all your qualifications and there's certainly a need on the island for building and repairs."

"Dad, I want to find my own house, something with a nice

size garden for Dot and the children."

"Well boy, when you lot go, me and Ada and Pixie won't want to stay on here. We shall look for something else as well."

"We've got particulars of one of The Dormy Houses down East Mersea," continued Daddy Peter, "Dot wants to go and have a look at it."

Dad had the last word.

"Goun have a look at it mate but them places weren't built to last, they were jest weekend and short holiday homes for golfers using the golf course. They're only lathe and plaster. To my mind, not a good investment."

Mum's brother Arthur had recently sold his bakery business in Hatfield and had returned to Mersea for his retirement. He'd decided to invest his money in property on the island and while he was visiting Nanna Saye, he saw Mum and told her about the latest properties he'd purchased. They were both large houses and would soon be going up for rent.

Craigmore was a detached property in Seaview Avenue and the other was a semi-detached house in Fairhaven Avenue, the two roads running parallel down to the sea.

Mum immediately thought of Peter and Dorothy and how they might be interested in one of the two houses. When she returned home, she told Peter and his father about Uncle Arthur's two houses.

"Mum, I know you mean well but I really want to own my own property," was Peter's response.

"How do you know that Arthur won't sell the property at a later date once you get established with yer business?" asked Dad, "I think you should at least take a look at them. You never know."

"P'raps you're right dad. It won't hurt to go and have a look."

They went to see Uncle Arthur who gave them the key to

look at the four bedroom semi in Fairhaven Avenue. Although it needed work done, Peter and Dot agreed it was just what they wanted, an ideal place to bring up the family.

An agreement was made on the rent with an option to buy at a later date. The house was named 'Lynton'.

The next big surprise came when Mum and Dad decided to rent 'Craigmore' – just a footpath's walk away from Peter, Dot and the two grandchildren.

CHAPTER 13

Electric light, flush toilets and the price of being nosey

OVERLEAF: *Terry Farthing in his tweed coat and plimsoles.*
ABOVE: *Jim Farthing spraying the strawberries.*

At last the day arrived for us to move into the new house. I had very mixed feelings of sadness and excitement. I was sad to think that I would never again be sleeping in the comfortable and safe surroundings of the bedroom at Waldegraves Cottage that had accommodated me for the past few years. I knew I would miss the familiar sound of the cockerel crowing as he woke us up in the mornings and as I stood there gazing around the sitting room, the emptiness stirred my emotions and nearly reduced me to tears. But then the thought of a new house and the excitement of the move cheered me up. The promise of a proper bath with hot and cold running water and a toilet that flushed at the pull of a chain was enough to make anyone excited. No more oil lamps - electric light immediately available at the click of a switch - and we even had our own telephone! Yes, 'Craigmore', our new house in Seaview Avenue, would be alright.

The garden was large, stretching into a vast orchard of fruit trees. I knew Dad had plans for the vegetable garden and also wanted to plant raspberry canes and strawberry plants. It wouldn't be long before we were self-sufficient again.

Our move was now to be a shared experience. I think that Mum and Dad must have been destined to share whatever they had with other people. Just as we were due to move to the new house, Mum received a letter from her sister, Auntie Lily, to say that misfortune had struck their family a terrible blow. The business venture that Uncle Harry was involved in had gone badly wrong - he had lost virtually everything including the house they lived in.

Uncle Harry was notorious for negotiating deals that 'couldn't go wrong' and many of them didn't. In fact, some had proved to be very lucrative indeed but their family lifestyle went up and down like a yo-yo depending on the stability of his business at the time.

Mum and Dad felt that they should offer Harry and Lily, and their children Bill and Muriel, the opportunity of living with us, just until they were on their feet again.

The offer was accepted gratefully, with the whole family arriving in a matter of days. One of the sacrifices that had to be made due to the extended family was that I now had to share a bedroom with Mum and Dad. This was something I kept to myself as I felt a bit embarrassed about it all. I had to try and forget about having my own room with Dorothy coming over to sleep at weekends as this certainly wasn't going to happen for some time.

It wasn't long before we got to know most of our neighbours and it was a pleasant surprise to discover how many young people lived close by. There was Carol and Mary Fulcher next door - both older than me, but very friendly. Next to the Fulchers was the Straw family. Jean Straw was about my age. She had a younger brother John and an older sister called Geraldine. Opposite the Straws lived the Wakefields. Susan Wakefield was about my age and she had an elder sister, Judy. (Judy was ill and sadly died).

As for us, two families living together seemed to be working out reasonably well, with just an occasional difference of opinions. It was good having Auntie Lil around as she was able to encourage Mum to let me have a bit more freedom and take part in more activities with other young people. Mum and Dad were very protective as far as I was concerned. However, this was changing gradually as I was slowly liberated into a world of adventure.

* * *

Carol and Mary, the two girls from next door called for me in the mornings and we cycled to school together. We began through the folley that led into Fairhaven Avenue. We would then cross the unmade road, hitting the bump on the other side which would bounce us off our saddles if approached too quickly. If there had been any rain during the night, we would encounter large puddles which reached over the top of our pedals. I remember the days when it had been raining heavily all night, giving us a 'deep puddle day'. Carol cycled ahead of us, ploughing through the deep water at the same time lifting her feet high off the pedals to avoid getting her shoes wet. We did the same thing, laughing and shouting as we bumped along the rough tracks that overlooked arable fields bordered by hedges and blackberry bushes.

The first house we came to stood on the corner of Empress Avenue and was owned by the Winches. It was called 'Bracken' and had the most beautiful gardens. It was here that the track widened into an unmade road suitable for motor vehicles to pass through to Prince Albert Road. Next we passed 'Meadow Croft', where Michael and Malcolm Wheeler lived. A sharp right-hand turn into Queens Ville Road took us past the eerie derelict building called Gorse Cottage - a sad reminder of the war and the sort of damage that was caused by 'The Doodlebug'.

We had to form a single file now as the track narrowed down to just a footpath. We followed the narrow track past the sandpit, emerging again in to the unmade Queen Anne Road. We raced down the steep hill into Rainbow Road, ringing our bells as we passed number one to let Dorothy know we were about. We approached the busy main Kingsland Road with care, heading left down to the school. This unsupervised journey of fun was far removed from the journey I had been used to on the school bus.

Daddy Peter, Auntie Dot, Susan and Terry were living at 'Lynton' in Fairhaven Avenue which was only a short distance through the folley, making it easy for Mum, Dad and myself to 'just pop in', which happened all the time. The moves were specially planned so that the two Farthing families were living within easy reach of each other. Mum now had two grandchildren, but Terry had a special place in her heart. It was as though she had her own son all over again.

It was a lovely sunny morning and I was playing ball against the wall of the house, when Mum called, interrupting my game.

"Pixie, I want you to go and collect Terry. Dot would like me to have him for the morning and he's going to stay and have dinner with us."

"Do I have to?" I replied.

"Yes please. It's time you stopped thumping that ball against the wall. It will give you something else to occupy your mind."

I did as I was told and was walking quickly back home through the folley with Terry trotting by my side. As we emerged into Seaview Avenue I could see there was a funeral procession moving very slowly up the avenue. Taking hold of Terry's hand I pulled him back gently to the edge of the bushes where we could wait unobtrusively for the cortège to pass.

The men in top hats and tailed coats looked a sombre sight as they marched at a dignified pace up the road. I am not sure how it happened but as I bent to catch hold of Terry's hand, I realised to my horror that I was on my own.

No Terry! Where was he? I glanced behind me and to the side of me - I was in a sudden panic. Where could he be? Then, as I looked up the road, trailing behind the men in their morning suits and top hats was Terry, trying very hard to imitate their slow, precise movements, swinging his little arms

134

up and down wearing his scruffy plimsolls with no socks and tweed coat - which Auntie Dot insisted he put on in case the weather changed - hanging half off his shoulders.

With a few quick steps, I reached out to catch hold of his arm but the little terror wriggled away from me and continued with his marching. I made another grab at his coat and this time successfully held on to him and dragged him back on to the footpath where we walked the short distance home. When I arrived indoors and told Mum what had happened and the embarrassment that Terry had caused, she said,

"Well, if you had been looking after him properly in the first place it wouldn't have happened."

He could never do anything wrong. I might have guessed it would be my fault. I always seemed to take more than my fair share of the blame. However, there were times when blame could well have been directed at me, especially when I allowed myself to get involved with some of the older kids in the street. I was only allowed to join the gang if I promised to keep my mouth shut. After all, I was the youngest there.

One afternoon we all met and decided to investigate an old shed which stood at the rear of a spare plot of ground stretching between the Straws' house and 'Lenora' where the Fulchers lived. The land was very overgrown with shrubs and blackberry bushes but there was a rough path which we managed to help each other through, pulling back brambles as we went along. When we reached our target it appeared to be a sort of summer house standing strangely alone - not even in a proper garden. We found the door unlocked and it opened after a sharp tug on the handle.

We all looked inside and found there were old tools going rusty, deckchairs and various bits and pieces. There were even tatty curtains hanging up at the window. One of the older girls thought we should clean it up and even find some better curtains from home. This could be our secret meeting house!

"Ssh!" said one of the girls, "I think I can hear voices."

We all stood silent and apprehensive, not wanting to be caught. After a few minutes of silence we decided it was safe enough to move on. We went along the rough pathway, back on to the road.

"Hey, mate, I know where there's another one of them summer sheds," said one of the boys.

"Where?" asked Carol.

"Go round the edge of the next two cornfields and it's all overgrown at the bottom of the gardens. I saw it when I went rabbiting with me Dad."

Tomorrow would be the day to explore our second derelict summer house.

We all met up at the agreed time of four in the afternoon. 'Strict Secrecy' was our motto. We moved quietly and carefully in to the 'backfields' that backed directly onto the gardens in Seaview Avenue. After walking further down the fields, we came to a tall boundary hedge which had several gaps in it, making it relatively easy to see what was hidden on the other side.

The second summer house came in to view – much larger than the one we discovered the day before. There was a verandah with steps that led up to the door. Again, the door opened easily. We went inside, noting that as well as the same sort of items stored in the other summer house, there were old chairs, suitcases and a large wooden chest. I felt quite uncomfortable about my friends rummaging in this property, although I shouldn't think that it had been used or touched for years - probably since the start of the war.

The next thing that happened to us was the worst thing that could happen to anybody. Someone - I can't remember who as I was too distressed to think straight - decided to open one of the large chests. The metal catches on the chest had become rusty over time and were refusing to budge. A few knocks with an old hammer soon released the catches enough for the lid to be prised open. There was a gasp of horror as we all looked on.

Inside the chest were human bones. The skeleton looked complete. The lid of the chest was shut with a bang. We were all frightened out of our wits and ran terrified from the scene of horror. Silently and quickly we ran through the fields to the safety of the main road. Sitting in a row along the raised curb of the pavement, a very dejected group of kids discussed what should be done about what they had witnessed.

"I think we should keep our mouths shut," said one of the older boys, "We shouldn't have been there in the first place, and if we hadn't been so nosey we wouldn't have seen anything," he added.

The discussion went on for some time. At one stage the police were mentioned but at the end of the debate it was decided to pretend that the event had never happened. I didn't utter a word the whole time. No one would have listened to me anyway. Eventually, the group broke up and we all went home. I wasn't very hungry at tea time. I just couldn't eat. The horrors of the afternoon kept coming back to haunt my mind. Mum asked if I was feeling unwell.

"No, I'm OK," I replied.

Bedtime arrived and I got into bed with a feeling of fear and unrest - I knew I wouldn't be able to sleep, there was too much on my mind. For once, I was pleased to be sharing my parents' bedroom. Long after Mum and Dad got to bed I was still tossing and turning.

"What is the matter with you, Pixie? I'm sure you must be sickening for something," said Mum.

I didn't reply. I just buried my head under the covers, wanting the next day to arrive. I awoke in the morning,

137

having spent a very restless night. I picked at my breakfast but insisted that I was alright for school. I was actually better at school as my mind was taken off my worries. I wonder if any of the others were going through the same torment as I was? I was too scared to even mention it to them.

A few days had passed with me being not quite myself. Mum and Dad were in the sitting room. Mum looked at me and said,

"There's something wrong, young lady and I think it's time you told me and your Dad what's going on."

"There's nothing wrong," I said.

"Yes there is. Are there any problems at school? I know when something's troubling you - you know you can tell me and your Dad, whatever it is. However bad it may seem to you, we would really like to know."

CHAPTER 14

Confession time, Sunday School and Uncle Bert

OVERLEAF: *Peter and Jim, been fishing, at the beach hut.*
ABOVE: *Peter French teaches the children, c.1960s.*
Originally 'Sunshine Corner', later 'The Beach Club'
or 'Sunday School on the Sands'.

The worry of the past days had been weighing down so hard on my mind that I felt I must confide in Mum and Dad. I started right from the beginning, explaining about exploring the first summer house, moving on to the second summer house and the horrors that lurked inside. I waited anxiously for their reactions after I had told them the whole story. Mum was looking at Dad who appeared to have an unmistakable twinkle in his eyes. He looked at me and said,

"Well, I hope you've all learnt a lesson - not to intrude in other peoples' property, however derelict or unwanted it may appear."

"Aren't you cross, then?" I exclaimed.

"Not really, me little ol' love. If only you had told us before, we could have put your mind at rest," said Dad.

He then went on to tell me that the summer house with the fearsome secret belonged to Doctor Grant and the bones in the wooden chest would almost certainly be the artificial kind used by medical students to study human anatomy. The relief I felt on hearing this explanation was overwhelming. I didn't know whether to laugh or cry. I had to justify my behaviour to Mum and Dad.

"I didn't tell you Dad because the others all decided we must keep quiet."

"Mum and I will keep your secret as long as you want us to," said Dad.

* * *

Sunday School had become an enjoyable part of my weekend. Roast dinner was at one o'clock on the dot every Sunday which gave me time to change into my Sunday best clothes and be at the Assembly Hall by two o'clock. My Sunday clothes would include a Panama hat and shiny black patent leather shoes.

Dorothy had dinner with us today and she was dressed in much the same way. We gathered together our Bibles and money for the collection box. Auntie Grace, Mum's sister from London, had just sent me a Bible that had beautiful coloured illustrations. I couldn't wait to show it to Miss Glen, my Sunday school teacher.

The Assembly Hall was just a five-minute walk from our home. As we approached the building we could hear the organ being played by old Mr Brand, accompanying the happy voices singing the chorus of 'Wide, Wide As The Ocean'. We collected our hymn books from Peter French at the door and then went quietly to our seats, joining in the singing with the rest of the congregation.

Doctor Grant was Superintendent at the Assembly Hall. He did most of the preaching and dealt with important things like weddings, baptisms and funerals. Although he was a kindly man, there were occasions when his talks became so boring that some of the girls and boys would get fidgety and begin to giggle. Today, I couldn't wait for him to finish.

At last, Mr Ken Bacon got up to announce the next hymn and lead us with the singing, after which we would all go to our classes. The tiny tots would run to their class where they would be taught - and entertained - by Mrs Daphne Bacon who had a very special way with the young children and could hold their interest with stories from the Bible.

After about twenty minutes of Bible Studies we returned to our seats in the hall where the service was concluded with another hymn. All the young people at Sunday School had been well behaved, maintaining their concentration for well over an hour, so there was a lot of powerful energy ready to burst out when they emerged into the bright sunshine. There was loud shouting and squeals of laughter.

The 'clip-clop' of Uncle Fred Farthing's horse and cart could be heard as it approached Seaview Avenue. Wilfred Bacon and some of the older boys took the opportunity to grab a lift back home down west. Uncle Fred (one of the thirteen Farthings) had been in the navy most of his life. He now worked for his brother Manny at the dairy, A.G. Farthing & Son. Fred was on his return journey from Waldegraves Farm where he had been to collect milk for the following day.

The most memorable events at the Sunday School were the summer outing to Walton-on-the-Naze and the Christmas party and prize-giving. The summer outing occurred at the latter part of the summer season when everyone who attended the Sunday School was taken to Walton for the day. It was always a wonderful day out at the seaside resort with its pier and amusements. Walton wasn't too far away - about twenty-five miles from West Mersea. We all met at the Assembly Hall where one or two Moores' buses from Kelvedon were booked to take us on our trip. Also included would be younger brothers and sisters, mums and dads and even one or two aunties and uncles.

The journey was a happy one with lots of enthusiastic singing and guessing games to keep us amused. On arrival, everyone was at liberty to choose how they would like to spend their day. Children who were not accompanied by their parents were supervised and cared for by their Sunday School teachers.

Everyone spent some time on the pier enjoying the rides and amusements and at the end of the day we all met at a cafe where arrangements had been made for tea. We sat down ready for tea. Dorothy and I sat together while Mum decided to sit with the adults. Sitting opposite us on the same table were some of the older boys.

Our vocabulary was soon to be enhanced to a more adult standard of understanding. What a good job Mum wasn't sitting next to us! Dorothy and I exchanged nudges as we listened to the jokes that the older boys were telling each other. When the waitress wearing her pretty white apron arrived to pour out the tea, she filled the cups. Stephen French, sitting opposite took a sip of his tea and said,

"It's as weak as gnat's piss."

This really made me laugh as I had never heard weak tea called 'gnat's piss' before. After the hilarious tea party, it was time to go to the buses and start the journey home.

The next major Sunday School event would be the Christmas party and prize-giving. There would be games, the wonderful party tea and a magic lantern show where slides were projected onto a big white sheet accompanied by a story told by the man who was projecting the pictures. Last, but not least, came the prizes for good attendance to Sunday School.

I must not forget to mention 'Sunshine Corner' - the Sunday School Beach Club - held on the beach every weekday for a fortnight during the summer holidays. Everyone was welcome with no age limits. A huge banner reading 'SUNSHINE CORNER' was securely attached to wooden posts and dug into the sand so that it could be seen up and down the beach. It attracted a large audience.

The activities at Sunshine Corner included games, competitions, prizes, Bible stories and singing accompanied by an organ, with the organist pumping bellows furiously with his feet whilst playing. The sound of the music and the singing could be heard far along the beach. Every day Susan, Terry and myself would go down to the Beach Club with Judy the dog following closely by our heels. Judy was a white terrier and for most of the time was very obedient and didn't need to be on a lead.

On one particular day we arrived early so the crowd hadn't yet gathered. The waves were lapping on the seashore and the sun shone brightly overhead. It wasn't long before the service began and we started to sing the first song. Everyone was singing at the top of their voices. The sound of the organ rang out and could be heard well into the distance. Suddenly, there was a terrible howling noise. The sweet sound of the organ stopped and the voices tailed away to nothing but the howling persisted. No, it wasn't exactly the Devil at work - it was poor old Judy with her snout stuck in the bellows.

After the dog was rescued we couldn't stop laughing but I don't think that the organisers were too impressed with us or Judy. I'll bet that if God had been looking down on us he would have thought it was better than a Punch And Judy show.

Auntie Lil and Mum had been to see Uncle Bert, their youngest brother, who was ill in a London hospital. When they arrived home they were both very upset and tearful. I sat listening quietly as they told Uncle Harry and Dad the events of the day. When they had asked the nurse when Bert would be coming home she gave them a strange look and asked them to go in to the office where she would like to talk to them. When she heard that they were his sisters, she said,

"Mrs Saye has asked us to keep your brother here at the hospital as she is unable to look after him at home. I'm afraid he doesn't have much time left."

Ada and Lily decided there and then that they wanted their brother at home. They could look after him and make whatever time he had left happy and comfortable. They told the nurse they would be taking him home as soon as they could arrange transport. Then they returned to the ward to tell their brother he would be going home. He was overwhelmed with emotion. They said they would keep him at 'Craigmore' until he was strong enough to return home to his wife Ruby and Donald, their youngest son. Bert was never to know that he wouldn't be returning to his own home.

This conversation about my Uncle Bert was really frightening me. I didn't want him to die. I heard Dad and Uncle Harry agreeing that Auntie Lil and Mum had definitely made the right decision and between them they could offer Bert a good chance to enjoy whatever time he had left.

"Is Uncle Bert really going to die?" I asked Mum, who looked at Auntie Lil and then said,

"We hope not, dear. Perhaps we can make him better."

I really hoped that this would be so.

Transport from the hospital was organised for a couple of days time which allowed for a single bed to be put up in our sitting room and the furniture re-organised. Everything had been done to make Uncle Bert's stay with us comfortable.

His arrival was quite distressing as the journey had been very tiring and he did look desperately ill. He was helped into his bed and after a good night's rest looked much brighter. A week of special care and good food made a noticeable difference to the patient. Instead of wearing a green dressing gown all the time, he was now getting dressed and being his usual funny self, joking and teasing and pulling my leg most of the time. At meal times, Uncle Bert always organised it so that I sat next to him. I know it was so he could good-naturedly torment and tease me.

"Come on, Pixie - you come and sit right here next to me," and he would pull my chair next to him.

Teatime was the time I had to keep my wits about me. Home made jam was always put on the table, usually raspberry or strawberry. I knew the chances of having the sticky jam paper stuck to my face were high, especially when a new jar was started. There were occasions when tea was nearly over and I would think that he wouldn't catch me today. I would be off my guard then, with a slap, he's put the sticky jam paper round my 'Jars' or 'Kisser' as he referred to

146

my jaws and mouth.

He would then laugh and say, "Gotcha!"

If not the jam paper, it would be the cardboard top of the milk bottle covered with thick, yellow cream right in my face.

We used to sit and play 'I-Spy' and if it took me too long to guess what it was, he would say, "C.C". I then had to say "Credda Cook" and he would say with a chuckle,

"Yes, you're right. It's your turn now."

The curious 'C.C.' was in fact someone called Credda Cook, who lived on the Island. Or he might say, "D.R." and I had to say,

"Doctor Ruddock," and I would get the same reply - "It's your turn now."

I didn't know who Credda Cook and Doctor Ruddock were and they certainly were never spied in the room, but they got me my turn at 'I-Spy'.

The other thing that Uncle Bert did was to rename our two black cats. He called the biggest one 'Mrs Royal Pluphin' and the other smaller one just plain 'Mrs Pluphin'. We all got so used to their new names that we forgot what they were called in the first place.

Mr Leggett would call from time to time to see Uncle Bert. He lived in East Mersea where he ran a small clothing business from his home in 'Green Gates' in Shop Lane. His stock and fittings were contained in a lean-to which was built against the side of the house. He carried a good selection of clothes in his van and delivered them to his customers where they were able to choose in the comfort of their own homes.

Uncle Bert had asked Mr Leggett to bring some jackets for him to have a look at. He arrived late afternoon with a choice of jackets for Uncle Bert to consider. It was through this jacket that I realised that my uncle was still very ill. He wasn't going to get better, he was actually going to die. I heard Mum and Auntie Lil talking to Mr Leggett in the kitchen while Uncle Bert was trying on the jacket in the sitting room.

147

"I don't think he will ever wear it," said Mum.

"He's getting weaker by the day," said Auntie Lil, "And he's in a lot of pain."

"Well, mate," replied Mr Leggett, "It doesn't matter if he never gets to wear it. Let him choose whatever he wants - it will be my treat."

They went back in to the sitting room, leaving me feeling quite upset at the conversation that I just had overheard. As Uncle Bert was a happy, cheerful person most of the time, I really thought he was getting better, although I should have realised that the injections he had to keep having were not good news. Meanwhile, Uncle Bert had selected his jacket. Not realising that it was to be a present, he had chosen the most expensive one there.

"Bert, mate, I shall need to have your ration book for the coupons but the jacket's a present from me," said Mr Leggett, "I've been doing quite well recently and can afford to treat a good friend."

Uncle Bert never did get to wear his new jacket. He died at the end of October 1947.

CHAPTER 15

'Berry's Imp', post war shortages and a freezing winter

OVERLEAF & ABOVE: *Bubbles, the musician.*

The sitting room had been changed back to the way it used to be and Uncle Bert's bed was taken away. I found it difficult to ignore the strange thoughts that crept into my head. Some of them were quite frightening. Apart from the ghostly thoughts, there was a horrible void - no more funny jokes, laughter and teasing. This amusing man had lived with us only a few months but he had left me with a lasting memory of his humour and much sadness which I knew would pass with time.

The year of 1947 produced a very hard winter with many falls of deep treacherous snow. We were unable to take our usual route to the village, shops and school via the fields and Prince Albert Road. Instead, the much safer alternative was along East Road. Mum's instructions when I left home were,

"Mind you come straight back home after school before it gets dark - you don't want to encounter 'Berry's Imp', do you?"

"No, Mum," I replied.

Berry's Imp was a strange, ghostly figure that could either be seen sitting on the gate by Moles' Grove (between Empress Avenue and Garden Farm) or on occasions would creep up on unsuspecting people travelling home by bike or on foot. His weird appearance was imp-like, exactly as his name suggested.

Mum and Auntie Maude were walking along East Road one very dark night, when Maude grabbed hold of Mum's arm saying,

"Ada, there's Berry's Imp".

Ada nearly jumped out of her skin, but replied,

"Don't be so daft - course it's not."

Out of the darkness appeared a figure with big, shining eyes. It was approaching them. Then the moon shone from behind a cloud, illuminating the apparition - it was just a lonely goat from a nearby farm. However, many an old Mersea-ite has claimed to have seen the ghost. I didn't want to be one of them, so I would definitely get home before dark.

Coal rationing was already adding to the discomfort of the bitterly cold weather and the shortage of coal meant that everyone was thinking up ideas to lengthen the life of the fire burning away in the grate. The smouldering remains of the coals would be left to go cold, only to be re-used the next day once the fire had been re-lit and got a 'good hold'.

One of Dad's economy drives was to sieve the coal dust that had been shovelled up from the coal-house floor and keep the pieces that were the size of small pebbles in a bucket ready to mix in with the larger coals. The dust would be sprinkled with water and put on top of a roaring hot fire to dampen it down so that it would burn more slowly and help preserve the coal. We had the luxury of wood cut from the trees in the orchard but for many people, wood was gathered from the shoreline of the beach where it had drifted in on the high tides.

The whole country was now feeling the after-effects of the war and rationing so when the American freighter the 'North Eastern Victory' was wrecked on the Goodwin Sands it wasn't surprising to see beachcombers searching all along the coast for the drifting cargo of the ill-fated vessel. The strong south-easterly wind steadily blew the booty off the Kent coast, along the Thames Estuary and into the River Blackwater. Sacks of flour, bales of cotton and casks of lard drifted onto the Mersea shore. It was like manna from heaven with many Islanders receiving and sharing some of the good fortune.

After drifting on the tide, the large sacks of flour formed a hard outside crust but, inside, the flour had been protected and preserved by the crust and the flour was perfect. Our family benefited from flour and a bale of kapok, both useful commodities during the hardship caused by rationing.

It was good news to hear that the entire crew of the North Eastern Victory were saved by the Walmer Lifeboat. The Goodwin Sands are some three and a half miles east of Deal in Kent and are known to be a graveyard to many fine ships and seamen. Still they claim man and vessel, even with modern navigation aids.

After many decades, the wreck of the North Eastern Victory can still be seen on a clear day and identified by her many masts and kingposts. On foggy winters nights she lies unseen as the strange eerie sounds of the bell buoy continue to warn of the dangers of the Goodwin Sands.

The winter snow melted and the warmth of the spring sunshine brought colour back again with snowdrops, daffodils, crocuses and primroses flowering in the hedgerows. We were now able to resume our short cut through the fields to school.

It still seemed strange at number one Rainbow Road since Nanna Saye had passed on to the realms of Heaven. Dorothy and I were now often given the task of putting flowers on Nanna's grave. We walked to the Barfield Road cemetery, clutching our bunches of flowers wrapped with newspaper, deciding that even when people were dead things could still be unfair. Some of the graves had huge amounts of flowers displayed in vases while others had no flowers at all.

Dorothy and I decided to share things a bit more evenly so we would take a few flowers from one of the vases that were full and put them on the graves that had no flowers at all. We would even use a few of Nanna's flowers as well. Our little act of godly benevolence took us quite a while as the watering can had to be filled again and again with water from the tap attached to a large, square post standing at the entrance by the large double gates.

We didn't tell anyone and we greatly enjoyed this secret squaring up of fairness in the cemetery - but we had an idea that our Mums just wouldn't agree with our logic.

Today turned out to be a very strange day. When we returned from our visit to the cemetery we were questioned about the length of time we had taken. Dorothy said quickly,

"We dawdled along, then we talked and we tidied the grave."

"Well, I've been waiting for you to go up to the Mill for me to get some chicken food," Auntie Tod said to Dorothy. "Ask for the wheat or corn sweepings from the floor - it will only cost a few coppers."

"I can't understand why you don't pay the full price and get decent food," Mum said to Auntie Tod.

"You would understand better if you was as hard up as I am," Auntie Tod replied.

"Can I go with her?" I asked my Mum.

"You can if you promise to come straight back," replied Mum.

Soon, Dorothy and I set off up Kingsland Road toward Mill Road. On the corner of Mill Road was Katy White's sweet shop and on the opposite corner was a toyshop. As we looked in the window of the toyshop, I saw a mechanical moneybox. I was so attracted by this toy that I told Dorothy I would go in the shop on the way home.

"I don't think we should go in the shop Pixie - not today, anyway."

We carried on up to the Mill for the cheap chicken food. Dorothy secured her purchase, placing the grain in her shopping bag. As the bag was rather heavy, Dorothy took

154

hold of one handle of the shopping bag and I held the other one. When we reached the toyshop on the corner, I again was attracted to the moneybox in the window.

"Pixie, we have to get home right now," said Dorothy.

Suddenly, the shop door opened and an elderly lady approached us.

"Hello, my dears, is there something that you like in the window?"

We both replied at the same time.

"No," said Dorothy.

"Yes," I replied.

The lady turned to me.

"What is it that you are interested in then, dear?"

"I really like the money box," I said.

"Well, come into the shop and I will get it out of the window for you to see," said the old lady.

"Come on, Pixie, we must get home," Dorothy urged.

Ignoring Dorothy, I walked through the shop door and waited by the counter while the moneybox was got out of the window. I was immediately impressed by what I saw. I had some money in my purse, but not quite enough.

"Just give me what you have got, dear - the rest doesn't matter," said the old lady kindly, as she handed me a paper bag containing my moneybox.

"Come on, we're late," said Dorothy, all agitated, "We'll be in trouble."

However, the old lady was determined to detain us for at least a few more minutes.

"I just want you to see my daughter," said the old lady, guiding me through a door, with Dorothy following behind.

In the room was a young lady playing a piano sitting with her back to us. The music stopped and the pianist turned round to face us. It was the pretty lady I had seen pushing the posh pram along East Road. Her face broke into a lovely smile as she looked at me and just said,

"Hello."

I smiled back. The old lady said: "My daughter is a musician and also a piano teacher. Would you like her to teach you to play the piano?"

I said that yes I would. They both agreed that it could be arranged.

"We really must be getting home now," said Dorothy, pulling me towards the door.

We made our way back into the shop and then to the shop door, which brought us back out into the street. The old lady wished us goodbye and invited us to visit them again, reminding me about the piano lessons. I was pleased with the moneybox and clutched the paper bag carefully in my hand. I couldn't wait to show my Mum what I had bought. My excitement soon turned to dismay at the reaction that we got from Mum and Auntie Tod as soon as they heard we had been in the toyshop. They exchanged looks of anger and dismay. Auntie Tod shouted at Dorothy,

" I told you never to go in the shop - particularly if you have got her with you," nodding in my direction.

Dorothy was near to tears as Auntie Tod dragged her upstairs. I looked at Mum, not understanding the reasons for their actions. I thought if I told Mum about the piano lessons, it may change things - she may feel more kindly to me and the ladies. However, it seemed to make things worse. Mum looked as though she was going to cry.

"Promise me you won't go there again."

I promised with a nod of my head. Dorothy came back downstairs. Her eyes were red, she had obviously been crying. In her hand was a large Bible, which she placed on the edge of the table. Looking straight at me she said,

" I told you we should go straight home, didn't I?"

Why was all the blame being directed at me? Mum then looked at us both kindly, and said,

" I think we should forget about what's happened today.

We won't talk about it ever again."

As I stood there I had a strange feeling that there was something I wasn't being told. Why was Dorothy cross with me, and what had made her cry? I knew it would be foolish to even consider asking any more questions. I concluded that it would be best to forget about what had happened today, just as Mum had suggested. I was still feeling fed up and miserable even after we got back home, so I asked if I could go and see Susan, Terry and baby John.

John was quite a character, full of mischief and growing up fast. Mum said I could go for a while but would expect me home again in about an hour. When I arrived, Susan and Terry were playing with the clockwork train set. They had it all set out on the floor including the station, signals, bridges and rolling stock. John was about to wreck their whole game. I grabbed him just in time but not quick enough to avoid him receiving a quick smack from his sister, Sue.

Susan was always considered 'The Boss'. Although I was older than Susan, she did seem to get her own way most of the time. John only cried for a short while as it was his bath time which seemed to take his mind off the smack. I helped Auntie Dot with his bath and got him dressed in his night-clothes, all ready for bed. It was time for me to go home. I had been gone for more than an hour and would soon be in trouble.

Just as I was about to leave I bumped into Diana Dawson, who lived next door at a house called 'Casablanca'. Diana was a couple of years older than me and an unbelievably attractive girl with dark hair and eyes. She could dance beautifully and was an accomplished acrobat. She later went on to marry the celebrated jazz musician, George Melly. Diana suggested I call for her at the weekend. I said I would, if Mum hadn't got anything planned.

The last time I went out with Diana, we took Susan with us

and happened to go missing all morning in the worst thunderstorm that I had ever seen. There was a large field adjoining Diana's house, occupied by two or three holiday shacks and caravans. After calling for Diana we wandered into the field to look for mushrooms. The sky overhead was getting blacker and blacker as the dark clouds gradually shut out the light. Then, we felt the odd spot of rain on our faces and heard the pitter-patter on the roofs of the old caravans.

"Quick, let's run home," I suggested.

"Don't be stupid, it's best for us to shelter," said Diana, who was fearless about the weather and very adventurous.

She suggested that we crawl under an old tarpaulin covering some wood at the side of one of the vans. As we struggled to crawl behind the protective covering, the thunder and lightning became more and more scary. The storm hovered directly overhead with flash after flash of lightening followed immediately by the heavy bangs of thunder. I began to think that if it didn't stop soon we could all die.

I was so scared that I could feel my legs shaking - the storm seemed to be lasting forever. Gradually, the lightening and thunder began to ease off, the sky became brighter and the sun appeared from behind the clouds although it was still drizzling. As we emerged from under our shelter we saw a beautiful rainbow.

"Come on," said Diana, "We can go home now. I said it would be OK."

I got into real trouble when we got home. Auntie Dot said we should have returned home as soon as it started to rain. Everyone had been very worried about us.

"You won't be allowed to go out with Diana again until you can act more responsibly."

New friends, dustbin cricket and boat trips

OVERLEAF: *Holiday chalets, from left:*
Mersea, Osea, Creeksea and Wallsea.
ABOVE: *The holiday gang. From left: (back row)*
Gertie Matthews, Barry Wicks, Flo Clench, Harold Matthews,
Minnie Wicks, Cynthia Clench, Harry Clench; (front row)
Nanny Matthews, Marion Wicks, Rodney Clench,
David Matthews, Pixie Farthing, Alf Wicks, Colin Matthews.

Mersea, Osea, Creeksea and Wallasea were four holiday bungalows situated between Fairhaven Avenue and Seaview Avenue. These chalets were insignificant to me until 1948. During this year I was introduced to a girl called Marion Wicks. She came to visit us with Auntie Lizzie and Uncle George Chitson - not my real auntie and uncle. Mum said they were a courtesy aunt and uncle - not real relations.

Uncle George was quite short in build, with hair that was fast receding. He had sparkling eyes and a cheerful grin and spoke with a London accent, as did Auntie Lizzie who was very tall, with lovely auburn hair. Uncle George was a talented pianist and entertained us on the piano. They had been friends of our family for many years and had met up with Marion's family during a previous holiday on the Island.

It wasn't unusual for George and Lizzie to take Marion out on excursions and today it was to Mersea Island. Marion and I spent the whole afternoon and evening getting to know each other. I was sorry when it was time for them to leave as we'd got on so well. The good news was that Marion was going to be returning in a few weeks time and would be spending a holiday with her parents just down the road in one of the four holiday chalets. This was the beginning of many wonderful summers for me.

It all began one afternoon with Marion calling round at our house to invite me to go and meet her family as they had now started their holidays and were residing in chalets down the road. Marion introduced me to her parents, Minnie and Alfie Wicks, who sat in deckchairs enjoying the hot afternoon sunshine. Her brother Barry was kicking a beachball about on the lawn and wasn't bothered about me or his sister. I noticed the people in the chalet next door were watching us as they sat on their folding canvas armchairs on the veranda. The lady wore a pretty floral dress and had a kind face. She gave me a friendly smile.

"Who is that?" I whispered to Marion.

"It's my Auntie Flo and Uncle Harry. They've got a young son called Rodney and an older daughter, Cynthia." Then pointing along the chalets, she said,

"In the third chalet are more of my relations, Uncle Harold and Auntie Gertie and their three sons, Michael, Colin and David. Our holidays were specially organised so that we could all have time together."

I gazed toward the third chalet and noticed an older boy in a wheelchair.

"Who's that in the wheelchair?" I asked.

"Oh, that's my cousin, Michael," answered Marion.

"What's the matter with him?"

"He got polio."

I felt sorry for this good looking young lad who appeared perfectly fit and healthy except from his legs which were supported by steel callipers fitted to his shoes. I watched as he wheeled himself with confidence across the short grass and onto the path. Seconds later he was followed by a teenage boy arguing with a much younger lad. They both ran across the road, pushing and shoving each other. The older boy jumped onto the typical seaside bench which stood on the grass verge leading to the beach. Another stride up and he was walking steadily along the backrest of the seat, arms outstretched to keep his balance.

Marion and I sauntered across the road where the boy was

performing his balancing act. I looked at him as he jumped to the ground. We stared at each other. I noticed he had the bluest eyes I had ever seen. When he ran away down the bank, I immediately asked Marion,

"Who is that?"

"It's my cousin, Colin," she replied.

"Well he looks really nice," I said.

Marion just shrugged her shoulders and laughed.

"He's OK, I suppose."

We followed on down to the beach. The tide was coming in so we all threw stones into the water, seeing who could make them skim and bounce the most. I was usually pretty skilful at this game, knowing how to select the right shape of stone for a maximum skim. Today, however, I had more than met my match with the two Londoners. Marion was beating me while Colin was better than both of us, being much bigger and with a stronger throw.

We hadn't been on the beach very long before Marion's Mum came down to ask if I would like to stay and have tea. I said that I would have to go home first and ask my Mum but if she agreed I would love to stay. Marion said that she would come up the road with me. We both got our bikes that were standing up against the white picket fence. Marion's bike was one that had been hired from Cornelius' bike shop, at a cost of 7/6d (35p) per week. It had a number painted in white, just below the saddle. This was a good indication that it was one of Snuffy's bikes.

On arriving home, we threw our bikes carelessly against the privet hedge and charged in through the back door, with me shouting out,

"Mum, can I stay at Marion's for tea?"

Mum appeared at the doorway leading from the hall and agreed that it would be alright for me to have tea with Marion and her family but I wasn't to be late home. Running off, we grabbed our bikes and raced back down Seaview

Avenue. By the time we arrived back at the chalet the table had been laid. A large plate of bread and butter stood in the centre of the table with a jar of home made jam, a plate of shop cakes and a home made fruit cake. There was a glass bowl containing half a cucumber and some tomatoes - these were the days of rationing. I stood there nervously, wondering where I should sit. Mrs Wicks looked at me and said,

"Come on dear. You can sit here."

She pulled the chair out, ready for me to sit down. I sat waiting for someone else to start - I couldn't be the first. Marion saved the day by leading the way. I then followed on by helping myself to bread and butter and the home made raspberry jam. They all shared a pot of tea which was kept hot with a colourful knitted tea cosy but as I didn't drink tea I had a nice cool glass of water. On this occasion there wasn't too much conversation, but Barry and Marion did a fair amount of arguing.

At the end of the day the beach became deserted as visitors made their way home, struggling up the steep slope carrying deckchairs, picnic baskets and string bags containing their damp, sandy towels and wet costumes. Some carried brown paper carrier bags with string handles. The strong sea air mixed with the sunshine had caused many red faces and tired, grizzling children. One tired child with a dummy hanging round its neck on a piece of string was quietened as his older brother shoved the comforter into its mouth with an expertise guaranteed to get the desired result.

In the evenings, when all the cars had moved out of the Seaview Avenue car park, the families occupying the four chalets would turn out for a game of cricket. The metal dustbin, bearing the initials, 'W.M.U.D.C' (West Mersea Urban District Council) in red paint would be picked up by the two metal handles and placed in the middle of the car park as an improvised wicket.

Everyone enjoyed their game of cricket. Michael in his

wheelchair would take his turn batting with his young brother David being his runner. I soon developed a close relationship with Colin. It was more like a brother and sister would be. He was always there to support me in any arguments and I knew that if there was a casting vote he would be on my side. I also knew that my chances at scoring more runs at cricket were much better if he was bowling. It was strange that we got on so well as he was at least three years older than me.

Susan and Terry wanted to meet my friends at the chalets and Auntie Dot said they could go with me, as long as they were good. We walked down Fairhaven Avenue with Judy the dog following behind. She went everywhere with us, prepared to protect us against any lurking dangers. It was ten o'clock on a beautiful morning with just a light mist beginning to lift across the estuary. It was going to be a scorcher.

With an afternoon tide, it was almost certain that Mr Tom Lungley would turn up on the beach with his boat 'The Nippy' to offer inexpensive boat trips around the racing marker buoy. If we wanted to go on one of the boat trips we would either have to use the ice cream money we had been given that morning or find some returnable Corona, Tizer or other empty bottles offering money back on return - as much as threepence each could be gained on the large bottles.

I was now telling our friends how we had learned the technique of earning from the day trippers and holiday makers who left their empty drink bottles on the beach or thrown under beach huts. We carried out this lucrative activity of collecting money-back bottles in a manner that didn't make other people on the beach too aware of our secret earner. We didn't want our profits to go down through too many people being in the know. After returning our find of empties to the shop, we calculated that we now had enough money for all of us to go on Mr Lungley's boat.

Returning to the beach, we knew we were in luck. There was already one boatload of people heading out for the buoy and a queue waiting for the next trip. There were now six more to join the motley crew - us three, Marion, Cynthia and Rodney. As the tide came in it brought with it a fresh sea breeze, creating waves which stirred the small pebbles on the sea bed, washing them up onto the shore. The tide was coming in fast, making many of the sun seekers retreat further up the beach, quickly gathering up small piles of clothes and the towels that they had been laying on.

The pleasure boat was now on its return journey, causing a small swell on the tide as she approached land. Mr Lungley steered the boat skilfully onto the shore, gently hitting the shingle on the beach. It would soon be our turn to stand on the old wooden crate that was used as a step to climb on to the boat. When we were all aboard, Mr Lungley collected the fares then headed out into the deep.

The sea was choppy, the boat hitting the waves making the water spray on my skin and the wind blew my hair across my face. Terry was clinging on to me happily but slightly scared of our exhilarating boat ride. Susan, showing no fear at all, was dangling her arm in the water. As we drew nearer the beach I could see another queue waiting to have a trip on 'The Nippy'. We all clambered over the edge of the boat and dropped onto the firm wet sand.

It was now time for an ice cream at The Fairhaven Café, owned and run by Mr Daly, a tall man with grey, nearly white hair. He always wore a smart white long sleeved overall jacket, reaching down to his knees. There were times when he had an angry look about him - it could have been the burden of the heavy workload of running the café and restaurant, helped by Mrs Dimmock his housekeeper, who at times didn't look much happier than he did. Mrs Dimmock was a short, plump lady with enormous bosoms, smiling only occasionally at the customers queuing up to be served. After buying our ice creams we went down to the beach to eat them, watching the tide gradually go out.

"I want to wee," said Terry.

"Can't you wait until we get home?" I said impatiently.

"No, I want to go. Badly," was his answer as he jumped up and down, squeezing himself with his right hand to avoid the inevitable.

"I want to go, too," said Sue.

We only had to go across the road to the public toilets. Terry had to go to the 'Ladies' as I couldn't take him in the 'Gents'.

Luckily, there wasn't the usual queue and the tiny vacant sign was indicated on one of the middle doors. I inserted a penny coin into the polished brass slot which released the mechanism on the latch and allowed the door to be opened. Terry went first, standing on his tiptoes to reach over the edge of the lavatory pan. Susan was next as I stood against the door, holding it ajar so that she didn't get shut in. I suppose I wasn't paying too much attention to Terry.

He did something that he'd always wanted to do - put money in the long wooden dispensing machine on the wall. The well-known name 'Southalls' was written clearly across the light coloured polished cabinet. The narrow panel of glass running down the centre revealed small cardboard boxes stacked neatly in a vertical line. Terry was convinced these little packages contained a 'prize' as in the fairground machines. With his money now in the machine, he was able to pull out the little drawer at the bottom. Opening the box retrieved from the drawer, disappointment showed on his face as he pulled out a feminine towel, followed by two safety pins.

"I'll take the pins home for Mummy, but I don't want this other rubbish," he said, angrily throwing it into the dustbin in the far corner.

The three of us trundled back down to the beach where Marion and the rest of them were playing a game of rounders.

We stayed for a while but it was getting close to our tea time and Susan and Terry wanted to go home to see children's television which was of course in black and white. The viewing time on television was still reduced. It had been closed all during the war years because it was feared that signals from the large transmitter at Crystal Palace could act as a guide to enemy aircraft. Programmes ran from three to four thirty and then again in the evening from eight thirty until ten.

Not everyone was lucky enough to have television (we didn't have one at Craigmore) but the radio, or 'wireless' was always very entertaining, with plays, serials, quizzes, concerts and, of course, the news.

CHAPTER 17

Kidddiesland, the Regatta and wayward fireworks

OVERLEAF: *'Kiddiesland'*.
ABOVE: *(Top) Peter Farthing and George Vince enter into the carnival spirit on Regatta day. Reckoned to be made from a plane's fuel drop tank, used during the war; Michael Matthews on Mersea beach.*

The morning was bright and warm. Marion called round for me early to see if I would like to walk to East Mersea Church with them - they were going to take the route along the beach. I hurriedly got ready, grabbed a cardigan and put on some sandals. Most of the time I ran about with bare feet but I knew we would be walking over rough ground. By the time we got to the bottom of Seaview Avenue everyone was ready and waiting for us - fourteen altogether.

We took the pathway from Seaview Avenue which ran through a small copse at the back of the beach huts. Michael's wheelchair had to be pushed carefully over the rough terrain. After crossing the bottom of Cross Lane we moved up the sloping land to where blackberry bushes and other hedges dangled over the edge of the cliffs that were gradually being washed away through the force of the tides. Now we were on the higher ground and could feel the strong sea breeze blowing across the estuary. Reaching the top of the sea wall it became more difficult with the wheelchair but the men managed to carry it over the worst parts. At last we arrived at Kiddiesland where the mile-long lane would lead us up on to the main East Mersea Road.

Kiddiesland was a landmark, familiar to the locals. In 1937, Mr Ingram, a wealthy gentleman from London, purchased many acres of land bordering East Mersea beach to build and equip a special children's resort so that deprived children could enjoy a day by the sea. An enormous bungalow-type building housed tea rooms and a play hall for

171

four hundred children, surrounded by a covered arcade for use in wet weather.

In its heyday it must have been rather splendid with its two hundred foot long swimming pool filled by healthy sea water each time the tide came in. In addition, there was three fifths of a mile of private beach. Beside the swimming pool stood six changing cubicles in a typical late 1930's cement construction design, now a strange feature of past years.

Unfortunately, just before World War Two, Kiddiesland was requisitioned by the army and used as a repair shop for aircraft engines. After the war, Mr Ingram reclaimed his property, hoping to return it to its original popular splendour but it was not to be as rationing and the shortage of petrol made it impossible to carry on.

We stood looking at the intriguing building, now derelict and surrounded by nothing more than the vast meadowland and memories of the past. We left the dreary sight of Kiddiesland and walked on up the lane until we came to the main road. It wasn't long before we reached Church Lane and East Mersea Church. On his way down the lane, Colin collected a number of burrs - a rough, sticky seedcase with little hooked spines - from the hedges. He rolled the burrs into a ball and in sheer devilment threw them into my hair. My freshly washed shiny hair became so tangled that it seemed almost impossible to get them out without cutting away a large chunk of hair. However, with a great deal of patience, his dad managed to unravel most of the tangles. My head was sore and my hair had gone frizzy.

I had never seen Mr Matthews get cross but today he was certainly angry with Colin. The rest of the party was a bit fed up as well. The mood changed when we reached the tranquillity of the church and Mr Matthews said a prayer as he usually did when we visited a church. We all knelt down and prayed with him.

We left the church and went up the road to the Dog and

Pheasant for drinks - lemonade for the youngsters and something stronger for the adults – and afterwards walked the three miles home by road.

Summer holidays were nearly over. Sad farewells had been said to all the London friends with most of us promising to write to each other. Mum said Marion could come and stay next Easter so we did have that to look forward to.

I am left with many happy memories of the holidays. Two days in particular stand out from the rest. The first was a four mile boat trip across the River Blackwater to Bradwell-on-Sea, a quiet, secluded village famous for its isolated chapel of Saint Peter-on-the-Wall which has been a place of Christian worship for over one thousand three hundred years. The oblong monument is clearly seen from the Mersea shore, standing barren and erect on the Bradwell peninsula.

It was a sunny, warm morning and we were all standing on the causeway waiting for Rupert 'Rue' Pullen to turn up with his motor boat 'The Pedro' to take us on the journey to Bradwell. There were fourteen of us all together including Michael and the wheelchair. After arriving on the Bradwell shore we had what seemed like a very long trek to get to see the historical chapel. We walked along weather-beaten tracks passing farmland and fields. To us youngsters, the chapel seemed no more than an old barn with a rough earth scattered floor and what appeared to be two rows of wooden kitchen chairs. We openly expressed our thoughts amongst giggles and laughter. However, Mr Matthews, said it was a place of worship and we should all sit quietly, while he said a prayer. We obediently did as he suggested.

Mr Matthews was at the time Assistant Diocesan Secretary at Saint Andrew's, South Harrow. He later went on to be

Chelmsford Diocesan Secretary and lived at Guy Harlings, Chelmsford, where we spent more happy hours playing cricket in the beautiful gardens.

I suddenly felt very humble and proud to be part of the historical Christian experience at Saint Peter-on-the-Wall. The serene atmosphere lasted only a few minutes as it was followed by our bursts of laughter. We emerged from the cool of the chapel to the warmth of the sunshine and the sounds of the seabirds. As I stood there, I allowed my imagination to dwell on the ghosts of the past.

In 2003 I revisited the chapel with my husband Alan, eldest son James and grandson Jack, together with my eldest daughter, Sophie. This time we travelled to Bradwell-on Sea by road - twenty six miles – and we were able to park within half a mile of the church. The walk was much the same as it was when I was a young girl. However, I was surprised and disappointed at the change to the interior. It now looked rather splendid, with a new floor and altar, bench seats and arrangements of fresh flowers. Sadly, my memory of how it was, has more appeal than the way it is now. I much preferred its rustic appearance of old.

The second outstanding day of my holiday had to be the visit to Colchester Castle Park and Castle Museum. We travelled to Colchester by bus. The journey was slow as the bus stopped at virtually every stop between Mersea Island and Colchester. As we approached the Roman wall on the edge of town it felt as though any minute we would hit the huge brick and stone supports which were part of the wall and protruded into the road. Our bus driver was Johnny 'Hats' Pavey and he had a reputation for erratic and unpredictable driving. He had on occasions given old ladies a very scary drive. His conductor was Norman Jaggard, who would call out,

"Pass along the bus please" when the bus got full, with

passengers standing along the gangway.

We arrived in Colchester High Street and got off the bus at Saint Nicholas' Church, just across the road from The Castle. When we first entered The Castle, a thousand years of history was all around us. It felt very cool after the heat of the midday sun outside. The light from one of the large windows fell on some Roman armour, attracting our attention and causing comments on the weight the Roman soldiers had to carry around. There was so much to look at and we all had different things to interest us.

Because of the large number in our group, we were approached by one of the Museum Staff who asked if we would like to go in the vaults as there was a guide available for a conducted tour. Marion's Dad accepted on behalf of us all. As we gathered at the entrance I felt a moment of panic. I really didn't want to go with them. I looked at Marion.

"I don't want to go down there, it looks horrible," I whispered, not wanting to look stupid.

"Oh, don't be daft," said Marion, "we're all going."

As we proceeded further into the dim tunnel, I felt an awful panic. My voice sounded louder than I wanted it to.

"I am not going."

I was going to wait with Michael as it was impossible for a wheelchair to go in the vaults but the adults were determined to persuade me that I would be alright. Mr Matthews suggested that I should hold Colin's hand. Colin put his hand out for me and I felt his hand firm and comforting, guiding me gently towards the brick steps that gradually descended into a dimly lit cave. The ground was covered with earth or sand and the atmosphere was cold, damp and smelt mouldy. I couldn't wait to get out again into the fresh air. The guide was saying that during World War Two these Roman vaults were used as air raid shelters.

When the tour was finished, I suddenly realised how nice it was holding Colin's hand...

Having got through the summer and with the school holidays nearly at an end, the last attraction of the year was The West Mersea Town Regatta held on Saturday. It was generally acclaimed as being the best Town Regatta for many years. The town had been gaily decorated with flags and bunting and the bright morning with a south easterly breeze made it a perfect day for sailing, with a record number of entries.

The scene on the river was picturesque with masses of boats in full sail including smacks, cruisers and winkle brigs, to name but a few. The sound of the finishing gun could be heard periodically as the winners passed the flag on the finishing buoy.

The afternoon entertainment started with the carnival procession parading through the main streets headed by the Alresford Silver Band. Children of all ages marched by the side of the band in time to the popular musical selections. People lined both sides of the streets until the procession passed by and then followed down to the waterfront.

I think our entire family must have turned out for the festive occasion. Our main interest was to see the entry made by Vince and Farthing Builders. It was the model of an aeroplane on a lorry. This was a skit on Councillor Charlie Priggs' campaign against the mosquito menace on the Island. Charlie was a 'rum ol' Mersea character' passionate in his fight on the local council to wipe out the gnats by spraying with insecticide so it was no surprise when George and Peter mimicked the operation by spraying the spectators with water cunningly concealed on the lorry.

There were shrieks of laughter and cheers from the crowds who were making their way down to the waterfront and onto The Hard. Many people had already arrived at the foreshore, some getting into boats ready to watch from the river. Others preferred watching from the land as they could then listen to the band playing on a small piece of walled green in front of Stone House. Stone House is a beautiful centuries-old house used in the late nineteenth century by local smugglers. Tales have been told of a secret passage beneath the floor, leading to a getaway tunnel under the river.

The water sports have always provided great family entertainment. The large speaking trumpet of the megaphone sent the announcer's voice across the river calling for the start of the first race. Fishermen, families and friends would all be competing against each other for the various cups and trophies. The 'Shovel Race' caused much amusement. Three people used shovels instead of oars to propel the boat along, the participants all struggling hard to win the race. They would occasionally try to balk the other competitors by splashing water into their faces.

There were many events but 'The Greasy Pole' was the hot spot of the day ('Admiral' Bill Wyatt's speciality). The event was won by walking a fifteen foot wooden pole - covered in grease - that protruded horizontally from the side of the Committee Barge. At the end of the pole fluttered a small red flag on a thin wooden stick - first to grab the flag was the winner. The stick would snap as the victor plunged into the sea ten feet below, where other less nimble competitors had gone before.

Inevitably a huge cheer went up from the crowds gathered on the shore and surrounding craft. The heat of the afternoon was taking its toll with numerous people jumping into the inviting water, the chill tide on their hot bodies making them gasp. Modesty didn't seem to be an issue to some of them as they cast off their top clothes down to underwear. Others jumped in with all their clothes on. It was all part of 'Regatta Day' and there was more to come in the evening.

The grand firework display would start at dusk after presentation of the prizes by Lady Joanna Crane on the forecourt of The Victory Hotel. The evening turned out to be much cooler with the wind now increasing. Thick woolly pullovers and jackets were worn by most of the crowds as they wandered along Coast Road to see the fireworks. Mum wasn't that keen on fireworks so I went with Dad. We cycled to Auntie Violet's and decided to leave our bikes in the back garden and walk the short distance down the road to see the display.

"Are you going to come with us, Violet?" asked Dad.

"No, boy, you go on down. I've got plenty I want to do home here. I've got me knitting and there's something on the wireless I want to listen to."

"Well, if yer sure that's what ya want to do mate, we'll be off then."

Auntie Violet hadn't been the same since Uncle Will died two years ago. They were such a devoted couple and the loss had been a major struggle for her to cope with. As we joined the crowds along Coast Road, there was a huge bang. This was the usual sign that the fireworks were about to start. We stood close to the Band Stand watching the colourful display being let off to the cries of 'Oh' and 'Ah' as the splendour of the firework stars fell from the skies. Suddenly the wind seemed to change, blowing the smoke into the crowded audience. Rockets fell among the people. Fear and panic suddenly took hold as some suffered burns.

CHAPTER 18

A close shave, a chocolate cake and the tea-leaf reader

OVERLEAF & ABOVE: *Mrs Lane the fortune teller.*
Pictured above from left: Rev. Derby,
Colchester United's Brian Woods, Lucy Lane.

Dad, being six feet tall could see what was happening. He grabbed my arm and said,

"Come on, dear, let's head for home."

We hurried up Firs Chase, followed by what seemed like hundreds of people all trying to escape from the danger. We left the crowds behind as we turned in to the darkness of Rosebank Road which was little more than a dirt track with two street lamps, one at either end of the road. Dad carried his old black 'Ever Ready' torch which he had taken off the front of his bike. Mersea only had street lights on the main roads so we were well used to carrying torches. Auntie Violet was surprised to see us return home so soon.

"Put the kettle on Violet, mate – I'm dying for a cuppa," said Dad.

I sat quietly watching the kettle boil on the hot coals of the open fire as Dad told of the horrible end to our evening.

"Oh Lor, what a ter do, boy!" exclaimed Auntie Violet as she removed the kettle from the fire, ready to make a pot of tea.

I couldn't wait to get back to school again. There were only a few days to go - but first, a trip in to Colchester to buy some new clothes! I'd grown so much during the holidays and Mum had promised to let me choose my own clothes this time. She had been saving up our ration coupons for some time. I was hoping there would also be enough for some new shoes. It was a special treat to go shopping in Colchester as we probably only went every six months to buy clothes. Most of our shopping was done on the Island and we had our own dressmaker, Mrs Bell, who made some of our clothes and did alterations.

Mrs Bell seemed to have hundreds of different patterns of clothes to choose from. If after looking at the various designs, we liked the top of one dress pattern and the skirt of another pattern, after taking measurements she would cleverly make up her own adaptations exactly to our requirements.

Terry had persuaded Mum to let him come to town as well. We walked excitedly to the top of Seaview Avenue where the buses passed every hour. We could never be sure if it was a single or double-decker bus.

"I hope it's a double-decker bus - if it is I want to sit right at the front," said Terry.

"You will sit exactly where you are told, young man," said Mum.

"Even if it is a double-decker, the front seat may be taken," I said to him, laughing.

Standing at the top of the road waiting, we could hear the familiar rattle of the bus engine coming along East Road. When it turned the corner and came in to view, we could see that Terry was in luck. A double decker with the front seats upstairs vacant! Herbert "Herbie" Mole, the conductor, helped us on the bus and when everyone was safely on board he rang the bell giving the driver the signal to move off. All the local drivers and conductors were well known for their little quirks and mannerisms. Herbie always called the bus stop at the Peldon Rose the 'Pelding Rose'. Another stop a few miles up the road outside the Abberton Lion pub was 'The Abberding Lion'. The local people all knew what he meant when he approached the stops. I'm not so sure that strangers to the area would have known what he meant.

After arriving at our destination in Colchester High Street, we got off the bus and walked down St Nicholas Passage with the church on the left and various shops on the right hand side. At the end of the very narrow walkway we could see the Co-op in Wyre Street. There was so much to see and buy in the Co-op. We went upstairs to the first floor where Mum tried on several hats but couldn't find exactly the one she wanted. Terry got a new pair of warm trousers ready for the winter and I found a fashionable Gor Ray skirt and button-through cardigan. Terry was getting fed up with buying clothes and wanted to go somewhere else. He'd been promised a trip to the ground floor in the lift and was now watching with interest through the grids of the metal sliding doors, waiting for the lift to reach our floor level. However, his treat wasn't to be as a smartly dressed lady walked across the shop floor with a notice in her hand that read 'Lift Out Of Order'. She hung it on the door handle by a piece of string.

"What does that say?" asked Terry.

I told him what the notice said and he replied looking at Mum,

"Nan, does that mean it needs some syrup of figs, because that's what we have to keep us in order?"

We all burst out laughing, including the lady assistant. Every fortnight Mum insisted we had a dose of syrup of figs. I quite liked the stuff but Terry hated having to take it. Mum would say to him,

"Come on now, it will keep your tummy in order."

If he swallowed it down, he would be rewarded with a sweet.

Mum was waiting for her change to be returned. It was to come by way of a capsule about the size of a small jam jar. I was always fascinated by this way of payment. The assistant accepted the money for the goods and placed it in the container which was then popped in a pipe that had a little door on it. When the door was closed a vacuum was caused and, with a strange hissing sound, the capsule was sucked up

183

the pipe then projected on to overhead cables suspended from the ceiling like a mouse-sized cable car. From there it reached its final destination - the office upstairs. The return journey was identical but in reverse. This time, the capsule contained the change and receipt for payment, which the assistant handed politely to Mum.

"Come on now, you two children. I want to go to Lucking's, then Sainsbury's and if you are both good, we'll go to Jacklin's for afternoon tea," said Mum.

Lucking's had a very good millinery department and my guess was that Mum would be trying on more hats. We padded up the luxuriously carpeted stairs to the first floor where the carpeting matched that which was on the stairs. It felt so soft as we walked across the floor.

"May I help you, Madam?" asked the very well dressed assistant.

"I would like to look at some hats," said Mum, walking over to the display of hats positioned on tall metal posts headed with mushroom shaped plates to hold the hats safely on display.

There were many more hats displayed on a shelf in front of a large mirror. While Mum was doing her thing trying on hats, I moved over to the large window to watch the passers-by and the traffic moving up St Botolphs Street. I turned round as I sensed movement behind me and there was Terry prancing about with a wide brimmed hat on his head embellished with a mass of roses. He had pushed the hat on his head so far that it had taken the elegant curve out of the crown and made a disastrous hump instead. Trying very hard not to laugh out loud, I grabbed the hat from his head and put it back on the shelf in front of the mirror - but not quite quick enough to avoid Mum seeing what had happened.

"You naughty little boy. You don't deserve afternoon tea. Unless you start behaving yourself, we shall go straight home."

Mum had chosen a good quality, but plainly styled hat.

She said,

"You can't have something too frimmicky in Mersea, it would look out of place."

The assistant packed the hat in tissue paper and placed it carefully in a Lucking's carrier bag.

"Madam, I am sure you will be delighted with your purchase," said the assistant, handing Mum her new hat.

"Thank you, I'm sure I will."

We now had to go back up the High Street to Sainsbury's. While Mum was dealing with the list of what she wanted, Terry was having a good look at what was available to buy. Suddenly, he shouted across the shop in a loud voice,

"Look Nanny, they've got some cheese just like your legs!"

Poor Mum had varicose veins and to a little boy, the blue cheeses must have been a close match.

There was just enough time to go to Jacklin's for our afternoon tea before catching the bus home. We climbed the stairs at Jacklin's, the wood panelling up the side of the stairs making the shop look dark but on reaching the top of the stairs there was plenty of light shining through the large windows, dressed with attractive, heavily draped curtains.

The table we selected was close to the window and overlooked the busy High Street. It wasn't long before the waitress came to take our order. She was wearing a black dress, white lace trimmed apron and matching lace headband. She wrote down our order on the small pad she kept in her apron pocket. Mum ordered a pot of tea, buttered scones and a selection of small tea-cakes. The waitress returned with our order, placing everything on the table from the large tray, including the plate of assorted cakes.

Then the argument started.

"I want the chocolate cake," said Terry.

"I want the chocolate cake," I said.

"Neither of you will have the chocolate cake, because I will have it myself," said Mum, reaching over and placing the cake on her plate.

We were never allowed to misbehave at the table so when Terry reached over and took the cream cake, I settled for the iced cake with a cherry on top. I saw Mum reach across for the cake knife and cut the chocolate cake in half. She then placed half on Terry's plate. I immediately thought,

"He's got his own way, as usual."

Then, the other half was placed on my plate, which made me feel very guilty as I ate the lovely chocolate cake.

"Hurry up now, you two. We don't want to miss the next bus home".

Returning to school after the summer holidays wasn't a problem for me as I enjoyed the camaraderie of the other children as well as the challenge of academic learning. I had to work hard to keep up with the brighter set of pupils because of my delay in starting school at six years of age, due to the war. However, I seemed to be streets ahead when it came to the more practical work, especially art, needlework and cookery - and I couldn't wait to work in the school gardens. Us Mersea children were more than privileged to have our own school gardens and the opportunity to help keep them in order. The older boys and girls had gardening lessons and learned mostly by practical experience to dig the gardens, mow the lawns and prune the trees. There was, of course, also some written work to be done.

On first entering the school gardens there was a feeling of tranquillity. Looking to the left there was a pond full of assorted coloured goldfish swimming around and hiding in the weeds at any hint of sound. Further into the gardens were canaries and budgerigars singing in the large aviary.

On the north side were two very large playing fields allowing two lots of sporting games to be played at the same time. Usually, the girls would be playing hockey, netball or rounders in one field and the boys football or cricket in the other. The entire boundary was fenced by six feet tall metal palings stretching right down beyond the playing fields to the kitchen gardens, where the vegetables were grown.

A healthy smell of pigs and chickens filled the air as well as the aroma that came from the huge mound of manure left to rot down as a natural fertiliser. There were times when some of the boys whose turn it was to muck out the chickens and pigs got bored with the task and had a 'pig shit fight'. Each weekend some of the older boys volunteered to feed and look after the animals and would be rewarded by having half a dozen new laid chicken eggs each.

It was Tuesday 14th September, 1948. Mum and Auntie Tod had arranged to go to a whist drive at the Women's Institute Hall and they said Dorothy and I were to go and meet them after we came out of school. The W.I. Hall was only a few minutes from the school and when we arrived we could hear the sound of laughter and conversation so we guessed it must be half time. We crept quietly through the door.

Luckily, Mum's table was close to the entrance. Lucy Lane was at Mum's table. She could read the tea leaves and was apparently very accurate with her predictions. Sylvia, her daughter, who was in the same class as me at school, once told me that her Mum had this very rare gift. It was because she was the seventh child of the seventh child. I thought it was all a bit exaggerated, but scary. She could also tell fortunes by reading the cards.

Now, here was Mrs Lane sitting at Mum's table, a lady with a friendly smile and eyes that twinkled, showing lines on her face that reflected hard working years. Her hands, as she picked up Mum's teacup, I noticed, had also been toughened by hard work. She looked into the tea leaves, exclaiming:

"Oh, my dear, there's some bad news on the way. It's right

at the top of the cup, so it's very close."

"I don't want any more bad news. We've had more than enough lately," said Mum.

"I'm sorry, my dear, I can't change what I see but I can say you will also be moving house in the very near future."

"No, that can't be true," replied Mum.

"We'll see," answered Mrs Lane with a knowing look on her face.

CHAPTER 19

Bad news comes quickly, a smacking at school and back to the tin bath

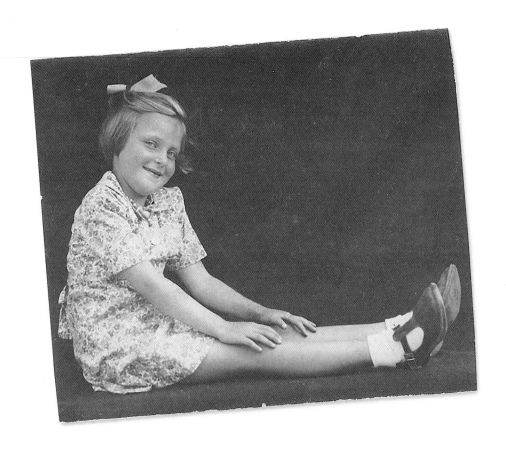

OVERLEAF: *Our fourth house 'High View', Victory Road.*
ABOVE: *Dorothy Hayward.*

The sound of the whistle being blown quietened the room and everyone returned to their seats ready for the second half of the whist drive to commence. The weather outside was rather chilly so Dorothy and I decided to stay inside and play cards on one of the spare green baize covered card tables. Dorothy placed all the cards face down in neat rows ready for us to play a game of 'Pairs'.

We hadn't been playing very long when the door opened, letting in the cold air. In walked Peter Jasper, one of the young men who lived with Auntie Violet. I watched as he walked to the table where Mum was sitting. I saw that she became rather agitated and gathered up her handbag and jacket which hung over the back of her chair. Peter went to the door, Mum following close behind.

"I've just had some very bad news," Mum was speaking in a whisper to us to avoid disturbing the people playing cards.

"Auntie Violet has died suddenly so I will have to go home to Dad. Auntie Tod will give you your tea and I will be round to collect you later."

Mum was speaking in a whisper to avoid disturbing the people playing cards. Curiosity made many of the people turn their heads to watch Mum as she went to the door. Her hand of cards had been taken over and was being played by one of the ladies who'd been washing up in the kitchen. I was finding it very difficult to concentrate on the game I was playing with Dorothy. The news of Auntie Violet dying was really upsetting for me but I couldn't cry in front of all these people.

"I don't want to play any more," I said to Dorothy as I held back my tears.

"Alright, we'll pack up now and call it a draw, shall we?" said Dorothy generously, who I think was probably winning.

I was silently wishing that the whist drive would soon come to an end. I just wanted to go home. It wasn't too long before the winners were announced and they went to claim their prizes from the top table. The noise of the chairs being dragged across the wooden floor and the chattering voices meant that we could now go home.

On entering Auntie Tod's living room we could feel the heat coming from the old kitchen range. The early part of the day was still very warm but by late afternoon there was a chill in the air. The tablecloth was on the table ready for tea but I had lost my appetite. Dorothy was having a sandwich made of soft brown sugar, mixed to a paste with margarine and spread on slices of bread. Post war rationing had made people think up all sorts of recipes and ideas to make food more tasty. We also made chocolate spread with cocoa powder, margarine and sugar, mixing the three ingredients to a stiff paste on the side of the tea plate, then spreading it on toast or bread.

Mum arrived to collect me at about seven o'clock. We had just listened to 'Dick Barton, Special Agent' on the wireless. It was an exciting fifteen minute programme of serialised episodes broadcast each night at six forty five, very popular with all ages. Mum and I cycled home, neither of us saying very much. Whatever was in our thoughts we kept to ourselves. I couldn't stop thinking of how things would be now Auntie Violet had gone.

There wouldn't be any more visits to her house. We would all miss her lovely chocolate walnut cake and coffee walnut cakes. She was a lovely Aunt - why did she have to die? Poor Dad would certainly be feeling the loss. I began to wonder about the three boys who had been living with her and Uncle Will, since they were youngsters. Paul had been like their own child, and then his two brothers, Peter and Jeremy went to live with them as well when their mother died. All three of them were virtually old enough to look after themselves - but where would they live?

The answers to my thoughts came on the evening after the funeral. Mum and Dad were in the sitting room talking when I arrived home. Dad looked up and said,

"Come on in, my little ol' love, we've got something we need to tell you."

Dad looked at Mum. I felt a strange urge to walk back out of the room again as I knew he was going to tell me something I didn't want to hear. He didn't beat about the bush, either.

"Auntie Violet has left me the house in her will. It is, however, rather complicated because she has made provision in her will for Paul to have the two west rooms on the ground floor and first floor, together with the furniture that's in those two rooms."

He paused while this information sunk in.

"We will have the rest of the house, together with all the furniture in those rooms. It will mean we will have Paul living with us, also Peter and Jeremy on occasions."

I would rather not have been moving but if we were going to move to Victory Road, I would be happy having the three boys living with us. My mind suddenly raced back to the horrible afternoon of the whist drive when Mum had her tea-leaves read and was told there was bad news on the way. The bad news certainly arrived that very afternoon and now the predicted move was about to happen. Mrs. Lane's accuracy with the tea-leaf reading sent a shiver down my spine. I knew then that Paul and his two brothers would be well looked after when we moved to 'High View' in Victory Road. Auntie Violet had anticipated this when she'd made out her will.

Uncle Harry had been able to get another of his 'can't-go-wrong-mate' business ventures off the ground. This time he'd opened his own photographic studio on the Island. He was especially talented as a photographer and his business was doing particularly well. Knowing that we would soon be moving, he had been able to rent a property called 'Oakdene' in High Street North for him and his family. 'Craigmore' was soon to go on the market to be sold, so Mum and Auntie Lil were busy packing household items into large wooden tea chests and cardboard boxes, carefully wrapping breakable items in newspaper and leaving out only the items that were necessary for our day to day use.

Moving house was no big deal for Auntie Lil. Her whole life had been spent moving around. She often used to tell me about the time she moved to France to work for Lord Bradbury as nursemaid to his children. Auntie Lil called him 'The Pound Note Man' because his signature was on the bottom of all the pound notes. On her return to England she could speak French fluently.

Dad came in the back door and said,

"Can someone make us a cuppa tea? I'm parched. I dunno what I'm gonna do with all the stuff I've got in the shed. I think I can make up a lorry load of tools alone."

A few more days and everything was packed, stacked and ready to go. Auntie Lil and Uncle Harry moved out a day ahead of us, leaving the house looking empty, eerie and quiet. I went up to the bedroom for a last look and to check that nothing of mine had been left behind. I hesitated in the doorway wondering if my angel would move with me - it came to me by the way of a bright light one night when I couldn't get to sleep.

I had been particularly naughty at school. It was the first lesson after lunch and I was talking to my friend while the register was being called. Mrs. South our teacher called,

"Quiet, please!"

194

I must have carried on chatting a bit longer, because she looked at me - anger showing in her face and eyes - and said:

"You girl, will miss games this afternoon. I told you to stop talking."

Games was one of my favourite lessons and when I saw the rest of the class putting on their black plimsolls, I was really fed up. Mrs. South then gave me fifty lines to write – 'I must not talk in class'. I had no other choice but to get on with my punishment which I thought at the time was very unfair. It didn't take me too long to complete my lines and then I became bored. I decided to have my own bit of fun. I got the chalk from the blackboard and wrote silly messages in chalk inside the lids of some of the desks. When the class came in to change from their plimsolls into their shoes, I quickly left my completed lines on the teacher's desk and made a hasty retreat. On the way home, one of the boys caught me up and said,

"You're gonna be in big trouble tomorrow. Mrs. South said she would deal with you in the morning."

"I don't care about grumpy Mrs. South," I said as I got on my bike and rode off.

It wasn't until after I had gone to bed that I started to worry about what I'd done and how Mrs. South would deal with me. I lay awake for ages. I even thought of pretending to be ill in the morning. It was then that I saw this very bright light. It was all around me and a voice came into my head and it said,

"If you worry, you die, and if you don't worry, you die."

The bright light faded away but I suddenly felt happy and relieved and quite ready to face up to whatever was coming to me in the morning. Just before I went to sleep I can remember thinking,

"That must have been either God or an angel."

I felt a bit apprehensive when I went in to the classroom in the morning and I didn't have to wait long before my punishment came to me. I suppose it was good to get it over with at the start of the day. I was called to the front of the class by the teacher, who asked me,

"Are you responsible for writing on the desks?"

My answer was short and sharp.

"Yes, Miss."

She grabbed me by the arm and said:

"You - are - a - very - naughty - girl," hitting the backs of my legs with her bare hands after each word she uttered.

The class was so quiet, you could hear a pin drop.

"Now, get back to your seat, and let this be a lesson to you."

I held my head up indignantly as I went back to my seat, hoping that her hands were stinging as much as my legs were. I made very sure not to shed a single tear.

I was suddenly brought back to the happenings of today by Mum's urgent call,

"Hurry up and come downstairs."

"Alright, I'm coming," I called back, running downstairs to the front door, which was wide open.

I could see the truck loaded up with the first lot of our furniture. I stood in the open doorway trying to sum up how I felt. I knew I had done this before but my feelings were a bit of everything - happy, sad, excited and apprehensive of what lay ahead in yet another new home. Dorothy was going to spend the first night with us at 'High View'. At long last, I had my own bedroom.

Dad had got my bike ready for me as I was to cycle down to pick up Dorothy and we would both bike down to our new home. When our next door neighbours - the Fulcher girls and their family - moved to Margate in Kent, our parents purchased their two bikes so my bike and Dorothy's were identical. We were both so pleased to have acquired these beautiful shiny black modern bikes with wire cable brakes and spent a lot of time going on bike rides. My bike ride today was taking me on a journey that would have everlasting memories.

When we arrived at my new home we stood our bikes against the tall ivy bush which acted as a screen hiding the outside lavatory door and offering extra privacy to anyone who wished to leave the door ajar for a bit of fresh air. The back door to the house was only a few paces away and opened directly into the scullery. Stepping into the kitchen, the open fire offered cheer to what otherwise seemed a gloomy outlook, with packing cases stacked up against the wall and furniture pushed to one side to make room for the next truck load of our possessions. Walking through the hall into the sitting room a similar scene greeted us. This time there were drawers resting on the settee, still full of Auntie Violet's things, waiting to be sorted. The carcasses had been taken upstairs ready for the return of the empty drawers. The tiny top drawers from the dressing table were full of trinkets and knick-knacks. I looked at Dorothy and said,

"Poor Auntie Violet."

"Never mind, Pixie," said Dorothy comfortingly, "At least she's with her husband now."

I wanted to get out of this room that held so many memories for me, especially the box of lead soldiers and army tanks. I ran up the steep carpeted stairs, grabbing on to the wooden bannister and gazing through the spindled balustrade at the top of the stairs which ran all round the landing. Dorothy was following behind me. I peered into the front bedroom, which would be for Mum and Dad. The bed frame had already been put up and I could see the chamber pot underneath the metal springs. The mattress and feather bed still stood against the wall. I never thought we would have to go back to having a po under the bed again. The luxury of a bathroom and bath with hot and cold running water was now just a memory. The horror of going back to a tin bath in front of the kitchen fire on a Friday night and just a single cold

197

water tap over the stone scullery sink made me wish even more that we had never moved. I looked at Dorothy and said:

"I don't want to live here."

"Well, Pixie, you know you will have to - you just don't have a choice."

"I know I don't, but it doesn't make me feel any better."

CHAPTER 20

Down West, *the inherited goat and more questions*

OVERLEAF: *Uncle Arthur in his back garden.*
'High View' can be seen, top right, rising behind the shed.
ABOVE: *Norman Smith's animal haulage truck with his*
daughter Mary climbing aboard. The house pictured
in the background is 'Brierly Hall'.

I walked dejectedly off into what was going to be my bedroom. Behind the door stood a double bed. There was an iron fireplace on the side wall with a wardrobe standing in one alcove and a mirrored dressing table - minus two drawers - in the other alcove next to the window. I gazed through the window onto the open field next door and, in the distance, between two trees, I could see the sea. I heard the truck pulling up with another load of our belongings and as I looked out of the window I saw Paul coming in through the back entrance with Bobby the dog. Bobby was an unusual dog - rather like a labrador but curly and dark ginger in colour. I stood at the window wondering how Paul and his brothers were going to feel about having a new family. I expect that he felt as lost as I did at that moment.

The day wore on with Dorothy and I exploring the gardens and all the outbuildings. There were large poultry sheds and brooders that I was pretty sure wouldn't take Dad too long to fill with stock, probably pullets. When Uncle Will was alive he had to abandon the idea of keeping any more chickens due to the rationing of the feeds. However, we had inherited a Nanny goat called Biddy. She was tethered in a field at the bottom of our extremely long garden. The one thing that wasn't rationed was the grass in the fields which Biddy ate and subsequently produced milk for the table. The day progressed with me having many high and low feelings but the worst moment came was when it was time for bed.

Mum had made up the large double bed in my bedroom

with our own bed linen. The sheets and pillowcases were crisp and white with warm woollen blankets, covered with a blue silk bedspread and matching eiderdown.

My bedroom, being directly over the kitchen, was heated only by the warmth creeping up from the kitchen fire downstairs penetrating through the ceiling. Mum had put two stone hot water bottles in the bed giving us a bit of extra comfort on this chilly night. Dorothy turned over with her back to me and snuggled down ready for sleep but as I lay there on my back looking up at the ceiling my mind began to work overtime with my imagination in top gear. Where did this bed come from? I knew we hadn't brought it with us as my bed was a single bed. So was this the bed that Auntie Violet had died in? It was then I began to wonder if this house was haunted by either Uncle Will or Auntie Violet. Fear was getting the better of me. I gave Dorothy a nudge, whispering,

"Are you asleep yet?"

"Well if I was asleep, I am not any more," hissed Dorothy.

"I can't get to sleep. Do you think Auntie Violet died in this bed?" I asked.

"How would I know?" said Dorothy. "I wish you hadn't mentioned it, now I won't be able to sleep either."

I decided to call Mum upstairs. She looked very tired. It had been a long day.

"What do you want? You should both be asleep."

"I am thirsty, Mum," I replied.

"I will go and get you a glass of water but mind you don't drink too much otherwise you will be getting up in the night and as the toilet is outside in the back garden you will have to use the pot under the bed."

Dorothy giggled out loud, knowing I hadn't been used to using the old 'gazunder' for some considerable time now. Unfortunately Rainbow Road hadn't been connected to the main sewers and Dorothy and her family still had to use the wooden lavatory down the garden and still had their chamber pots under the bed. After Mum returned with my glass of water, she asked if we had both said our prayers. We both replied with a yes. I knew I had got to ask Mum a question.

"Mum... did Auntie Violet die in this bed?"

"No, of course she didn't. What a question to ask! Now go to sleep the pair of you."

I still don't know to this day whether she did or not. Mum bent over and kissed us both goodnight. Although we both felt rather grown up, goodnight kisses were very comforting. Feeling reassured by Mum's words, I soon dropped off to sleep.

We had now been in our new home for a few days and I just knew we were going to be happy. Dorothy must have been feeling much the same as she hadn't even mentioned returning home. The village and shops were very convenient and easily accessible. The quickest way was to go through the folley directly across the road from our front gate. This unmade footpath was very picturesque with a spinney on one side where bluebells and primroses grew as spring approached. The other side was bordered by a tall hawthorn hedge, attracting many nesting birds.

On first entering the folley, the path quickly dropped away to a very steep incline and on reaching the bottom rose steeply again up the other side of the hill like a roller coaster. A short way on level ground led to a sharp left-hand bend. Right on the corner at the edge of the spinney stood Primrose Cottage where the Dinnin family lived. From this point the next folley could be clearly seen just across the road.

After making our first trip to the village on foot, we decided it would be fun to take our bikes down the steep hill of the first folley. This was just the beginning of many joy rides. I suppose it may seem strange that we were unfamiliar with these footpaths but children and adults living only a couple of miles away were not always aware of footpaths and woods outside their close knit home territory.

My three previous homes had all been situated towards the east end of West Mersea which was known to the locals as 'Upland'. Anybody living past the halfway mark of Mill Road were known as 'Uplanders'. I had previously been an Uplander but now I was living in 'The Yachting Centre' I was classed as being 'Down West'. Dorothy and I were privileged to be able to lay claim to every highway, byway and short cut on the Island, including the beaches and sea walls.

The weather was getting considerably colder and with Christmas only a few weeks away, we were beginning to make Christmas cards, decorations and small gifts at school in readiness for the big day. Rationing was still in operation though, making it difficult for families to be able to give the gifts of their choice. However, everyone had been so used to enduring the hardships of rationing that homemade gifts were both a joy to make and to receive. It's strange that I am unable to remember much about Christmas but I can remember Dad home curing a large piece of pork and Mum making a Christmas cake from one of Uncle Arthur's famous recipes.

Uncle Arthur Saye (Punch) was Mum's oldest brother and lived a little way down the road from us on the opposite side. He came back to Mersea to live with his wife, Alice and their three daughters after he retired and sold up his bakery business in Hatfield, Hertfordshire. He promised to ice and decorate Mum's Christmas cake so it would be the best. I never knew how to take Uncle Arthur. He was such a big tease. I remember when he once asked,

"Would you like some cherries?"

"Oh, yes please," I replied.

He laughed, saying,

"What a shame I haven't got any then."

Christmas dinner was much quieter than we were used to but we had roast chicken with vegetables and all the trimmings followed by Christmas pudding and custard. Mum, Dad and Paul had wine with their dinner and I had Corona fizzy limeade. In the afternoon, Daddy Peter came to collect us in the car and we went to 'Lynton' for tea. Paul decided that he wanted to stay at home and listen to the wireless. We had a lovely time at 'Lynton' with Susan, Terry and John. I missed being able to see them every day. We played with all the new board games, including tiddley-winks. After we got through all the games, it was time for tea.

In the centre of the table stood a huge snowball made of cotton wool and decorated with artificial holly. The snowball contained gifts, games and novelties and opened up at the top by some sort of spring action that forced the novelties to pop out onto the table. There was a great deal of fun and excitement. Everyone had been given a number on his or her tea plate and the novelties in the snowball had a corresponding number stuck to them. If the number on the novelty matched the number on your plate, you claimed your prize.

After tea we were all going to watch television. According to the newspaper there was going to be a special Christmas evening of entertainment. We all settled down for our Christmas viewing with bowls of nuts, home made peppermint creams and brittle toffee. The room had a haze of cigarette smoke wafting up to the ceiling because all the grown ups were smoking - these were the days when the hidden dangers of cigarettes were not recognised. The smell of alcohol was in the air as well as the occasional puff of wood smoke when logs were thrown on to the open fire.

The festive smell of Christmas was undoubtedly a lasting memory for me. Television viewing was finished for the evening and as the programme closed down, the television was switched off. I watched the round blob of light in the centre of the screen gradually reduce to the size of a pinhead and then disappear. The twisted wax candles on the Christmas tree were flickering as the wax ran down onto the brightly coloured holders which were spring clipped to the branches of the tree. Auntie Dot quickly blew the candles out, leaving only the glitter from the thin shreds of silver paper and cotton wool blobs depicting snow as the angel looked proudly down from the top of the tree. It was nearly time to go home.

Mum was collecting our things together ready to put them into the car. There was a heavy frost outside and Dad was calling for us to be careful of the slippery path. I got into the car, snuggling up to Mum for extra warmth in the back seat.

"Mate, it's cold enough to flea yer." said Dad, putting on his warm tweed cap. It had been a lovely afternoon and evening.

The start of the New Year and getting back to school again made me more aware, through conversations with the other pupils at school, that it was now time for me to recognise and admit to myself that I couldn't have two Dads. Roy Bloomfield, one of the kinder boys in our class, spoke up after listening to me discussing that I was bothered about calling two people Dad.

"Don't worry about it. So what if the youngest one is your brother? I've also got a brother who is very much older than me."

"So if Peter is my brother, Susan, Terry and John are my nephews and niece?"

"Yeah, that's right."

"What do you call your brother then, as he's much older than you?"

I never did get an answer from Roy as it was time to go back to our classroom and I didn't approach the subject ever again. I sat in the class turning over in my mind the best way to let Mum know that I was old enough to call 'Daddy Peter' just plain Peter. Another thought came to mind. Auntie Dot would simply be 'Dot'. Cycling home from school gave me even more time to prepare for the ordeal of explaining to Mum what was in my mind. When I arrived home, Mum gave me a cheerful smile and her usual greeting.

"Hello, dear. Have you had a good day at school?"

This made me begin to want to change my mind. I didn't want to hurt her or make her angry.

"Mum..."

"Yes, dear?"

"Why do I call Peter, 'Daddy Peter' when I have already got a Dad?"

Mum looked straight at me and said,

"Well, dear, when you were a baby you called him 'Dada' and then as you got older, it was 'Daddy Peter'".

"But Mum, he's my brother."

"Yes, dear, I suppose he is."

"I am going to call him 'Peter' from now on, Mum and Auntie Dot, just 'Dot'".

"I am sure that will be just fine. You can tell them next time you go round."

"Mmm..." was all I replied.

Peter and Dot were both very understanding about me wanting to address them in a different way.

"Darling, you're growing up so fast. Of course you must call us Peter and Dot. I have been expecting you to make this choice for some time now," said Dot.

Peter looked at me with a fleeting sadness, then his eyes sparkled as he gave me a quick wink and an affectionate cuddle. I was relieved to have a brother and a sister-in-law.

As spring approached, Dad began to renovate the large and rather dilapidated chicken houses ready for some young pullets. He had been thinking about putting these poultry sheds back in use for some time now. The roof had been repaired, the odd window wire meshed and re-glazed. There was little left to do except to purchase the livestock. A journey to the market in Sheepen Road, Colchester was arranged for the following Saturday. Peter had agreed to drive Dad to the market in the car. Norman Smith, the local haulier would be at the market as usual to deliver livestock for anyone requiring his services.

"I'd like to go with you to the market, Dad, if that's OK," I asked.

"Yes, you can come if yer like, so long as yer don't ask for anything." He knew what I was like as far as animals were concerned. I loved them all.

"I won't. I promise, Dad."

CHAPTER 21

A free bus ride, Marion returns and two go 'ebbing'

OVERLEAF: *Ray Cutts (left) and Jacko Hewes*
about to go 'ebbing'.
ABOVE: *My friend, Marion Wicks.*

Going with Dad to the Sheepen Road market on Saturdays was one of my favourite outings. Today was no exception. The sun shone as we walked around, viewing the pens full of young chickens. The pungent smell of animals filled the air and cattle became restless as they waited for their fate to be decided by the highest bidder.

We stopped at several pens with Dad picking up the pullets and feeling their rear ends to make sure that they were at the point of lay. He eventually decided which lots he would bid for. The first batch went for more money than he wanted to pay but he topped the bidding on the next lot and the auctioneer banged his hammer. Dad was now the proud owner of three hundred pullets. I was quite excited about his little venture and couldn't wait for Mr. Smith to deliver the birds.

Mum was less enthusiastic.

"I thought I'd seen the last of bloomin' chickens in large numbers but I suppose it will keep your father happy."

"Mum, you know it will make him happy," I answered.

After Norman Smith had delivered the chickens and they were installed in the chicken house, Peter came down to see how Dad was getting on with his birds. After talking to Dad, he came indoors to see Mum and have a cup of tea. He said,

"Dad's as happy as a pig in shit."

"I know dear, and I really wouldn't want it any other way."

Dorothy was staying the night as Dad's sister Elsie was coming round for the evening to play cards. We would either play Newmarket or Chips. I preferred Newmarket as you could win more money but as we only played a penny a time - a halfpenny in the kitty and a halfpenny on the horse - you couldn't exactly win a fortune. The horses were Jack, Queen, King and Ace.

If Auntie Elsie came to play cards on Sundays we had to play for matchsticks as she said it was wicked to gamble on a Sunday. She would have the box of matches and give us all six matches to play with. We placed one in the kitty and one on a horse.

When the game was over Dad would be persuaded to play some hymns on the piano and we would all have a singsong to some joyful melodies. Sundays also meant we could have a lie in. Both Dorothy and I belonged to the library so we could spend some time reading our library books in bed. The librarian, Mrs. Baldwin, would get quite angry if we returned our books late. She was a fierce old girl and glared at us over her horn-rimmed glasses.

"Pixie! Dorothy! It's time to get up," called Mum.

"Won't be long," I replied.

Dorothy slept on the outside of the bed, with me against the wall. Dorothy jumped out of bed and was first to use the pot that she grabbed from under the bed. I thought she was never going to stop weeing and got a sudden fit of the giggles. I made Dorothy laugh so much that she blew off, giving out a huge noise. I was laughing so much that I now needed the pot badly.

"Quick, get off, I am going to wet myself."

I was so desperate I gave her a shove, which nearly led to disaster.

"What are you two girls getting up to up there? Hurry up and come down for breakfast."

We quickly got dressed, went downstairs then washed and cleaned our teeth at the kitchen sink. When we sat down at the table we still couldn't stop giggling. Mum was making toast on the grill. Dorothy was eating her puffed wheat. I had poured my cereal into the bowl with the milk and had just taken a mouthful when I noticed the colourful advert on the box that said 'Shot From Guns' - it was illustrated with a huge gun shooting the puffed wheat cereal into the air. With my mouth full, I looked at Dorothy and said,

"Shot from guns."

I laughed so much that I shot the puffed wheat out of my mouth straight across the table. Dad was so angry with my bad manners.

"How dare you behave like that at the table. Take your breakfast in the other room. You can eat on your own."

By this time I was hysterical, despite being on my own at the table in the sitting room. I eventually suppressed my laughter, realising that if Mum got cross she might suggest that Dorothy went home and that was the last thing I wanted to happen. It was Sunday school that afternoon and I didn't want to go on my own.

After our Sunday roast we caught the two o'clock bus from the bus park in the High Street. It dropped us right outside the Assembly Hall. We'd met Miriam Bacon, Dorothy's friend, along the road and there were a few other young people on the bus as well. The bus conductor collected everyone's fare - except mine. I kept trying to catch his eye to let him know that I hadn't paid but each time he seemed to be taking someone else's fare and didn't take any notice. As the others were getting off the bus I was at last able to catch the conductor and tell him that he hadn't taken my money. He did the strangest thing. He just looked at me, winked, grinned and said,

"That's alright."

I got off the bus and said to Dorothy,

"He didn't take my money - it's strange - I wonder why not."

"I dunno," she replied, "perhaps he just forgot."

After Sunday school we caught the bus back home again and it was the same bus driver and conductor. Exactly the same thing happened - the conductor didn't take my money. When I got home I gave my bus fare back to Mum and told her that the bus conductor didn't take my fare. Dad sat in his easy chair reading his newspaper. He looked over the top of the paper and said,

"Didn't take your fare? Why not?"

"I don't know."

Mum said,

"What did the man look like?"

I described him the best way that I could.

"Jim, I reckon it was Harry Conway."

"Oh, I see," said Dad. He continued to read the paper but it seemed to have irritated him.

"Who is Harry Conway?" I asked.

"You wouldn't be any the wiser if I told you," said Mum, a sombre, mysterious air about her.

I knew it was best to refrain from pursuing the matter further - for the time being anyway.

I had been corresponding with my friend Marion ever since she returned to Harrow after the summer holidays. Now the Easter holidays were nearly here and Mum had kept her promise about Marion being able to stay with us for Easter. Only a few more days and she would be back in Mersea.

It was during this holiday that we both learned how to go 'ebbing'. This involved following the receding tide, walking miles out across the mudflats looking for oysters. Marion's uncle Ray Cutts was the best teacher we could have had. We already knew where to find the best cockles and winkles on the mud and it was while we were cockling that we met Ray Cutts and his wife 'Cuddy' - I never learned her real name.

They were on the ebb with Ray carrying his hessian sack over his shoulder.

"What are you looking for, Uncle Ray?" asked Marion.

"Spat and brood, gal," he replied. "If both on yer come 'ere, I'll show yer what yer gotta look for."

"Alright, but we're looking for cockles."

"Yer can do both but if you pick up spat and brood you'll be able to earn yourselves some pocket money."

"Oh really! Will you show us what to do then? We could do with some extra money," said Marion.

We followed Ray and Cuddy and they taught us the best technique for finding spat and brood. Ray explained that spat (tiny oysters) were worth less money than brood. Brood were much bigger which meant that they wouldn't take so long to mature and were worth more money. It was sometimes possible to find a fully grown oyster. They were like gold dust to us as they were worth a lot more.

We soon got hooked on ebbing and earned very good money by selling our catch to Ted Woolf - who at that time was the biggest oyster merchant on the Island and paid the highest rates. We must have walked many miles searching the shores for oysters, returning home again covered in mud and hungry but healthy and with money in our pockets.

The next morning we woke up wondering what to do. We were both lying in bed when I had an idea.

"Marion, do you think my room would look better if we moved the furniture around?"

"Yes, I do. It would be better if the bed wasn't against the wall, because unless I get out of bed first, you have to climb over me."

"Shall we do it after breakfast, then?"

"Yes, if you want to," said Marion.

I drew back the curtains. It was a lovely sunny day. The

birds were singing and our chickens must have been laying eggs as they were making the noises that chickens make after laying - 'Coop...coop...coop quark!' I think the sound of the hens must be partly responsible for our family name for them. Calling chickens 'coopies' has been passed down through the generations.

"Come on, you two girls - your breakfast is ready. It will get cold if you don't hurry up and come down," called Mum.

"Alright, we're coming," I replied.

We had a lovely breakfast of eggs, bacon, fried bread and baked beans. I whispered to Marion about the boys at school calling baked beans 'arsehole ammunition' - we both got a fit of the giggles and were told to behave at the table.

After breakfast we went back upstairs to put our plan of moving the bedroom around into action. It must have been one of the worst ideas we'd had for a very long time. First, we moved the bed across the window to allow enough space for the wardrobe to be moved. We then tried to move the wardrobe but with all the clothes hanging inside it was too heavy. So we took all the clothes out and laid them across the bed.

"We're getting in a bit of a muddle here," said Marion as we tried to find a space for the chest of drawers.

The heavy Wilton rug covering most of the floor was, by now, rucked up under the furniture.

"Your Mum is going to be really cross with us if she finds out," said Marion looking very worried and serious.

I just looked at Marion's worried expression and began to laugh, seeing the funny side of things. The very worst had happened. We were wedged in the bedroom, unable to get out and no one could get in either. I could hear the ominous sound of footsteps coming up the stairs. I was now also beginning to get worried.

"Pixie! What's going on in there?"

The brass knob of the door was being turned, but I knew

216

that Mum couldn't get in.

"Nothing really, Mum. We've just got in a bit of a muddle trying to change the bedroom round."

"Open the door at once!"

I looked at Marion, who shrugged her shoulders and whispered,

"What now?"

"I'm really sorry, Mum, but we're stuck. Everything's got wedged because we tried to move the bedroom round."

"I don't know what your father will say about this when I tell him."

We could hear her making her way back downstairs. The bedroom window was open and we could hear Mum calling,

"Jim... Jim," from the back door.

I looked through the window and could see Dad coming down the garden path.

"What ya want, mate?"

"It's the girls. They've tried to change the bedroom round and they've got all the furniture wedged - they can't get out and we can't get in."

Dad came heavy footing up the stairs. The sound of his feet on the stairs reflected the mood he was in. It was a wonder the doorknob didn't come off in his hand the way he was trying to push the door. It didn't move any more than about three inches.

"I don't know why you can't bleedin' well leave things alone." He departed back downstairs, closing the back door with a bang.

When I peered out of the window Dad was coming down the garden carrying a long wooden ladder. The only way in was through the window. After Dad climbed into the bedroom he was able to manoeuvre the furniture back to its original position. As soon as the door was free to be opened we scurried downstairs, no longer prisoners of my bedroom. Marion looked at me and said,

"I've never seen your Dad angry before."

"I know. He doesn't usually get that cross. He'll be alright later - let's go for a bike ride."

On our travels we met some of the local kids, played rounders on the beach for a while and then returned home for mid-day dinner. On the way home we passed the church, then into Church Road. As we rode along side by side I said to Marion,

"Let's see how far we can ride with our eyes closed."

"Okay," said Marion.

I began to cycle slightly ahead of Marion, cheating just a little bit because I kept opening one eye with a quick flicker. Suddenly, from behind me came an enormous bang, then silence. As I turned round sharply to see what had happened, Marion came crawling from behind the wooden gate of a house, her bike lying on the ground. As she pulled herself up a kind old lady appeared, having heard the loud bang of the bike hitting her garden gate.

"Have you hurt yourself, my dear?" she asked.

"No, I'm fine," said Marion rubbing her grazed knee as she picked up her bike.

Although I was sorry about Marion's accident, I just couldn't help seeing the funny side of her mishap and I started to laugh and laugh - so much so, that I thought I might wet myself. Marion also had a fit of laughter. How would our day end.

Mum had the dinner ready - stew and dumplings.

"What have you done to your knee, dear?" she asked Marion.

"Oh, I just fell off my bike."

CHAPTER 22

New classrooms, the Coastguard Cottages fire and more questions

OVERLEAF: *Fire destroys the coastguard cottages.*
ABOVE: *Ben Mole with his wife Patricia (Sylv) holding baby Veronica. They were rehoused after the fire.*

There was great excitement at school now the three new senior classrooms and modern on-site canteen were completed. I knew it would be a year or so before I moved up into the senior classes but I was looking forward to enjoying the new facilities.

Seniors had been in their new classrooms for some time and the whole school would soon be using the canteen. Dan Woolf, the school caretaker, was in charge of the new central heating system which supplied heat and hot water to the canteen and classrooms. The entire system was run from a large, new coke-fuelled boiler.

One afternoon at break time, two of the older boys, David (Moey) Mussett and David Stoker, who were notorious for getting into muddles, noticed the boiler room door had been left unlocked.

"Cor, look at this, Moey," said David Stoker as he opened the door wider.

"Ass more complicated than the old 'un," said Moey, gazing inside. "Let's see how high we can raise the temperature on that big ol' gauge, shall we?"

"How the hell are ya gonna do that, then?" asked David.

"Get some heat under it," said Moey.

"Christ, yes," said David, giggling mischievously.

As the boiler door was opened, the ferocity of the heat made them withdraw quickly. Undaunted, they used a small coal shovel and a poker to hook a few pieces of hot coal from the boiler, intending to hold them under the thermometer.

Suddenly, they were startled by the sound of a whistle being blown. Break time was over. So, it seemed, was their experiment. They dropped the shovel holding the hot coals and ran into the playground ready to return to the class.

What the two boys didn't realise was that the hot coals had landed on a pile of empty coal sacks. Slowly the sacks began to smoulder - it would only take a small draught to cause the lot to ignite. As Dan Woolf approached the boiler room he could see tell tale black smoke escaping through cracks and openings.

He knew it was going to be a job for the Fire Brigade. If he opened the door now and let the air in, the whole lot could go up. What the hell had these two boys been up to? He'd caught sight of them running from the scene when the whistle went.

We all sat down in the classroom whispering quietly as we waited for the lesson to start.

The murmur of voices was suddenly drowned out by the loud warning siren coming from the nearby Fire Station. Minutes later we heard the clanging of the fire engine bell. The sound of the bell stopped and the loud rattling of the fire engine's motor could be heard. It was here - at the school! The whole class began to chatter loudly, wondering what was going on.

"Quiet, please," shouted Mister Davis, "I'm sure you have all seen and heard a fire engine before."

An attempt was made to get on with school work but our concentration seemed to be lacking. It couldn't have been too serious as it wasn't long before we heard the fire engine moving off. No one seemed to know exactly what had happened. The next day there were various tales going around the school about the reason for the Fire Brigade being called out. It was alleged that David Stoker and Moey Mussett had accidentally caused a small fire in the boiler room. After morning assembly Mister Cotgrove, the headmaster, said,

"I would like David Stoker and David Mussett to come to

my office, please."

The two boys went to 'Ol Cotgrove's' office. The accusations had been dealt with the day before. The boys had owned up to their 'accident' and now they were faced with the punishment - six of the best with Cotgrove's cane. As they stood there nervously waiting, Mister Cotgrove spoke.

"Well, Stoker, do you want to bend over or do you want to hold out your hand?"

"On the hand sir," said David.

"Come on then boy. Put your hand across the desk."

David put his hand across the desk, holding his breath, and just as the cane came down he pulled his hand away. The same thing happened two more times. This infuriated Mister Cotgrove so much that he shouted at David,

"Bend over that desk, boy. I'll not have any more of that nonsense."

David bent over the desk and got six lashes with the cane across the bottom.

"Come on Mussett. Bend over. Your turn next."

Moey didn't get a choice. He took his punishment. Six whacks but not a tear from either lad. As the boys walked across the playground Moey looked at David and said,

"Cor, my bloody arse is sore. What ya have to take yer hand away for?"

"Jest so you could get yer arse hit so shut up moanin' will ya? Mine's sore as well."

Two dejected Davids walked back into their class and sat down very carefully on the edge of their chairs. Hopefully, it wouldn't take too long for the pain to go away.

I lay snuggled warm in my bed. It was just after six o'clock on the morning of 28th October, 1949. I was awakened suddenly by the sound of the siren going off. I knew it meant there was a fire but at that moment I was too tired to give it much thought. I must have drifted off into another light sleep because the next thing I was aware of was the sound of the bell ringing on the Fire Engine. It couldn't be far away as I could hear the bell clearly. Almost immediately there seemed to be more than one fire engine as I heard more bells ringing.

Dad was always up early in the mornings. It was difficult for him to change the habit of getting up at dawn ready to start his day's work. He'd managed to adjust to some extent but he did enjoy his own company first thing in the morning. His first job was to switch on the electric kettle ready for Ada's cup of tea in bed. Mum looked forward to her cup of tea which Dad always made sure was in a China cup with two McVities Rich Tea biscuits in the saucer. I heard him come upstairs with Mum's tea and as both our bedroom doors were open I heard most of their conversation.

"I've just been talking to Bo Saye. He's off out today so he's delivering the milk early. He's just told me that the Coastguard Cottages have all bin burnt down. The fire started about six o'clock this morning."

"How terrible, Jim. Has anyone been hurt?"

"No mate, I don't think so, but they're all homeless."

So that's why the siren went off and no wonder I was able to hear the bells so clearly - the Coastguard Cottages were only a few minutes walk away from our home. I thought that if I got up early and went to school the long way round I'd be able to see the extent of the damage caused by the fire. There must have been at least eleven families living in the cottages with many children of school age attending our local school.

Laying in bed thinking about what would happen to the homeless families began to upset me. I felt scared for them. How would I be feeling if it were us? I got up, dressed and ran downstairs to find Dad enjoying his fried breakfast. He needed his quiet time in the mornings without Mum bustling about. During the cold winter months, after lighting the kitchen fire, he would often bring the oil stove in from the scullery, place it on a chrome tray on the kitchen floor and fry his breakfast in the warm while the fire was getting up.

I remember Mum coming downstairs one winter morning when Dad hadn't time to clear away the newspaper which he'd placed on the lino floor under the chrome tray and oil stove. The newspaper was spattered with tiny oil splashes from the frying pan.

"Jim, have you been frying on the kitchen floor with the oil stove?"

"No, mate," Dad answered with a chuckle as he picked up the newspaper quickly.

"Well I hope not. It's not the thing to do."

Mum's early morning cuppa usually avoided a confrontation in the kitchen. She knew what he got up to but couldn't condone his 'fry-up'.

As planned, I left for school earlier than usual. Dad had already got my bike out of the shed and it stood at the back entrance by the ivy bush. Rosebank Road was full of ruts and puddles as we'd recently had some bad weather so I kept close to the hedge, pushing my bike into Victory Road. I crossed over the road into the first folley, got on my bike and whizzed down the hill and up the steep incline on the other side. It was here on the level ground approaching the end of the folley that the air contained the horrible smell of burning.

Entering the second folley I had to get off my bike as there were a number of people standing around talking about the early morning tragedy. Eventually I was able to see what was once a row of houses, now just a ghostly shell of outer brick walls showing large square openings where the windows had once been. The chimneys stood tall and square, their enormity exaggerated by the absence of the roof. The Coastguard Cottages had gone. It was hard to believe that as most of the Island was still sleeping in the comfort of their homes, all the residents in Coastguard Cottages were fleeing from the life threatening flames that were fast engulfing everything they owned.

Ben Mole was the first alerted to the fire by his young son, Alan. There was a small hole in the ceiling of the boys' bedroom, where they had accidentally pushed the handle of a broom which at the time was being used to make an indoor tent. Alan was suddenly awakened by strange crackling sounds coming from the attic. Looking up at the ceiling he could see a flame licking through the small round hole. Jumping out of bed he ran to his parents' room shouting,

"Dad... Dad, wake up, there's flames in the attic."

"Goo away, boy. Yer bin dreamin'"

"I ain't, Dad."

"Bugger off."

Alan hastened back to his room. The fire had really taken hold. Sparks and debris were falling onto his bed. Alan screamed at Terry to get out of the room, then ran back to his father, shouting loudly,

"Dad, it's real. I am not dreamin' – there's a fire in the attic."

Ben threw back his bedclothes and jumped out of bed. He was still putting on his trousers as he ran to the boys' room, his wife following close behind him. Looking up at the ceiling he realised how serious it was. It wouldn't take long for the fire to spread through the whole roof as it was all open space with no partitioning walls separating it into individual attic space.

"Get out all of yer. There's a fire in the roof."

Mrs Mole, fearful for her children, was shouting to the girls to hurry up. Her voice was high pitched and shaky as it carried through the house.

Geraldine, the oldest of the girls, had snatched her six month old baby sister Veronica from her cot, cradling her protectively in her arms. By now the tiles were beginning to fall through the roof, crashing down dangerously.

Joyce grabbed her brand new overcoat, putting it over her pyjamas, leaving her new shoes by the bed. As she ran outside to safety she felt the cold of the ground on her bare feet and wished she had put her shoes on. It was too late to go back inside as the fire was now burning fiercely. Ben stood next to his wife, checking that all his family were safe outside. Geraldine, baby Veronica, Young Ben, Alan and Terry. Yes, they were all out safely.

He ran to check if anyone needed help. Charlie Gundy was trapped inside. Ben managed to pull him through one of the windows - his escape through the door had been cut off by the fire. All the families living in the cottages were experiencing the same horrors. They were all having to flee for their lives with no time to save any possessions. The fire had first started in the end house next to Willie and Florence Pudney. Arthur, their son, had risen early for work and had just turned on the wireless when he saw sparks flying past the window. He only just had time to alert his sleeping parents who managed to get out safely but the flames had already spread across a vast area of the roof.

The speed at which the firemen worked to try and contain the fire couldn't be matched by the efficiency of the water drawn from the inadequately small pipes coming directly off the mains supply. Sheer frustration and despair was beginning to show on everyone's faces as the firemen wrestled with the supply of water. It looked as though the homes were surely doomed.

However, every family had miraculously got out of the burning inferno. The Island hadn't suffered as great a loss as this during the whole period of the war. It was ironic that just a faulty electrical wire could be the cause of this devastation.

When I arrived at school I put my bike in the bike shed and joined a group of friends gathered in the playground. The main topic of conversation was the early morning fire. Everyone was concerned for the unfortunate families and what was happening to them. It was rumoured that some had been offered temporary shelter at the Church Hall in High

Street North while others had gone to friends and relations. Help with food and clothes would certainly be a top priority.

I was now passing through a difficult stage in my life, not knowing what was happening to me. One minute I felt so happy I could almost move a mountain, the next minute I felt like bursting into tears. One afternoon as I came out of school, I noticed Mum had come to meet Terry and was waiting on the opposite side of the road talking to some of the other Mums. I looked at Mum and realised she looked older than the other mothers. My gloomy mood suddenly took over and I began to think to myself,

"I hope she doesn't go and die yet." In the event, she lived until she was nearly ninety years of age.

I kept this morbid thought to myself, never telling anyone, but when I got home I began to cry, tears rolling down my cheeks.

"What's the matter, dear? Why are you crying?"

"I don't know," I answered.

"There must be some reason. Has something gone wrong at school?"

"No, I don't know why I am crying. I can't stop."

"Come on, dear, dry your eyes before your Dad comes in, you don't want to upset him."

I did as I was told and gradually began to feel better. Stupid things would often reduce me to tears. The mood swings went on for a long period of time. Auntie Tod said it was my hormones and not to worry as most young girls went through the same thing. I would like to think that one of my hormonal swings was responsible for an altercation I had with Madge. She was one of the pupils from Peldon and travelled to Mersea School by bus every day. At times it was rather, 'them and us', or 'The Peldon Lot'.

Madge was bigger than me and also a bit older. She was

being offish with me, laughing and giggling with her friends. At one point she stood close to me, glaring into my face. I wasn't normally aggressive or unkind, but today I retaliated and gave her a piece of my mind. At the same time I gave her a shove and said,

"Go away, Madge Baldwin. You're adopted."

"No I'm not."

"Yes you are. So there."

I knew it was an unforgivable thing to say and I wish I had kept quiet - I still feel guilty today. I had heard Mum and Auntie Tod talking one day and Madge was described as the adopted daughter. We both stamped off in different directions, Madge with her friends and me with mine. The next day in the playground, Madge approached me with her friends following behind her and spoke in a loud voice so everyone could hear.

"Anyway, Pixie Farthing, I told my Mum what you said and she said that you're adopted."

"Oh no I jolly well am not, so you can clear off right now."

I really wanted to hit her, but walked away with these words turning over in my mind…

'…why would her mother tell her lies?'

Dot was getting bigger and bigger. We knew that it wouldn't be long now before the baby arrived. The birth was to be at home and Mum said she would be there to help as soon as they needed her.

CHAPTER 23

A *new arrival,* the beach hut bungle and senior school

OVERLEAF: *A school play. From left: (back row)*
Jennifer Mills, John May, Pixie Farthing, Dawn Forster,
Dorothy Carter, Sheila Sibley, Roy Bloomfield; (front row)
Billy Kettle, Sylvia Lane, David Carter, John Chatters.
ABOVE: *West Mersea County Primary School teachers, 1954.*
From left: (back row) E. Hucklesby, J. Jowers, B. Jowers,
M. Davis, Miss Aldridge, Mr Ambridge; (front row) I. South,
F. Keene, Mrs Cheshire, Mr Westcott (Headmaster),
G. Johnson, J. Chesney.

On the 11th April, 1950, Timothy Farthing was born. He was a strong, healthy baby, wanting the usual attention that all babies require.

Terry was spending even more time at our house now. It was one less little person for Dot to look after. Dot reminded Peter that the baby's birth should soon be registered. He agreed they should sort it out but he was in a hurry to get off to work.

During the morning he was passing the Council Offices and popped in to check which day the Registrar would be there. His luck was in. He could register the baby today and the Registrar would be available in a few minutes. It wasn't long before he was invited into the main Council Chamber. The Registrar sat behind the large oak desk with two other chairs positioned in front of him, but slightly to one side.

"Good morning, sir. How can I help you?"

"I would like to register the birth of my son."

The Registrar was completing the form, asking all the relevant questions, and then he asked,

"Baby's name?"

"Timothy Farthing."

"Baby's second name?"

Peter hesitated for a moment, realising that they hadn't really settled on a second name.

"Er, um - James."

"Are you sure now?" said the man at the desk.

"Yes, of course. James will be fine."

The birth certificate was finally signed and handed over. Peter paid the fee and left the office. After he got into his vehicle parked outside, he realised that Terry's second name was also James. The boys would both have identical initials - T.J.

"What a bugger!" he thought.

Smiling to himself, he folded the certificate neatly and placed it safely in his wallet. He'd have to wait for the right moment to tell Dot about Timothy James.

Dad was self-employed and had always been his own boss. He was still a very hard working man. His love of the land, animals and outside life meant he took on varied jobs. There was always someone at the door offering him work. And on occasions he would work for Peter. Beach huts were becoming popular again on Mersea and many were being built all along the beach.

Peter was extremely busy with building and decorating and had plenty of work still coming in. The firm was having a job keeping on top of it all and Dad had been collared to paint one of the huts. Most of the beach huts were numbered and he had been given strict instructions - which hut and the exact location.

He was armed with all the equipment he needed - sandpaper, undercoat, green topcoat, brushes, turps and cleaning rags – all packed into the very large saddle-bag on the back of his bike. He went everywhere on his bike, as did nearly everyone else in those days.

It was a hard working day with just one break from one until two o'clock for his dinner. During the latter part of the afternoon, Jacky Wells, one of the other workmen was sent down to the beach to see how Dad was getting on and if he required any help. What happened next would have been good material for a comedy sketch.

"Christ, Jim, it's the wrong bloody hut," said Jacky,

laughing hysterically.

"It ain't, mate. It's the one I've been instructed to do."

"I was with Pete when he priced up the job, Jim. It's the hut next door." Jacky literally rolled on the ground laughing.

"You mean to say I've spent all day painting the wrong bleedin' hut?"

"Yes, mate, ya have," said Jacky, still laughing.

"I bet a shilling they won't get me painting any more unless they can manage to give me the right number."

I now knew I had failed the entry exam to attend The Girls' High School in Colchester. I knew when Mr. 'Popeye' Davis our form teacher selected us that I would be a borderline case. The school had a large number of both boys and girls entered for the grammar schools this year. The boys who passed would attend the boys' Grammar School.

The results had been announced in school assembly. There was a round of applause for those who had been successful. I must say I was slightly disappointed but also relieved that I would be staying at Mersea School and would be moving into one of the new senior classrooms.

Mr Davis gave the class basic music lessons combined with singing, which taught us the value of counts to each note, the tonic sol-fa, doh-ray-me etc and the ability to sing in tune, following the music on printed song sheets. Occasionally on a Friday afternoon, he would bring his large harp and play it to the class. I found this a real treat and loved listening to this beautiful instrument. Not everyone enjoyed it as much as I did.

We had just finished singing the song that included the lyrics,
'Some talk of Alexander and some of Hercules,
Of Hector and Lysander, and such great names as these...'
Sylvia, my friend sitting at the desk in front of me, must

have been fooling around, or not paying attention because suddenly Mr Davis shouted,

"Sylvia Lane! Tell me - who or what is Hercules?"

She looked around with a puzzled smile on her face.

"Come on now. Answer the question."

Giggling to myself, I whispered to her,

"A bicycle."

To my surprise, she actually repeated,

"A bicycle, sir."

"Come out here, girl."

The weather was cold and the two ends of the long scarf she was wearing hung over the back of the chair. Earlier, I had tied the loose ends to the chair. When she got up to move to the front of the class, she dragged the chair across the floor with a loud clatter.

"I am really sorry, sir. I don't know how this could have happened."

She spoke in an apologetic voice, turning around to look at me. The whole class was laughing hysterically. Fortunately we were saved by the bell as it was time to go home.

With the summer holidays over and the start of the autumn term, it would be strange without the 'brainy ones' in class. The one I missed the most was Jennifer Cock. I was also going to miss Dorothy who went to East Ward Secondary Modern School in Colchester. She wanted to do business studies, including shorthand and typing. East Ward was able to offer these facilities.

There were a lot of new pupils having to move up from Langenhoe Junior School to West Mersea Seniors. Langenhoe was about four miles from Mersea and these pupils came by bus every day. Right from the very first day at Mersea School, Dorothy Carter from Langenhoe came to sit next to me and she became my best friend, sharing difficult times, jokes and secrets. We and some of the others in the class had so much fun that I never wanted an excuse for time off.

Our class was large with twenty-eight pupils. The teacher was Mrs Johnson. We could tell by the look on her face that she was going to be strict – 'a right old honey'. Mrs Johnson, apart from being our teacher, was the school's main needlework teacher, in charge of all the sewing machines and dress materials.

We had been making some small felt toys, decorating them with coloured beads and sequins. I'd begun to stuff my pink and grey horse with cotton wool when Dorothy said,

"I could do with a haircut. I think I'll have it cut into another fringe."

I looked at Dorothy's hair and could see the fringe had virtually grown out.

"I'll cut it for you, it won't take long."

"Well you can't do it now."

"Yes I can, I've got the scissors," I said, clicking them open and shut and giggling quietly.

Mrs Johnson had her back to us. She was helping someone sort out their sewing machine.

"Have you got a comb?" I asked Dorothy quietly.

"Yes, it's here in my bag."

"Let's have it, then."

Dorothy handed me the comb.

"Quickly, put your head down, so I can comb the front hair forward."

Mrs Johnson was still very busy. I combed Dorothy's hair into place and quickly snipped away, leaving her with a very uneven fringe.

"Oh, it does suit you," I said, and began to laugh.

"What's it like?"

"It'll be OK."

My giggling and Dorothy's whispering must have reached Mrs Johnson's ears. She turned round and shouted,

"Quiet please!"

I grabbed the loose hair off the desk and held it in my hands. Dorothy picked up any hair that was still on the desk, both of us scared of being found out.

"What are you going to do with it?"

"I don't know."

I looked at the felt horse, my brain working overtime. I had to get rid of the handful of hair. I knew where it was going. I stuffed as much as I could in the horse. Dorothy had a half empty packet of Smiths crisps in her bag and was able to put the remainder in the crisp bag. Luck was with us as Mrs Johnson called out,

"Right, it's nearly time to pack up. Will you please put your things away."

"Phew, that was a close shave."

We both started to laugh again, this time with relief.

"Pixie, it's all very well for you to laugh - my Mum's gonna kill me when I get home."

Being a 'Senior' and associating with boys and girls of up to fifteen years and over meant the naivety of the 'Junior' years suddenly disappeared. We had to face the responsibility and reality of growing up. It was certainly no less enjoyable though. Academically I was now achieving good results but my sense of humour and failure to control my laughter sometimes got me in trouble. There was one occasion in particular when I had to spend a whole afternoon outside the classroom door. Dorothy whispered to me, her hand shielding her mouth,

"I've got a joke to tell you later."

"Oh, go on, tell me now."

"A lady had a wooden baby. Her husband was a Pole."

I began to laugh. It had a spontaneous effect, making Dorothy laugh as well. She had been suffering for some days with a bad cold and as she laughed a string of long yellow snot dangled from her nose. Her embarrassed horror and quick fumbling for her handkerchief made me laugh even more. Mrs Johnson, hearing the laughter, looked at me and said,

"Ann Farthing, get out of this class immediately. You can do your laughing outside."

As I got up, I let my chair drag across the hard floor, making as much noise as possible. I knew everyone was looking at me but at the time I couldn't care a damn. I hadn't planned to upset the class and if Old Ma Johnson had spoken to me in a nice manner I would have said that I was sorry. I had been taught to respect grown-ups even if I thought they were wrong.

Time was passing quickly at school. I was now in Mr 'Jankers' Jowers class, just one away from the leavers' class. Dorothy and I remained close friends - we were still allowed to sit together, sharing the same desk. Mr Jowers was a good teacher and could at times be good fun. However, he was always in control of the class, particularly with some of the more challenging pupils.

One day, Alan Weaver - or 'Tary' or 'Bucket' (as in 'Tarbucket') - was laughing and talking in class. The eggs had just been collected by the two boys doing their week's chicken duty. The eggs were in a basket on the front desk. Mr Jowers reached across, picked up an egg and threw it, aiming at...

"Weaver!" he shouted loudly.

The slimy contents and broken eggshell slithered down the back wall. The class roared with laughter.

"That's enough now, you rowdy lot. Weaver, you can go and clear that mess up."

* * *

I now moved up to Mr 'Hucks' Hucklesby's class - my final year before leaving school. Huck was a good teacher. His teaching methods were unconventional but often got marked improvements from pupils who previously had poor results. Part of a literature lesson would be taken up by Huck sitting at his desk reading one of the chosen classics to the class. He would read in such a manner that even the most boring tales would keep everyone interested.

The same would apply to his poetry reading. There were times when he would hold us spellbound by a scary ghost story he had made up himself or even some true World War Two stories from his experiences while fighting for his country. This tall, bearded man gave a lot to the school and we all respected him.

He did dish out occasional punishments, mostly to the boys. In the large, walk-in cupboard behind his desk lay the two items he used for administering punishment - a very large slipper and a fid, which is a long, tapered wooden tool used for splicing rope. If anyone had done anything bad enough to be punished, Huck would give them a choice.

"Do you want the slipper or the fid cake?"

The answer would almost certainly be,

"The slipper, sir."

CHAPTER 24

East Coast floods, Bert Stock's Fair and the £500 armchair

OVERLEAF: *Houseboat Peggotty.*
ABOVE: *Don Bland and his wife Ruth.*

It is Monday 2nd January, 1953. During the weekend there were the highest tides ever recorded along the East Coast of Great Britain and the biggest on the Island for sixty years.

Mersea Island suffered a lot of material damage but thankfully there was no loss of life. Newspapers, the radio and television reported fatalities in many areas including Jaywick and Canvey Island. I found it remarkable that gales from the North of Scotland could cause a surge so great that it raised our tidal waters to such an extent.

The damage along Coast Road, a short walk from our house, was unbelievable. Boats lay across the road, houseboats had broken adrift and turned over on their sides and there was even a broken up old smack blocking the road by The Causeway - with debris laying everywhere. The saddest sight was the beach huts. Some were completely broken up while some had been taken out to sea by the tide. Others were badly damaged, leaving their contents open to the elements and unscrupulous pilfering. Only a few survived and were left standing, ready for the next season.

This year, the caravans from Bert Stock's Fair were to be parked in the field next to our house. The fair arrived every year in time for the regatta and was normally held in the Victory field adjoining the Victory pub. Usually the caravans, amusements and stalls had enough room to park on one field but this year the fair was bigger and better than ever and needed more room to park the caravans. Mr Bert Stock came to visit Dad to ask if it was possible for us to supply the people living in the caravans with drinking water.

Dad agreed that it wouldn't be a problem. Our scullery was a wooden extension built onto the back of the house and sometime in past years a hole had been drilled through the wood just large enough to take a piece of rubber hose pipe. Every day the large galvanised tank that stood against the wooden wall would be filled with water from the hose connected to the indoor cold water tap. The water was used for the chickens or to water the garden.

The 'Caravan People' would be able to put the hose directly into their water containers. Mr Stock was pleased with the arrangement and promised there would be very little interruption to our day as he was aware that someone had to be at home to turn on the tap. Bert Stock's caravan was very large and was one of the first to arrive on the Victory field. The fair travelled slowly through the village - a picturesque convoy of large trucks and assorted caravans.

One by one they arrived at the Victory field with the large open two-tiered trailers displaying an assortment of amusements. The brightly coloured dodgem cars - despite being held securely in place - jogged from side to side as the large trailer bumped over the high kerb then crossed the grass verge and pathway to get onto the field. Mr Stock's caravan stood right at the back of the field, sheltered by a tall hedge and overhanging trees. It had an elaborate air about it - an aristocratic traveller's home.

Soon it was to be surrounded by other vans, not as posh but just as important to the opening night of the fair. The site became cluttered with vehicles, all waiting for the time to unload the amusements, rides and side stalls. In the meantime, just up the road, family caravans were beginning to arrive on the field next to our house. Not long after they arrived the older children were off out on their bikes, not a bit tired after their long journey. They had obviously completely adjusted to this way of life.

Two days later, the gentle westerly wind blew the sound of fairground music across the Island. It drew the crowds, all wanting to enjoy the fun of the fair. We all walked down the road - Mum, Dad, Terry, Cousin Dorothy and myself. The sight was awesome.

Brightly coloured lights lit up all the stalls and rides. A loud siren blasted from the dodgems when each ride came to an end. The carousel revolved with twisted brass poles taking the elegant horses up and down, their manes blowing in the wind as the ride gradually built up speed. The swinging boats were at the right hand entrance to the fair field. Some of the older boys on the swings were pulling and synchronising the long thick ropes so well that they were swinging high enough that it almost looked as though they would fall out.

Mum and Dad were trying their luck at a stall offering some very attractive prizes - dolls, teddy bears, electrical goods and tea sets. To win one of these wonderful prizes you had to match the name on your purchased ticket to the name lit up on an electronic board. Participants would wait expectantly, looking for the light to stop on their name.

Dorothy and I decided to go and look at the dodgems while my parents were trying to win a prize. The dodgems were where all the teenage boys were so we decided to see if we could match their skills. We were having a wonderful time, each of us taking our turn at driving. We got into a couple of scrapes where an assistant jumped on the back of the car to turn the steering wheel hard to release us from a tangle of crashed cars. We were well under way when Mum and Dad beckoned us to come off. It was just as well because we were both running short of money and there were a lot of things we still wanted to go on - especially the horses.

Terry was very excited as he had won a complete tea set. Mr Jack Mole, who lived just up the road from us saw Terry win his prize and said,

"Terry the Tiger, the Tea Pot Winner!"

After Terry's win, whenever we passed Mr Mole in the street he would call out,

"Hello, Terry the Tiger, the Tea Pot Winner!"

There was now only one more night of the fair and they'd soon be packing up ready to leave. Mrs Bert Stock came to the house to visit Mum and thank her for her kindness in supplying water for the people in the caravans. In return, Mum was invited for afternoon tea at their caravan. I was having dinner at home and listened to Mum telling Dad about her invitation.

"Jim, I really don't think I want to go to their caravan. I don't think it's my type of thing. Do you?"

"You go, Mate. You might jest enjoy yourself. You can't be rude and let the woman down."

"No, I suppose not. I'll go after I've met Terry from school."

Poor Mum. She thought she was having tea with a Didicoi.

After collecting Terry from school, the two of them walked down Victory Road to the fairground. The afternoon was hot, with the sun beating down from a cloudless sky. Walking through the fairground, they felt the cool of the shade created by the tall striped canvas stalls. Ada Farthing followed by her grandson approached the Stocks' grand-looking caravan. The maroon coloured exterior was shiny and dust free with a highly polished brass handrail leading up the steps to the door. Mrs Stock was waiting at the door ready to greet her.

"I'm so glad you were able to come. Do come in, my dear."

Mum was taken aback by the grand interior of the mobile home. The soft furnishings were very well chosen, blending together to give the room a tranquil feeling. The afternoon tea was a complete success with the two genteel ladies drinking tea poured from a teapot that matched the beautiful china tea set.

They were both able to relate to being used to having a tasteful environment. At the end of the season, which was now approaching, Mrs Stock would return to her lovely house in Norfolk for a well-earned, comfortable winter rest. Ada couldn't wait to tell Jim all about her afternoon. It was far from being how she imagined at first - a bit rough and ready. She was so impressed, anyone would think that she had been to tea with the Queen.

The nineteen-fifties saw a period on the Island where many of the local men began to enjoy their spare time in activities which usually involved going to various pubs - not forgetting the Two Tides Club situated at the bottom of Seaview Avenue.

Here gathered a motley crew of the 'in crowd'. Nearly all of them had their own businesses and were for the most part hardworking and generous with their voluntary help and financial donations to the community. There were times however when they lacked sense and would lapse into moods of sheer boyish devilment, playing practical jokes on each other. Peter hadn't changed over the years and he usually either knew or was directly involved with at least some of the harmless fun. The same applied to Bert Carter, Frederick Smith, Dudley Cock, Alan Jowers and cousin Bill Farthing, to name but a few.

Bert Mussett was one of the local oystermen. He was a very quiet, unassuming man, married to Uncle Arthur Saye's daughter, Madge. They had two sons, Peter and Paul. Early one morning, Bert went to the window and peered outside to see what sort of a day it was going to be. He was taken aback to see one of his fruit trees completely covered with worn out old shoes dangling from the branches by their laces. He never did find out who was responsible.

Bert had the reputation of being one of the slowest drivers on the Island. It was a well known joke between the locals that if there was a long, slow-moving trail of traffic stretching a few miles back along the road to Colchester, you could be sure you were either following a hearse or Bert Mussett.

Another tale worth mentioning is the one about the old brown armchair. It started its travels by arriving at the front door of Frederick Smith's house 'Millcroft' in Upland Road. The road was unmade and full of deep ruts and bumps making it difficult to drive without being heard. Nonetheless, the chair had been successfully delivered during the night. Fred discreetly disposed of it by leaving it at his brother-in-law's, Bill Farthing. Bill was so embarrassed at the condition of the old relic that he put it in his shed right away so it would be out of sight until he could get rid of it. He knew just where it would be going.

The next morning, Bill put the chair in the milk van, arranging the crates of milk so that the chair could be easily removed and left at Peter's when he delivered the milk. It was quietly put outside the door before anyone was up and about. Peter guessed right away that Bill had something to do with the mystery object but decided it had to go elsewhere.

The poor chair continued its journey around the Island, eventually arriving for the second time at Fred Smith's. Fred, with the help of his son Alan, left the monstrosity at Don Bland's. Don had now had the shabby object on his doorstep twice and was pretty fed up. He decided to put an axe through it before burning it on the bonfire. After he'd smashed the axe through the wooden frame a few times, he noticed a small, neat bundle of white paper fall to the ground. Letting the axe drop, he bent to pick up the bundle. To his utter surprise and delight he discovered that there were at least one hundred large old five pound notes.

He couldn't believe his luck. Five hundred pounds reward for disposing of an old armchair.

* * *

Everyone was getting excited about the latest family acquisition - well, almost everyone. Mum and Dad had reservations.

"Jim, why on earth do they want a houseboat?"

" I don't know, mate, but it ain't a mite a good you worryin'. It's up to them what they do."

"I can't bear to think about the children walking up that long gangplank, especially at high tide."

"Look here, Ada mate, them kids have got more sense than you give 'em credit for. They ain't daft enough to goen fall in the water."

"Well, I hope you're right, Jim."

'The Peggotty' stood proudly in her mud berth. Her past history as an Auxiliary Schooner was just a memory but she still had an important role to fulfil on the water as a unique home - either as a houseboat for permanent accommodation or simply as a holiday home. The family had joined the quaint but unusual community of 'Houseboat Owners', where there were at least twenty other boats.

I was impressed with the unexpected luxury on this floating home. The conversion of the additional deckhouse was very large with windows facing all directions giving beautiful views of both the land and sea. The comfortable, large upholstered settee and armchairs, with the tasselled rug covering the floor, made it feel as though you were not really on a boat at all. This was until I climbed down the hatchway to the saloon - grabbing onto the handrail with my feet cautiously feeling for every step until I reached the safety of solid wooden floors beneath my feet.

I looked around the room which was much larger and more luxurious than I expected. The low ceilings and sloping floor made for a strange feeling of being slightly off-balance but it was obvious that The Peggotty had in the past been a very fine ten-berth sailing boat. Built in Brixham in 1902 by S.J. Dewdney, she was sixty eight feet long with a fourteen feet beam.

Dot was in the large, well equipped galley sorting through the kitchen utensils and checking that the cooker was in working order ready for the family to have overnight stays on board ship. The bunks in the various cabins had already been made up, including Peter and Dot's double room. They were all probably very comfortable but I knew I wouldn't stay on board overnight. I was one for my creature comforts and sleeping in a cabin with very low ceilings and only the portholes for fresh air on a hot summer night wasn't for me.

However, I was to enjoy many hours on and around the boat throughout the summer holiday. Peter bought a ten-foot wooden dinghy which was moored alongside the houseboat and we all learned to row up and down the creeks.

CHAPTER 25

Farewell Peggotty, the Ray Island adventure and school prefects

PRIMARY SCHOOL ...SEA COUNTY SUMMER TERM 1954

Headteacher

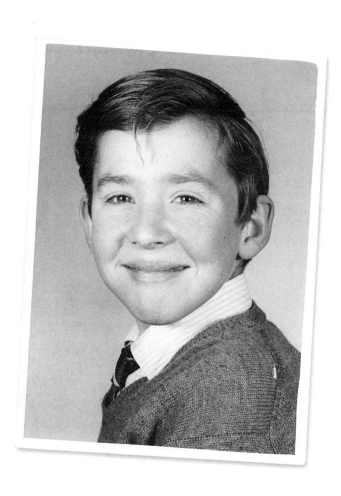

OVERLEAF: *School prefects, 1954. From left: (back row) Victor ponder (Vic), Geoffrey Carter (Geoff), Roy Bloomfield (Bloomers) Alan Weaver (Tarry), John Frost, Johnny Baldwin; (front row) Daphne Hewes, Brenda Pettican, Pauline French, Helen Proctor, Lilian Mills, Ann Farthing (Pixie).*
ABOVE: *Tim Farthing.*

One afternoon, as the tide was beginning to come in, Terry and John decided to go for a row in the boat. It was Terry's turn to row and he quickly built up some speed but, not paying attention to the depth of the water, he suddenly hit the mud. The impact caused John to bounce out of the dinghy and hit the soft, sludgy mud from where - against every law of physics - he bounced straight back in again. Fright and anger made John retaliate.

"It's all your fault, Terry. Look what you have made me do."

John stood up, ready to give Terry a push, nearly capsizing the boat. That brought them both to their senses and quietened them down. Peter was watching from the deck, where he was getting ready to do some fishing.

"Hey, you boys, watch what you are getting up to, otherwise you can bring the boat in."

"Alright, Dad. I'm sorry," shouted Terry.

It looked as though there was going to be a fairly high tide. I decided I'd better get home, as the tide was coming in fast and would soon cover the gangplank, leaving me stranded on board. The boat was now afloat. It was a calm day and the water was gently lapping against the sides. The electric cables that ran from all the boats to the main electricity supply had plenty of slack to allow for the movement of the boats at high tides.

Mum's worst fears about one of the children falling into the water very nearly did happen. Tim had just been kitted out with new clothes. He couldn't wait to put them all on and show them off to the world. Vainly taking a last look at himself in the mirror, he left the boat and walked quickly and proudly along the gangplank, taking care to hold on to the handrail. He was followed closely by John and Terry.

For some time, there had been a small gap where part of the wooden handrail had broken. It's not clear what happened next to make Tim fall into the mud. Was it the broken handrail that made him lose his balance or was he purposely nudged by his brother John who wanted to see him fall into the mud with his new clothes on? Terry was of the opinion that John pushed past him, bumping into him at the break in the handrail. When Mum heard about Tim's fall into the mud she said,

"I knew no good would come of young children living on a stupid houseboat. Next time it could be worse - you mark my words."

She was full of gloom and doom.

During the winter months, The Peggotty was broken into by some thoughtless young burglars who stole a lot of valuable items and left the interior in a complete mess. Friends, family and relations had all enjoyed many happy times on board the boat but nothing stays the same for ever. It was probably the break-in that made Peter and Dot decide that it was time for The Peggotty to have a new owner. Avril Copping, a lovely lady, wanted to buy her as a permanent home for her and her daughter, Janice. The sale was agreed and Avril now owned The Peggotty. It was her home.

The little dinghy was now moored down at 'The Hard'. Virtually anyone was allowed to use it as long as they put it back where they found it. The rules for us were to only row between The Victory Pub and The Causeway - a safe distance for anyone to be seen and rescued, should a mishap occur.

One afternoon after school I said I would go for a row with Susan and her friend, Roslyn Greaves. It was a lovely warm afternoon and we'd changed into T-shirts, shorts and plimsolls. We waded out to the boat, pulled in the anchor and took turns with the rowing, occasionally rowing in pairs. Roz was quite happy to let us do the work. After a while, we got a bit bored with rowing up and down the set boundaries we'd been given. Sue and I were rowing together and started to row past the Causeway in the direction of Strood Channel. The water was flat calm and we were quite excited about moving out of our usual territory.

"It doesn't look very far to get to Ray Island," I said to the girls. "Shall we row up the channel in that direction and have a look?"

"Okay," said Sue, laughing.

"What will your Dad say?" said Roz, nervously.

Sue and I both agreed that he probably wouldn't mind too much so we continued to row up Ray Channel, getting more excited as we approached the Island. At last we were there. We jumped out of the boat into the shallow water, dragging her safely up on to the soft sand.

Just a short distance away lay an old wreck, partially buried in the mud. The Island was deserted apart from us girls. The only sounds were the rippling waves and calls of the sea birds. There was an eerie feeling about the surroundings and the famous story about the Mersea salt marshes 'Mehalah' must have been on all of our minds. It was written in 1880 by a local rector, the Reverend Sabine Baring-Gould - he also wrote the famous hymn 'Onward Christian Soldiers'. In the story, Mehalah lived on Ray Island with her mother until their cottage was tragically burnt to the ground.

The combination of curiosity and the unknown drew the three of us further onto the Island. There were plenty of bramble bushes, rambling roses and even an apple tree. Then, we came across the remains of some sort of building with red brick footings. This surely must have been where Mehalah had lived! By now, the sun was hidden behind the clouds, shutting out some of the light and reminding me that we had got rather carried away and should start to return home.

"Come on you two girls, we'd better get home, otherwise we'll be in trouble."

We made hurriedly for the sandy beach and were horrified to find that the tide had gone out. We were in danger of being marooned on the Island - but there was still a little water left.

"Quick, Sue. We've got to get that boat into the water right now."

The three of us pushed and pulled the boat across the mud until she touched the water to float. We only managed to row a short distance before we ran aground again. We were getting very anxious. The only way we were able to make any headway was to get out of the boat and drag her along the mud until we found enough water for her to float again. We had to continue like this until we reached deep water. It had been a very tiring and stressful journey back. In the distance we could at last see the Causeway with a small gathering of people standing at the far end. As we got closer, I could see Peter standing amongst them.

"Where the hell do you think you've been? We were about to launch a search party."

"Sorry, Dad," said Sue.

"You should bloody well have more sense, Pixie."

"I am really sorry, Pete, but the tide went out. We nearly got stranded at the Ray."

"You shouldn't have gone there in the first place."

It was no good arguing. We were in the wrong. I was just realising how worried they must have been when they realised the boat was missing. Sue and I weren't the only ones to get into trouble today. Terry also copped it from Dad.

It was early evening and Terry asked,

"Granddad, can I have a go with the air gun, please?"

"Yes, mate, as long as yer careful."

Dad took the gun from its hiding place and handed it to Terry. I stood by the back door and watched as Terry took one of the lead pellets from the little square cardboard box and loaded it into the gun. He looked about him, eyeing the hedges for something to shoot at. Overhead flew a couple of starlings, heading over the tall hawthorn hedge.

"I'll get the little f*****s," said Terry.

I couldn't believe what I had just heard! I wasn't aware that Terry knew such a word. It was probably a new one he had picked up at school. Just as Terry was about to pull the trigger, Dad interrupted his concentration shouting,

"Don't you dare use that sort of language, young man. Now give me the gun."

He strode over and took the gun from Terry.

"Goen see your Nan and tell her I am ashamed of yer and there'll be no more shooting today."

The sudden death of the headmaster, Mr Cotgrove, during the summer of 1953 was a big shock for everyone. Pupils in the top class were contacted and asked if they would like to pay their respects by attending a memorial service at the Wesleyan Chapel, Mill Road. It was a warm day and I was wearing a colourful summer dress. I cycled to the chapel and stood my bike against a nearby brick wall. Walking through the chapel door I left the sunshine behind and an uneasiness swept over me as I saw the coffin resting on wooden stands.

I wanted to run away but someone was giving me a book and guiding me to a seat that was far too close to the coffin. I had never been to a funeral before - I thought I was just going to a service. I began to feel hot and uncomfortable. I knew I had to control myself. Looking around, there were some other school pupils there and if they could cope, then so could I.

I couldn't wait for it all to end. I wanted to get back out into the sunshine. At last it was all over and the coffin was being carried outside. The relief I felt was overwhelming. The ordeal I had faced in the afternoon returned to my mind after

I had gone to bed. I had a job getting to sleep and then faced a restless night.

Returning to school after the summer holidays we had a temporary headmaster whose name was Mr Goodfellow but in January 1954 we had a new permanent headmaster, Mr Westcott. He made a big difference to the school with many changes and was popular with the teachers, pupils and parents. Prefects were introduced into the school under a new system.

I was among the names of the pupils put forward but stupidly nearly lost the opportunity through something I did in assembly. We were all singing one of my favourite hymns, 'All Things Bright And Beautiful'. I knew it off by heart and didn't need to look at my hymn book. I happened to notice I had two dress-making pins stuck in the lapel of my jacket. Sylvia Lane, my good mate, stood directly in front of me. I took one of the pins out of my jacket and stuck it in her bum. She screamed loudly. Turning round, she looked directly at me, laughed, and said,

"It was you!"

I laughed as well - I couldn't help it. We were both told to go outside.

After assembly we followed the rest of the pupils back to class. Mr Hucklesby called the register. Then, a message was received for Ann Farthing to go to the headmaster's office. I knew exactly what it would be about. I ran across the playground to 'The School House' where the headmaster's office was. I knocked on the door.

"Come in."

I entered his office. He sat on the opposite side of a large oak desk.

"Good morning, Ann."

"Good morning, sir."

"There's no need for me to tell you why you are here."

"No, sir."

"What on earth made you do it?"

I couldn't help chuckling.

"I don't know, sir."

I knew he was slightly amused as he had a twinkle in his eye.

"Look here, Ann; I really would like to see you become a prefect. Your academic achievements are excellent, you have proved to be a good all round sport - especially with field events - and you're in the netball and hockey teams, as well as the success you've had with the discus."

He paused and looked down at the floor. When he looked back up, he was very serious.

"However, even with this glowing record I can't guarantee that you will get the teachers' votes, especially after what happened in assembly. Your behaviour has to be impeccable - an example to others. Do you understand?"

"Yes, sir."

"Very well. You may go now."

I was about to go out the door when he said,

"Your spontaneous fun isn't always undesirable, Ann."

On returning to the classroom, I heard a ripple of laughter as I returned to my seat.

"Settle down, please," said Mr Hucklesby. "Young lady, I don't want to see you in trouble again."

"No, sir."

The staff room over in the School House had now been moved upstairs to make way for the new system of introducing prefects into the school. They would be able to occupy the old staff room. A table tennis table had been installed for the prefects to use in their leisure time. A whole week passed before an announcement was made in assembly on the selection of prefects. Mr Westcott was facing the school pupils. The hymns and prayers were finished.

"And now we have come to the final decision on who has been chosen to be prefects."

I stood and waited as the names were called out.

"First, we have the Head Boy, David Vince. Head Girl, Pauline French."

After the applause for Head Boy and Head Girl, he went on to name the prefects. As each name was announced, I hoped I might be next.

"Roy Bloomfield; Alan Weaver; John Frost; Michael Webb; Geoffrey Carter; Jennifer Mills; Shirley Fenn..."

At this point, he hesitated. I was holding my breath - would there be one more? And then he said,

"... Ann Farthing - better known to everyone as 'Pixie'."

I was there! I would be able to play table tennis - and the rest, of course. My last year at school was memorable – a little bit sad - but certainly one of the happiest. It was only sad because I couldn't make up my mind which boy I cared for the most. I had been spending time with one of the other prefects, Alan Weaver. He was good at table tennis and we teamed up as partners. Alan was also a good footballer and played for Mersea Island Football Club.

Peter 'Skipper' Vince was the treasurer of Mersea Island Football Club. He was also a linesman and attended to any first aid needs. Peter saw me talking to Alan Weaver at one of the home matches.

"I'll tell yer mother what yer getting up to when I see her on Tuesday," he said, laughing and joking.

"For Christ's sake, shut up, Peter, it's not like that," said Alan.

"What is it like then, mate?"

We both walked away, knowing without any doubt he would say something for a joke to wind everyone up, including Mum.

CHAPTER 26

First aid, a scatty wife and the Champions Cup

OVERLEAF: *Pixie and Alan, receiving the North East Essex Sports Champions Cup.*
ABOVE: *From left: Wendy Westcott, Pixie Farthing and Pat Lord helped put out a motorcycle fire.*

Peter delivered our bread on Tuesday, Thursday and Saturday, working for the local baker, Fred G. Smith. There was no other bread like it. Often, it was so fresh it was still warm when it was delivered. Many times I'd been in trouble with Mum for peeling off the top of the lovely crispy outer crust and eating it, just as it was, without butter. One of Peter's tricks to boost his sales would be if we were not at home to leave a box of fancy cream cakes on the kitchen table next to the bread. Every time this happened, Mum would say,

"That leary young devil has left cakes again without me ordering them. Well, he can take them back next time he calls."

They were always eaten before he was due to call again.

Saturday was 'Football Day' so Peter's day had to start at four o'clock in the morning. He had a great and willing helper in his young son Terence who could only have been eleven or twelve years old. Nothing stopped for football. Peter was so well trusted and respected that all the local shops and businesses had extra keys cut so that he could let himself into their premises to deliver bread and cakes early on Saturdays meaning he could finish work in time for the match.

Danny Cock, who managed the Fairhaven Café for his father, Glenny, even had a bread and cheese snack ready for them to eat. Fred Smith also sold and delivered animal feeds and Saturday was the day they delivered a hundredweight each of oats and bran to the local riding stables, owned at the time by Patricia 'Catchie' Catchpole. This was one of the jobs that neither Peter nor Terence liked because Fred Smith had promised that the feeds would be put in the feeding troughs ready for the horses to have their food. Often the horses were frisky, which made the job a bit tricky.

Peter took after his father, Arthur (known as 'Old Skipper'), who also liked his football.

Basil Underwood was one of the players. His father owned Underwood's Garage and Underwood's Buses and Coaches. Basil was the coach driver for away games and usually drove the coach right to the touchline so that 'Old Skipper' – who had poorly legs - could see the game from the coach.

I had become quite friendly with Alan Weaver and often supported the Mersea Island football team. On one occasion there was an away match at Whitehall Road, Colchester, with Peter in his usual role of linesman. It was becoming an exciting game when suddenly, Bob Fitch, one of Mersea Island's strong players, got injured, suffering a very deep gash to his leg. He managed to hobble to the sideline, helped by one of his team.

Peter ran to assist with the first aid box. Looking at the open wound he very quickly undid the box, took out the iodine bottle and poured the entire contents into the gash on Bob's leg.

"That'll be alroight, mate," he said, not wanting to sacrifice one of their best players.

Bob went back on to the field saying,

"I am bloody well safer out there on the pitch, mate, than I am with you."

A few months passed before Mr Westcott, the new headmaster, was finally able to get his family settled in Mersea. It was strange to hear they were living in what was once our old house 'Craigmore' in Seaview Avenue. Mr

Westcott said his daughter Wendy hadn't got to know anyone yet so I offered to call round to the house and introduce myself to her. We were to become very good friends.

Mrs Westcott soon became a frequent visitor at our house and got on very well with Mum. They often chatted over endless cups of tea. Betty Westcott was quite a character - not at all the sort of person you'd expect a headmaster's wife to be. She tried to avoid getting involved with the school although there was one occasion she went to visit Marie Davis because her husband, Myrdden (Popeye) was away on a teacher training course. Betty called to see if Marie and the children were OK. She took a large bag of apples from the garden, thinking they could be baked in a pie.

"How terribly kind of you, my dear," enthused Mrs Davis.

"Oh, that's alright, they're just windfalls," said Betty.

"Really! Is that a special make?"

Betty was amused that this well spoken, but scatty lady didn't know what a windfall was. She worked round it by saying,

"They are very good cookers, Marie."

They sat down for a quick cup of tea then Betty said her goodbyes and cycled up The Lane. She struggled up the steep hill - the road was then rough and unmade. At the very top, after a sharp right hand corner, the road ran straight and levelled out, allowing time for a breather. Betty then bumped along the rough ruts of Rosebank Road to call in at our house for a chat, a laugh and a cup of Mum's special tea, brewed to perfection in her China teapot.

I had my friend Pat Lord staying with us for half-term week. Pat lived in Hatfield, Hertfordshire and loved coming to the Island whenever possible. We first got to know each other when Pat's mother came to stay next door.

Wendy Westcott said she would call round for us at ten

o'clock. It was a warm, sunny day and we decided to go down to the beach for a swim as the tides would be just right. Mum wasn't too happy as she said that she didn't think that it would be warm enough. However, we managed to persuade her otherwise. Pat and I got our swimming gear together before cycling to Wendy's to get her stuff.

Mum was right. Although there was plenty of heat in the sun, the water was still very cold and being a morning tide, the sun hadn't been shining on the mud long enough for it to get hot and warm up the incoming tide. None of us wanted to stay in the water for very long. We came out shivering and quickly got changed between the beach huts.

After dinner, we decided to cycle to East Mersea. We had just turned into East Mersea Road when we came upon a young man who seemed to be having trouble with his motorcycle. Just as we got close to the bike, it burst into flames.

"What shall we do?" I called to the girls.

"Get help!" said Pat.

The situation was urgent. Petrol could easily explode. We cycled quickly to the nearest cottage, threw our bikes down on the grassy bank and banged frantically on the front door. When the man opened his door I shouted,

"Please can you help? There's a motorbike on fire just up the road."

He grabbed a watering can and a galvanised bucket and filled them both from his water butt. All four of us ran quickly to the scene of the fire where a car had now stopped and the driver was trying to help. The water immediately put out the flames and the man from the cottage said the motorcyclist could leave his bike at his place until it could either be put back on the road or disposed of.

After our little adventure we carried on to East Mersea, past the Old Club House, which was once part of the Golf Course and on to the sea wall overlooking Brightlingsea.

* * *

I suppose it was inevitable that I would be drawn into a close relationship with Wendy's older brother, David. He was a very likeable person and we got on well together. However, I did get a fair amount of teasing from the boys at school about 'The Headmaster's Son'. He then began to get too serious. I was feeling smothered by all the loving attention I was getting from him. It was making me feel uncomfortable because I wasn't ready or committed enough to return so much affection. Holding hands in the pictures, a goodnight kiss and cuddle to show we were special close friends was all I was ready for.

David knew there was something wrong when I kept making excuses about seeing each other so much. He went very quiet and moody. Gradually we saw less and less of each other. Mum asked me why I wasn't seeing so much of David.

"Mum, he's getting too serious."

"I suppose you're messing around after that Weaver boy again."

"No, I'm not," I answered - not altogether truthfully - as I'd met up with him a few times round the village.

I was kept busy at school. I wanted to get some good results in my exams, especially as this was my last year. At an interview, I had been promised a place at The North East Essex Technical College and School of Art on a full-time secretarial course, subject to my school exam results being good. Brenda Pettican and myself were the first pupils ever to be accepted from a Primary School as students normally came from Secondary Modern Schools. Thanks to our new headmaster we were to be a test case.

Sporting activities were now taking up a lot of my time. The school was competing for the prestigious North East

267

Essex Sports Champions Cup and we were in with a chance to win it - but nothing comes easily and it meant lots of hard training after school. I had been selected as captain for the girls' team. Alan Weaver was the captain of the boys' team.

The Championship was held at the Garrison Sports Ground in Colchester and when the big day arrived the weather was fine but not too hot. At morning assembly, Mr Westcott wished us all good luck and said he knew we had a good team. He would, of course, be there to support us. Returning to the classroom, we were all given numbers which were pinned to our T-shirts. Mine was number twelve. The sight of the numbers made it all seem more real and very exciting.

The contestants from the senior classes gathered at the school gates together with the teachers who were ready to lend their support. It was just a short distance to walk to the bus stop in Barfield Road as we were to catch the Eastern National Service bus that would only take twenty minutes to get there.

We were probably one of the smallest schools to enter the competition but here we were at the sports ground listening confidently to the voice coming over the loudspeakers telling us where to gather for the various events. It wasn't long before the sound of the starter's gun signalled the start of the first race. There were a few races before our events began but the afternoon couldn't have been more exciting as we watched our team gaining first, second and third in different events.

I soon had to take part in the hurdles and was getting a bit nervous. We were short of sports equipment at school and didn't have enough hurdles to practice properly. The scores were being put up on the board and West Mersea was soon in the top three. Even the teachers were getting excited. Would it happen - could we win the cup?

If we won the last event - the relay - we would definitely take home the cup. The relay race was about to begin and we all moved into position and waited for the sound of the starter's gun. Bang! We got off to a good start. I turned round and watched as the baton was handed from runner to runner - all perfect passes. The baton was now passed into my hand. I was running well and gaining ground fast. The race was ours! I had only to pass the baton to the last girl who would take it across the winning line.

We were the winners - the cup was ours. We had to wait for the final confirmation of the winners. Then it was announced over the loudspeakers,

"... West Mersea County Primary School"

Alan Weaver and myself, as captains, proudly received the cherished cup. Next morning in assembly, Mr Westcott, with a broad grin on his face, announced the good news to the school, adding jokingly,

"I wonder if this cup will end up on the same mantlepiece."

There were hoots of laughter and loud applause. What a happy memory for our last year at school!

Most of the prefects were gathered in the recreation room, sitting around chatting about the changes that had taken place over the last year and how Mr Westcott had moved the school forward to modern standards that pleased everyone. We agreed that we'd all had a good time over the years.
Then we began to recall memories of school. One was of Robin Cook 'Cooky' having an unusual talent involving the use of his bottom. He could, in fact, fart to order. There was one occasion on the school field before cricket practice when one of the boys said,

"Come on, Cooky, how many times can you fart?"

They reckon he did a hundred. Each time he was tapped on the bottom with a cricket bat he produced wind.

Alan remembered being on playground duty when one of the little juniors was cheeky and rude.

"I picked the little bugger up and was about to duck his head in the water butt when Jo Westcott came up behind me and said quietly, 'That's not the way for a prefect to behave.'"

The laughter in the recreation room was beginning to get louder.

"Shh, we're making too much noise," said Pauline, the head girl.

Everyone quietened down, then Lillian Mills recalled the time when some of the girls went swimming down Stoker's Beach after school. One of the girls, Dorothy Saye, was so cold she ran out of the water, put on her woollen cardigan and then went back into the sea again.

And Roy Bloomfield remembered the time he ate an apple and left the core hanging on the tree because no one was allowed to pick the apples. His punishment was to stand in the middle of the school field all afternoon.

CHAPTER 27

College, *a motorbike ride and identity problems*

OVERLEAF: *Alan dressed in police uniform, outside his mum's house on Barfield Road.*

ABOVE: *Police football team at Layer Road. From left: (back row) Alan Weaver, Dick Bird, John Kerridge, Cliff Bareham, Bert Turner, Len Jones, Fred Hagon; (front row) Les Bennet, Les Brown, Supt. Simpson, John Page, John Fitzjohn.*

Lying in bed I could hear the clock at the side of my head ticking in the quietness of the night. The distant sound of a disturbed curlew drifted across the marshes. I was tossing and turning. Tomorrow was my first day at college and so much was passing through my mind. Should I have turned down a place at the Agricultural College in Chelmsford? I felt I wasn't ready to leave home yet and to go there I would have had to become a boarder at Chelmsford.

Art School was what I really wanted to do but it was a four-year course. Mum and Dad said four years was a long time and being a bit old fashioned didn't think that being an artist was the right sort of career for a girl. Were they right? It certainly didn't matter now - I had made a commitment for the next year. Sleep must have eventually overcome all my doubts. I could hear a voice calling,

"Pixie! Pixie, wake up, it's seven o'clock."

Daylight poured into the room as Mum drew back the curtains, making the curtain rings rattle against the brass curtain rail. I quickly threw back the covers knowing that I didn't have much time to spare. I had to catch the ten past eight bus. Catching the bus was the easiest part of the day. The rest of it was likely to be difficult and full of surprises.

Joan Cornelius, the little girl I had sat next to on my very first day at school was now - after ten years - sitting next to me on my first day at college. For the past few years she had been attending a Secondary Modern School in Colchester and we'd lost touch. It was so nice to see a familiar face. Of course the other familiar face was Brenda Pettican, the only other girl from Mersea School. Us two ol' country gals were going to find this course very challenging.

We were at a disadvantage because everyone else in the class had previous experience with both shorthand and typing. The other subjects were English, Accounts and Office Training. English seemed to be covering a wide field of study including how to speak properly and how to enhance a sentence. An example would be describing stars in the sky as 'a firmament of luminaries'. I could just imagine saying to one of the local lads,

"Look at that firmament of luminaries."

Their reply would probably have been,

"What the hell are you talking about?"

After a few weeks, Brenda left the college. I found it a struggle but I was determined to carry on with my studies to the end. Every night I stayed up late, doing homework. It took me twice as long as everyone else but I had to keep up with the rest of the class.

Mixing with the other students made me aware of the protected environment we had enjoyed as children on Mersea Island. The girls at college were fun to be with and their conversations enlightening. Most of them were 'street-wise', often being met outside the college by Americans who were stationed at Wethersfield air base and who were usually in large, flashy cars.

The only time I could lay claim to any sort of vehicle attraction was during one lunchtime. I had met Alan in the town centre and was walking back to college when Alan's mate, Roger Sheldrake, pulled up beside us on his big black motorbike. The three of us were talking together at the top of North Hill. Roger was revving up the bike to keep it ticking over. I was already late getting back and said,

"I must go now as I'm late."

"Git on the back, gal, I'll give yer a lift."

I glanced at Alan, who nodded as if to say, 'Give it a go.'

I felt the excitement as I lifted my leg over the pillion and clutched Roger's waist tightly as I sat down. He stood there, roaring the engine loudly and then we were off, driving down North Hill, my hair blowing in the wind.

"Stop here!" I said.

"I can't, mate," he shouted, "Me brakes ain't working properly. Hold on tight."

I was so scared. The hill looked very steep. I tucked myself against his back hoping we wouldn't crash. Suddenly, his foot went out as he brought the back wheel round into a skid, turning left into the wide driveway of The Technical School (we were still part of the school until the new college building was completed). Pupils stood to one side as we passed, admiring the big black motorbike that dared to go up the drive. Climbing off the bike, my legs still felt wobbly.

"Cheerio, mate!" and Roger was off.

During the afternoon break, I was approached by one of the tutors who had heard about the motorbike incident.

"It's people like you, doing stupid things that could give the college a bad reputation."

I apologised and said it wouldn't happen again.

I had permission to leave college at lunchtime. It was a glorious day as I walked up North Hill with a lightness in my step. My year of hard work and studying was now nearing its end. Turning into the High Street, I stopped to check my reflection in a large shop window. I wanted to look smart for my interview with The Youth Employment Bureau.

Arriving at the offices in Culver Street, I entered the reception area and walked cheerfully to a seat, joining the queue of other young people. The chain of events that occurred over the next hour were so poignant that I will carry the memory for the rest of my life. I sat there, patiently waiting my turn. A voice called out,

"Next, please."

I walked confidently to the desk, where I was asked,

"Name, please."

"Ann Farthing."

The receptionist began to sort through the index cards that were neatly filed in a long filing drawer standing on top of the desk, all in alphabetical order. She seemed to be having some difficulty in finding my records because she went through the whole file, systematically checking each card individually. Then, she looked in the file that her colleague was responsible for. She looked up at me.

"You did say your name is Ann Farthing?"

"Yes, that's right."

"Well, according to our records dear, you don't exist," she said, chuckling. "Would you like to go and sit down again, please?"

I moved to one of the spare chairs, where people were still waiting to be seen. The receptionist walked off into one of the back offices, returning later to ask me my date of birth. Sitting there, I was feeling very lonely and uneasy. I knew there was something wrong. The minutes were ticking by. After about twenty minutes, I was confronted again, this time by a smartly dressed, well spoken lady, who said in a kind voice,

"Would you come to my office, please?"

I stood up and followed her in to her office, where she drew up a chair for me.

"Sit down, my dear."

"Thank you," I replied, sitting down and anxiously wondering what was coming next. Looking at me from the other side of her desk, she began to speak.

"I have made numerous telephone calls to help trace your birth records and I am truly sorry but we cannot trace anyone called Ann Farthing with your date of birth. Now - could you be known under any other name?"

"No, I don't think so," I answered.

"Look, my dear, I can imagine this is very stressful for you. I am going to leave you on your own for a while to give you some quiet thinking time. Maybe you could cast your mind back. Can you think of anything at all that may suggest you may at sometime have had a different surname?"

I sat in this unfamiliar room, wishing I had never turned up for this appointment. If only…

I don't know what made my mind suddenly return to a day long ago when I was sent out to do some shopping. Mum said I could have some sweets and handed me the ration book. At the shop, Mr Mills took the shopping list and gathered the items together, placing them all on top of the glass counter.

"What sort of sweets do you want, my dear?"

"I'll have a quarter of a pound of pear drops, please."

He took the large glass sweet jar down from the shelf and weighed the sweets onto the brass scales. Then, he slid the sweets from the scoop into a paper bag.

"Can I have your ration book, please?"

I handed over my ration book, but not before noticing that where my name should be, instead of saying, 'Ann Farthing,' it said, 'Ann Smith'.

Mr. Mills packed everything into the canvas shopping bag, including the ration book, and handed it back to me over the counter. When I arrived home with the shopping, I said to Mum,

"Why does my ration book have 'Ann Smith' on it?"

"Oh, does it, dear? They must have made a mistake. I'll have to get it sorted out."

Some time went by before I saw the ration book again and this time the strange thing was that the cover was missing.

"Where's the cover to my ration book, Mum?" I asked.

"It must have got lost. Don't worry, I'll stick it back on again if I find it."

At the time, I didn't question these explanations. Did the

ration book have the clue to who I really was? I was feeling emotionally empty and my mouth had gone dry but I felt I must be strong. I had a horrible situation to deal with. Deep down, I now knew that I would be found under the name Smith. Less than ten minutes had gone by since the lady walked out of the door but to me it seemed an eternity. I could hear her high heels as she returned along the corridor. The door opened and the smartly dressed lady entered again.

"Sitting on your own for a while - has it helped you to recall anything that may help us find your records?"

"Yes, I have thought of something. One day, my ration book arrived and it had the wrong surname on it. Please could you try looking under the name of Smith?"

"If you would like to come back to reception, I will check through the records again."

Flicking through all the cards, she stopped, took out a card and said,

"Yes; here we are - Ann Smith."

I couldn't wait to step out into the fresh air and sunshine. Everything seemed so normal with the hustle and bustle of the town in the busy lunch hour. They say that every cloud has a silver lining. As I began my lonely walk down Culver Street I could see my cousin Dorothy and her boyfriend Michael coming along the road in my direction. Never in all my life have I been so relieved to see a familiar face.

"Hello Pixie," said Dorothy, "is everything all right? You look serious."

"No, not really. I have just been to the Youth Employment Bureau to register. There was a problem with my identity and the name I am registered under."

"Oh dear. That's worrying for you," said Dorothy.

"Dorothy, who is my real mother?"

"Auntie Ada is, of course! Look, Pixie, I have got to get back to work now but I'll see you tomorrow lunchtime. Let's go to Wash's for lunch."

"Alright. You may be able to help me sort out the mystery. It will be nice with just the two of us. We can have a good chat."

Dorothy and Michael both went back to work leaving me alone with my thoughts. Did Dorothy know more than she was admitting? I decided not to return to college for the afternoon. I wouldn't be in any mood to concentrate so I went to have a look in Woolworths.

One of the counters had been specially adapted to sell a popular confectionery product. The four glass sides of the counter contained a huge mountain of bright yellow lemonade crystals. The crystals were sold loose from one ounce upwards, scooped into a paper bag and put on the scales to be weighed. The sticky mix was sold mainly to young people who liked to dip and lick their fingers in the sugary, sharp mixture. The very smell as you passed the counter made your mouth water.

The temptation was all too much for a young lad out shopping with his mother. She stood very close to the counter chatting to her friend and holding tightly to her young son's hand, oblivious that her little boy was stretching up with his free hand and dipping his grubby fingers into the bright yellow gritty mixture. It was turning his fingers and tongue bright yellow as he licked away at the free and delicious treat. I wondered if there had been any other dirty fingers sampling the pile of lemony powder.

Travelling home on the bus gave me more time to reflect on the past and how I should deal with the future. There was one thing I was absolutely sure about and that was how much I loved my Mum and Dad. Whatever the name said on that card, I was still Ann Farthing. I looked just like the Farthings. Many times in the past relations had remarked,

"She's a real Farthing - she looks just like her Dad."

So why 'Smith'?

I didn't want to think about it any more.

"You're home early today dear," said Mum.

279

"Yes, the lesson was cancelled."

I hated lying, but it wasn't a real lie. I had to cancel the lesson because I felt circumstances were beyond my control. I was looking forward to meeting Dorothy the next day. This gave me a feeling of relief. I had someone I could talk to and trust. I knew I could share my secret and it would be safe.

The next day, over lunch, I told her everything. However, I did have a feeling that she was holding something back.

"Why don't you talk to Auntie Ada. Tell her all about what happened yesterday. She may be able to tell you what's going on."

"I can't because I don't want to hurt either Mum or Dad. They have been protecting me from something for all these years and I'm sure they must have done it thinking it was best for me."

"Well, I'll have a talk with Mum when I get home this evening and if she tells me anything, I'll let you know," said Dorothy.

"Dorothy, I have a feeling that Peter could be my real Dad. I always called him Daddy Peter when I was young, didn't I?"

"Yes, I can remember that," she said quickly, glancing at her watch. "I must go now, otherwise I'll be late for work."

Dorothy chose the moment to end our conversation. I don't think she wanted it to go on any longer so we both left the restaurant to go in opposite directions. I met Alan returning to the Police Station in Queen Street, smartly dressed in his new uniform. He was in a hurry to get back to the station so he couldn't stop and talk.

Alan and another young man called Dick Emeny were both lucky enough to pass the high standard exam to enter the Police Force as cadets. Out of a large number of applicants, only two places were available in the area. A few weeks went by before the letter he had been anxiously waiting for arrived on the doormat. He had the offer of a place at Colchester Police Station. This time the uniform was issued free.

When he passed the scholarship at eleven years of age to go to the Boys' Grammar School he was unable to attend the school as sadly his Mum couldn't afford to purchase the uniform.

Courting days, Cadder and Brassy Mussett and the Sea Cadet donation

OVERLEAF: *Pixie's and Alan's courting days.*
ABOVE: *Mersea Island Sea Cadet Band on the field behind The British Legion. In the centre of the picture is Alan Weaver, far right is Douglas Humm.*

I'd been going out with Alan officially for some weeks but not exactly with Mum's approval. Like most mothers, she thought I could 'do better'. I had been friendly with other boys - just platonic relationships. Holding hands in the pictures and a goodnight kiss was as far as I wanted to go. Alan was becoming rather special to me. I was even prepared to bend the truth a little so that I could see him for a little while in the evenings. Mum would do all she could to keep me in and I would do all I could to get out. I didn't know if Dad was on my side or not, but I would go to him and say,

"Dad, I am going to take the dog for a walk. Would you like me to get some tobacco from the shop?"

"Yes please, dear. Get me an ounce of Digger Honeydew and a packet of blue cigarette papers."

Now, even if Mum decided the dog didn't need to go out for a walk, I still had a good excuse to go to the shops and I would be able to meet Alan.

Brothers Cadder and Brassy Mussett owned the village shop in the High Street, almost opposite the end of Yorick Road. It was open all hours and sold more or less everything anyone might need - including poultry food. Cadder would also double up as a hairdresser. The floor had been repaired in places with old bits of tin.

The locals would gather outside the shop for a yarn. It was a well known meeting place. Strangers would return to the shop again and again just to meet these two rum ol' boys, particularly Brassy, who would tot up the prices of the goods purchased, give you the grand total and wait expectantly for the customer to part with their money. If it was a ten shilling note or a pound note, he would grab the note from the customer, screw it up in a ball in the palm of his hand and then straighten it out flat on top of the counter, brushing out the creases with both hands. When he was paid in coins, the silver coins were placed between his teeth, presumably to make sure it wasn't fake money, then he would check along the edges before throwing them into the till.

One day, Brassy stood outside his shop admiring a baby in a pram. A lady came by and began talking to the baby.

"Tell the lady you can't talk, dear" interjected Brassy.

Brassy is long gone. He was one of the many eccentrics who lived on the Island.

Even at the age of sixteen I was still expected to be home by nine o'clock. If I was out with Alan and we were late home, Dad would be at the gate looking for me. When we came down Victory Road we could see Dad standing in the shadows of the tall hawthorn hedge.

"That's your father. I'll be off now."

Alan would then leave me to face the music and would hurriedly retreat back up the road. I told him he was being a coward and he said,

"No I'm not - I'm just being sensible."

Mum was realising that however hard she tried, she wasn't able to keep us apart. One of Dad's old sayings was,

"Love'll pull ya further than gunpowder can blow ya."

As Alan had now plucked up enough courage to call for me at the house, perhaps Dad had been right. On Wednesday and Saturday evenings we usually went to the pictures at the British Legion Hall. It was a popular choice of entertainment for all ages with two performances, one at four thirty in the afternoon and one at seven thirty. Both were usually well supported.

The first house tended to be noisier as it was full of youngsters who were obliged to fill up the front seats first. The seating was very basic with rows of hard wooden chairs. A central passageway separated the left and right hand rows of seats. Ruth Carpenter, the usherette, came round with ice creams at the interval. She would take care to watch the young lads when they had finished as some of the less well behaved boys would throw their empty cartons at people across the hall.

Occasionally, the projectionist would come hustling down to give them a warning. If anyone continued to misbehave he would grab hold of them by the collar and shove them out of the double swing doors. During the cold winter months the hall was heated by a large open coal fire, surrounded by a brick fireplace. It added a romantic warmth to an otherwise draughty hall.

One disadvantage was when it was time for more coal to be shovelled on to the fire. If the wind was blowing in the wrong direction it would cause a sudden downdraught in the chimney and smoke would billow out into the hall. Those who had pushed and scrambled to get close to the fire would either end up coughing through the film or going home smelling of smoke.

Today was the very first time I had been in Alan's house. I must have been seen walking down the steep garden path as the front door opened just before I had time to knock.

"Hello, dear, I expect you've come round for Alan. I'm afraid he's not quite ready yet. You'd better come in and wait for him."

I stepped into the hall and was shown into the sitting room

287

which was very small and neat. There was just enough room for the smart three piece suite - a two seater settee that stood under the window and two armchairs, one either side of the fireplace. A modern radiogram stood against the space left on the far wall.

"You'll have to excuse me dear, I am just getting the girls' tea."

Mrs Weaver went off leaving me on my own. It wasn't long before I heard Alan come downstairs and I heard his mother say,

"Pixie's waiting for you in the other room."

He came into the room and the surprise showed in his voice as he said,

"I didn't know you were here."

"I've only been here for a few minutes."

There was an uneasy silence - neither of us quite knowing what to say next. Then Alan said,

"Would you like to hear Freddie's new radiogram?"

"Yes, I would. It looks very posh."

Sorting through the records, he selected 'We're in the Jailhouse Now' sung by Webb Pierce. He put the record on. The quality and tone coming from the built-in speaker was unbelievable. At home we were still using an old wind up gramophone where the needle had to be changed after every few records. Paul had once shown me how to find mature thorns from the hawthorn hedge which made a cheaper and adequate substitute when we ran out of gramophone needles.

"I'd better put it off now before Freddie comes in from work. He might have a go at me, especially if I don't ask his permission to use it first."

Alan turned off the power and put the record back in its place.

We were going round to Peter's to watch the television as

there was a good programme on that night. When we arrived, we knew there was something wrong. Terry and John were in real trouble. It had just come to light that a plan they contrived to make pocket money weeks ago wasn't exactly above board.

Mrs Pointing and her daughter Valerie no longer lived in the house next door and it had been empty for a long time. The garden was overgrown with weeds but the spring bulbs had still managed to push their way up through the undergrowth. Tight green buds were waiting to open up in the sunshine. Mr Hutley's house further down the road looked derelict. No one had lived there for a very long time either.

Terry and John crept quietly round the side of the Hutley house and into the back garden where they found a rickety old garden shed. Pulling open the door they saw a lot of wooden boxes that contained a large quantity of flowerpots. Some were cracked and broken but others were perfect, apart from being dirty. The boys now had everything they needed to start a plant stall. First, they went home to get a container for the flowerpots. They returned to collect their hidden find and brought their haul home to the back garden where the pots were scrubbed and cleaned in the water butt.

While the pots were drying, the boys got a spade and fork out of the shed and put them over the fence. They then climbed through a gap in the hedge at the bottom of the garden where the bulbs were growing. The small number they needed would never be missed. It didn't take the pair of young rogues long to finish their digging. Soon, the filled plant pots were standing neatly on a table by the roadside.

Up until late afternoon only a few sales had been made. Disappointed at their turnover of stock they decided to take some of the plants round to sell at peoples' doors. Their door to door sales patter was to be their downfall.

They were doing quite well until they knocked at the door of a particular bungalow at the top of Fairhaven Avenue. The door was opened by a friendly, elderly lady.

"Would you like to buy any pot plants?" asked Terry very politely.

"Are they being sold for charity?"

"Yes, for the Sea Cadets," answered John as quick as a flash.

"What a lovely idea! I expect you know my husband, Mr Cass. He helps a lot with the Sea Cadets."

They both thought it prudent to keep quiet about Mr Cass. They knew he was a Councillor but were unaware of his involvement with the cadets. The boys beat a hasty retreat down the road after selling the last two plants and shared out the money. If only John hadn't lied about giving money to charity things might have been different.

Several weeks later, long after Terry and John had spent their profits, Mr Cass knocked on the door wondering what had happened to the money that the boys were going to donate to the Sea Cadets. Peter was obliged to loan his two sons the money that Mrs Cass assumed was going to be donated to the cadets. They were then told to go and pay it to Mr Cass and apologise for being late with handing over the cash.

Their punishment was to be grounded for a week for telling a lie and then each week money was deducted from their pocket money until the debt was paid off. Apparently on the day the whole episode took place, Dot had gone into Colchester shopping with Tim, and Peter was at work, so no one knew exactly what the boys were getting up to. Alan and I were amused at their resourcefulness and couldn't help but laugh at the outcome.

After watching television at Peter and Dot's we walked home through the fields. Alan wanted to get home early as he wasn't feeling too well. He had a cold coming and was beginning to feel shivery. I wasn't surprised when he didn't catch the bus to work in the morning but two days passed and he was still off work. I'd made up my mind that if he wasn't on the bus on the third day, I would call round and see how he was that evening.

With only a few more working days to go at college I had been busy but I was looking forward to getting home, having an early tea and going round to see if Alan was feeling better. I cycled round to the Weavers' at 6, Barfield Road and leant my bike against the picket fencing that ran along the side of the kerbed path and main road. I knocked at the front door and heard a voice shout,

"There's someone at the door."

Then another voice said,

"No, you answer it."

Then Mrs Weaver came to the door.

"Hello dear. Have you come to see how Alan is?"

"Yes. Is he feeling any better?"

"Well, his cold began to get steadily worse then it turned into pleurisy. The antibiotics are now beginning to work as the pain seems to be easing. Would you like to go up and see him?"

"Yes I would, if that's all right."

I followed Alan's Mum upstairs to the bedroom, where there was a double bed and two single beds. Alan was half-asleep in one of the single beds. When he saw me standing there he said,

"What did you want to come round here for?"

"She's come to see how you are, dear."

"Well, she shouldn't have bothered, 'cos I'm all right."

I stood there feeling very uncomfortable, not knowing what to say next. I was beginning to wish I hadn't come.

"Would you like me to go, then?"

"No - you might as well stay now you're here."

"I'll leave you two to talk then," said his Mum, leaving us alone in the room.

I looked around the bedroom and could see that all the

other beds were covered with heavy old army, air force and navy overcoats. They were being used for extra warmth instead of eiderdowns and bedspreads. At that moment I became very aware of the struggle the family must be having financially.

"So why did you have to come round and see this lot?" Alan said downheartedly.

"Alan - I came to see you and to find out how you were. I don't care that you've got coats on the beds. It's better than getting cold."

He put his hand out and took hold of my hand.

"I'm pleased to see you and I am glad you came."

I wanted to reassure Alan that I wasn't bothered by their circumstances, but I didn't quite know how. I could say all the wrong things and sound patronising. I decided to say nothing.

CHAPTER 29

Two jobs, two bosses and the sack - twice

OVERLEAF: *Pixie Farthing.*
ABOVE: *Postman Bill Pontyfix (pictured left)*
outside West Mersea Post Office, June 1953.

College had come to an end and I was looking forward to having a break. My first job interview was at two o'clock. It wouldn't have been my first choice but I had to start somewhere and I wanted to work in Colchester. Over the past year I'd got used to the busier lifestyle the town offered, although it was nice to return to the peace of the Island in the evening. The one o'clock bus would get me there in plenty of time. The job description in the advert said:

Secretarial Work, hours from 9.00 am to 5.30pm
Mon to Fri good rate of pay.
Franks of Colchester
Tyre Specialists, Crowhurst Road

Approaching the place where I could be working, my hopes of an office with even a modicum of style were immediately shattered. I walked into a large yard stacked with old tyres ranging from enormous agricultural tractor and lorry tyres down to standard car tyres. Ahead of me was a directional notice saying 'Office'. The door was opened and a tall, smartly dressed and well spoken gentleman said,

"Good afternoon. You must be Miss Farthing."

"Yes, that's right."

"Do come in. I'm Hugh Franks, the proprietor."

Sitting at a desk directly opposite me was a very pleasant lady who I was introduced to as Valerie Orrin.

"Valerie comes in every afternoon and looks after the

books as well as other office duties."

Mr Franks sat at the spare desk and invited me to sit down on the chair by the side of the desk. My whole interview took place in front of Valerie as this was the only office. The rest of the building was a tyre warehouse. I answered all the questions about my qualifications then Mr Franks got up from the chair and picked up a book.

"Now Ann, I would like you to go and sit behind that typewriter and type me a couple of paragraphs from this book."

Valerie kindly handed me a sheet of paper and I proceeded to type a few paragraphs from the book. I handed him the typing which he looked at and appeared to be satisfied.

"I would also like to dictate a short letter for you to take down in shorthand."

He picked up a spiral notepad and pencil from Valerie's desk and handed them to me. I was very nervous about the shorthand and when he said 'Michelin tyres' I wrote 'Michelin' in longhand as I couldn't think how to do it. I read the letter back to him and again felt I had his approval. He stood back as if he was considering, then said,

"The job's yours if you want it and the wages are two pounds, twelve and six per week. What do you think then?"

He was direct and to the point. The money was more than I was expecting and I was a bit taken aback. In fact, it would make up for me not having fulfilled my dream of a stylish office with thick wall-to-wall carpeting.

"Yes - I would like the job."

"Can you start in a week's time?"

I hesitated for a moment, disappointed at the thought of being unable to have some time off during the summer holidays.

"Yes, a week's time will be alright."

Shaking my hand and looking at me with a friendly smile he said,

296

"I'll look forward to seeing you at nine o'clock next Monday."

I left the office with an element of doubt in my mind - pleased that I had got the job, but wondering if it was the right job for me. Only time would tell.

My first day at work was different to anything I had experienced before and not at all the sort of thing we had been prepared for at college. No one told us what it was like to be working with and around all male company. Virtually all the customers were men and the sales representatives were men. In fact, I was lucky to even hear a female voice over the phone. I was glad to see Valerie in the afternoon. She made me feel at ease right away and became a close and trusted friend.

I don't think I would have survived working in the job if it hadn't been for her coming in to work every afternoon. We had more than a few laughs on the first afternoon of working together - one of them being about the toilet. There was just one facility shared between all of us, male and female - a boxy type shed, just across the yard from the office, with a flushing system that echoed noisily, offering little privacy to whoever had 'just been'. It was definitely a space to avoid if you possibly could, especially during the cold winter months when I was told the whole lot froze up. I enjoyed my work and continued to work for the firm for over a year.

I had just arrived back from my lunch break one Friday afternoon when my boss came in to the office and said he had some important news to tell us as it was likely to affect us all. One of the sales representatives who had been working for Dunlop Tyres was going to join the firm as a partner. There were going to be some future changes but for the time being everything would be operating in the same way.

Less than a week had passed since the announcement of the changes. I arrived at work early and was having a chat in the yard with Jack, the tyre fitter, when Mr Franks called to me across the yard, saying,

"Ann, I'll be in the office in a moment and I'd like to have a talk with you."

"Sounds ominous. I wonder what's up," I said, walking off hurriedly.

I got to my desk, put my handbag on the floor and was about to go through the untidy stack of mail which had been left earlier by the postman when Mr Franks came into the office, walked across to the chair behind Valerie's desk and sat down. I thought he looked a little uneasy. He then looked straight at me and said,

"Ann, I am so sorry but I have to tell you that we won't be needing you to work for us any more. I must stress it's nothing to do with you personally, or the standard of your work, but my new partner's wife will be taking over your job."

Not having the experience of being sacked before, I didn't know what I was supposed to say. Yes, I was shocked at the news, but my pride and stubbornness stopped me from showing any emotional reaction.

"Well, I'll miss working here, but sometimes an unplanned situation such as this does help you move on to something better."

The half-hour bus journey home was always a good opportunity to sit quietly and resolve a problem. My problem today was how I was going to tell everyone at home that I no longer had a job. I could feel the anger and humiliation welling up inside me. The bus jolted suddenly, braking to avoid a dog that had run into the road. This momentarily disturbed me from my anxious mood and put me into a more positive frame of mind. I was now wondering what my next job would be.

When I arrived home, Mum was reheating my dinner which she'd saved from their main midday meal. The plate of food was standing over the saucepan of steaming hot water covered with the lid. I lifted it to see what I was getting. Lamb chops, mixed garden vegetables and gravy.

"Mum, I am starving. Is it ready yet?"

"Yes dear. Go and sit down and I'll bring it to the table."

It was tea-time for Mum and Dad and they had a choice on the table of cheese and celery, a plate of bread and butter, raspberry and strawberry jam and a plate of fancy mixed cakes.

When we were all settled round the table I thought it would be a good time to tell them about my unfortunate day. After I had told them what had happened at the office, Dad looked at me across the table and said,

"Well mate, it ain't a mite a good you worryin'. It won't take ya long to find another job, that I do know."

Then Mum added,

"You have gained experience over the past year. You can't blame yourself for what's happened. You may find something else advertised in the local paper."

Searching under the headings of 'Job Vacancies' in the Essex County Standard, I found a job that seemed to be just what I was looking for. It was with a television rental firm in Colchester requiring someone for general office duties. I walked to the telephone box at the bottom of the road and phoned the number advertised to make enquiries about the job, and to find out if the vacancy had been filled.

"Hold the line a moment and I'll get the manager to come to the phone. He'll be able to tell you all you want to know."

After a fairly short conversation I was given an interview that was to be at twelve thirty the next day. The firm's name was 'Good Listening'. I wouldn't have a problem finding it as it was virtually next to the Regal Cinema. It didn't take me long to get back up Victory Road hill. I could soon be working again!

Alan was playing badminton this evening. He played for the Colchester Police Team. I decided to stay in and have an

299

early night as I wanted to be up early in the morning. I must have been very tired. I can remember switching off my bedside lamp and the next thing being woken by the sound of the Bill Pontyfix the postman, delivering the first post in the morning - we had two deliveries of letters in those days, eight in the morning and then the second post at midday. It was the thud of the letterbox that woke me.

My first thoughts were about the interview. I would catch the eleven thirty bus to make sure I got there in time. After breakfast I spent even more time getting ready, changing from one lot of clothes to another and leaving an untidy pile mounting up on the bottom of my bed. I eventually chose a tight yellow skirt and yellow tone top. I had recently treated myself to a tan-coloured designer blouse. I put it on, leaving it loose with the buttons undone. It gave me a smart but casual look. All I needed now was my high-heeled shoes. I always wore high heels as it helped exaggerate my usual height of five feet and two inches. Looking in the long wardrobe mirror I was satisfied that I looked alright for the interview.

When I got downstairs I asked Mum if I looked alright.

"Yes dear, you look fine but you had better hurry up otherwise you'll miss your bus."

I grabbed my handbag and ran out calling,

"Goodbye! I am off now."

"Bye dear. Good luck!"

I arrived for the interview with five minutes to spare. It gave me time to look through the large plate glass window displaying televisions of various sizes. One thing I noticed was the thick wall-to-wall carpeting. Nervously, I opened the door and walked over to the desk where a man stood talking on the telephone. I stood back and waited until he had finished his conversation.

"I have an interview at twelve thirty."

"Ah yes, you must be Miss Farthing. Would you come through to the office please?"

I followed him into the office at the back of the shop where he explained exactly what I would be expected to do. Then he asked me to add up a long column of figures - pounds, shillings and pence - which I did correctly.

"I know you can do both shorthand and typing. There won't be much shorthand, but there will be a lot of copy typing and then, of course, you will have to do some shop work."

The interview was rather hurried as people were coming into the shop to make their television payments. I could see the interruptions were irritating him and his patience was wearing thin. Then he suddenly said,

"If you can start work on Monday at nine o'clock, the position is yours."

I stood for a moment looking through the shop window and could see the large shop fronts opposite. Crouch Street was busy with shoppers bustling about with their shopping bags filled with carefully chosen purchases. This was a complete contrast to the area where I had previously been working. I had to make a decision right now, and my answer was yes! I would be on a month's trial as from Monday.

The first day at work went well. I picked up the systems and working procedures with no real problems. I was introduced to the engineers who serviced and repaired the televisions. They came in and out of the office at various times during the day, picking up new instructions on breakdowns and making deliveries to new customers. The firm promised a same day repair service or a replacement set until the repair was completed.

Week two saw me settled into a job I was beginning to enjoy. I was now competent and able to cope with all the work in the shop and with the customers.

Early on the Friday afternoon of the third week I was working in the office when the manager came in, fiddled about with what appeared to be wage slips and suddenly out of the blue said,

"Well, Ann, it's not really working, is it?"

"What isn't working?" I was puzzled. I had no idea what he meant.

"The job, this work. You really aren't coping, are you?"

I can't describe exactly how I felt. At first I thought that he was joking but he didn't look or act as if it was a joke. It took only a matter of seconds for the full impact of his words to hit me. I went hot with embarrassment, then uneasiness, followed by the anger which was going on inside me, but I was able to keep it to myself.

"I thought I was managing alright," was all I could think of as a reply.

"No, not really. In fact at the end of the four weeks I think we will have to call it a day. I must hurry now. I need to catch the bank before it closes."

After he had gone I sat down at the desk to stop my legs shaking. It was hard to concentrate on doing any work. Sitting there, I began to wonder if I was really that stupid to think that I was getting on alright when in fact I wasn't doing very well at all according to my boss? No! That couldn't be right - I knew that I wasn't struggling with the work.

The shop door opened and two of the engineers came in to see if there was any work for them to catch up with. I handed them the jobs book and thought that I might as well tell them now.

"While you two fellows are here I want to tell you that I will be leaving here soon. Next week is my last week."

"Fed up with us already are you, Ann?"

"No, not at all. It's the boss. He doesn't think my work is good enough and I am beginning to wonder myself now."

"I can't believe that," said the youngest man as he walked out of the shop to the work van.

Joe, the older man, said,

"You mustn't blame yourself for what's happened. I know you're perfectly capable and able to do this work. What I am about to tell you must be kept just between ourselves. He knew when he gave you the interview and the job that you would only be here for a month. I know for a fact he'd already given the job to an older person but she had to give a month's notice before she could leave. He just needed someone to fill in for a month."

"You have no idea how much better you have made me feel, Joe. I really began to doubt my own integrity."

When I told Mum and Dad about how I had been treated at work and that I had only one more week to go, Dad was furious.

"I am not going to have you treated in that manner."

"Please, Dad, just leave things as they are. He will know something's been said and we can't get Joe into trouble."

"She's right, Jim," said Mum.

"Have it yer own way, but I don't hold in with the way he's treated ya."

I continued working for one more week, happily leaving it all behind me at five o'clock on the Friday afternoon.

CHAPTER 30

Ashes by post, the strange toothpaste and the truth

OVERLEAF: *Pixie in her 'pixie' bonnet*
ABOVE: *Wedding of Frederick Smith to Winifred Farthing.*

Two weeks later, I started another job. This time it was as a Post Office counter clerk in High Street, Colchester. I had reservations about the career change but it certainly couldn't be any worse than my recent experiences. I liked the job and the girls I worked with.

A few weeks passed, then I was asked to sign a government Secrecy Act form. Once I had signed the form I was allowed to make entries in the National Savings Bank account books. It was a revelation, making me laugh to myself, how dear little old ladies, who were poorly dressed and often pleaded poverty, would produce a National Savings Bank book containing deposits amounting to hundreds and sometimes thousands of pounds.

One afternoon I was serving a customer who I had got used to seeing each day. He usually came in about a half hour before closing. He had his usual large canvas sack full of neatly wrapped parcels, all tied up with string. I took hold of the packages by the string and weighed them on the large metal scales indicating the correct price per item. I called out the price of each one which was one shilling and sixpence (7½p), stuck the stamp on and stamped it with a large rubber parcel stamp before piling them carefully up for the final pricing. The next parcel appeared to be exactly the same as the others, but it was slightly heavier.

"Oh, that one is one and ninepence," I said with surprise.

"He must have been a big fellow. You're only little. You would probably be tuppence ha'penny."

Connie and Diana, the girls working next to me, both laughed. My customer looked at me and said,

"You don't know where I work?"

"No, I'm sorry, I don't."

He laughed, saying

"I come from W.H. Shephard, the Funeral Directors down the street. You've been weighing up peoples' ashes in the urns."

I was appalled at the thought of peoples' ashes being weighed on the Post Office scales, chucked into mail bags, collected by the mail van, then doing another earthly journey on the train before reaching their final destination.

This story is nearly as bad as the one told by an elderly aunt who went to stay at a friends. She forgot to pack her own tooth powder and assumed it would be alright to use some of the powder that was in a container standing on the washstand, next to the toothbrush jar. To her utter horror she later found out later it was Uncle Percy's ashes.

My Post Office work became permanent. I learned everything there was to learn regarding business done over the counter at the Post Office. It was varied and interesting and I eventually got to know all the customers. I didn't miss my office work one little bit.

The time had now come when it was important for me to actually hear someone confirm who my real father was. Deep down inside me I knew. I had known for what seemed a very long time but I had managed to ignore the obvious and carry on pretending. I felt the one person who would tell me the truth would be Auntie Tod.

It would have to be the right moment when no one else was about and when the mood was right for both me and Auntie Tod. Only a few days went by when we found ourselves alone. Mum was upstairs getting ready as they were both going to an evening whist drive at the British Legion.

I felt now would be a good time to ask my important question.

"Auntie Tod, I've got something I want to ask you. I know it might be difficult, but please will you be truthful? Is Peter my real Dad?"

She looked at me and hesitated before speaking, then said,

"I've been saying to Ada for a long time that she should be telling you but you know what she's like - too proud for her own good sometimes. Yes dear, he is your father, but don't tell her or Jim that I've told you. It's just between us."

"What about my birth mother?"

"Look dear, I've said enough for now. I'll talk to you another time. There's a lot you should have been told."

We could hear Mum coming downstairs and the subject was dropped immediately.

Some weeks later, Auntie Tod was leaning over her front gate talking to a passing neighbour. I was riding past on my bike and stopped to say hello. The neighbour carried on up the road.

"Would you like to come in for a few minutes? I am all on my own and I want to have a little talk with you about the question that was left unanswered regarding who your mother is."

I leant my bike against the brick wall separating the garden from the main road and followed her indoors, wondering exactly what I was about to hear. Auntie Tod began by saying,

"I know the problems you have had to face over the past couple of years about your identity and how many things have been kept from you about who your real mother is. Jim and Ada should have told you a long time ago, but for some reason they have thought it best to say nothing."

I listened intently as she continued,

"Can you remember the day that you and Dorothy went to the toy shop in Mill Road? Dorothy tried to get you to come home but the ol' gal - wicked ol' sod - enticed you into the sitting room where a young woman was playing the piano."

"Yes, she was playing it beautifully. The old lady asked me if I would like to learn to play the piano. When I said that I would, she said that her daughter would be pleased to teach me."

"That woman's name is 'Bubbles' Smith."

I caught my breath. I knew…

"Auntie, you needn't say any more. I know now who my birth mother is. As soon as you mentioned the name 'Smith' I just knew it had to be her."

Everything was beginning to come together. In that very instant my mind returned to scenes of the past. Again, the ration book came to mind. My unexplained but very strange attraction to the pretty lady we used to see along East Road when I was just a little girl. All the other puzzling times when things didn't quite add up.

"Auntie, now I know the truth I must leave all that in the past. It's best left alone for everyone's sake. I had a wonderful childhood, filled with love and everything else a child could wish for."

"Well, it could be said that you was spoilt, although Ada and Jim wouldn't admit it."

And there the matter was to be left for some years, with the conversation between us being kept a secret.

I was going to ballroom dancing classes at the school this evening. Alan had absolutely no interest in dancing whatsoever so Geoffrey Hewes became my dancing partner. He was a good dancer and picked up the steps very quickly - we were a good team. Alan usually came to meet me when the class was over but tonight he was playing badminton for the Police Team so I thought I would call in at The Legion and meet Mum and Auntie Tod. The whist drive was nearly over. Mum and Auntie Todd were sitting at the same table as Charlie 'Tiddler' Mole and girlfriend, Jean.

Tiddler sat back on his chair and was considering which card to lay down next. Then he said,

"When I get home tonight, I'm gonna hev a fried snowball and a glass of wind."

Auntie Tod said,

"Well done, mate. I'll hev the same!"

After the whist drive there was still plenty of daylight left and it was a lovely evening. All three of us cycled home along Mersea Avenue. Auntie Tod had decided to come home with us for a night cap.

When we arrived home Dad was just sharpening his cut throat razor on the strop that he had conveniently hung over the brass door handle. He was going to do Sam Webb's pigs first thing in the morning. Doing Sam's pigs meant castrating screeching pink piglets, depriving them of their 'manhood'. Dad was the next best thing to a vet for many of the smaller farmers on the Island. He would perform various small operations like docking dogs' tails and castrating both tom cats and pigs. Once, he operated on a chicken, removing a large growth from its neck. It made a full recovery, living a long and healthy life, which was surprising seeing that it had been stitched up with a needle and cotton from Mum's workbox.

I can remember the day a fully grown blackbird was in the garden trying to fly but was ending up in a heap with its wings spread along the ground, a terrified look in its tiny round eyes.

"Come on, ol' mate, what's happened to ya then?"

He picked up the bird and showed me its broken leg. I was handed the bird.

"Hang on to it for a minute, will ya?"

He went indoors and came out with a box of matches and some thread. His large hands gently used a match to make a splint for the bird's leg and it was then secured with the thread. It was like magic as the bird became able to fly again.

Another memory, a very amusing one, was the time Ted

Woolf, who lived next door, had been encouraged by Dad to make some home made wheat wine. He gave Ted one of his recipes which included using wheat and raisins. Ted had got to the stage of draining the wine and was left with the wheat and raisins which he threw on the lawn for his ducks to eat. Later we heard his voice at the back door shouting,

"Jim, Jim! Come quickly, there's something up with my ducks."

"What ya mean, mate?" asked Dad as he followed Ted next door.

He was faced with an unbelievably comical scene. There were about a dozen ducks laying on their backs, paddling their webbed feet in the air.

"Well help me Bob if they ain't all drunk. They've taken in the alcohol from the wheat and the raisins. Mate, there's nothing we can do, only wait for 'em to get over it."

Over the years the Island and its people have kept many hidden secrets - some beautiful, some sad and some meant never be revealed. Today I have at last been able to piece together the hidden and secret love of my real parents.

Bubbles Smith was a pretty, fair-haired teenager, barely sixteen when she first started going out with Peter Farthing. Although he was three years older than her, they seemed a well-matched couple. She was an intelligent teenager and also a very good musician. Nothing would keep her from the man she loved. She was drawn to Cross Farm, down Cross Lane at every opportunity, especially if she was able to find an excuse to get away from her mother, who was a tyrant at the best of times.

Cross Farm was just a short walk from the sandy beach and the tall, rugged cliffs - now washed away forever by the pounding waves from the sea. They offered a very private and romantic setting for courting couples. The tops of the cliffs

were surrounded by farmland, wild shrubs and blackberry bushes - another favourite spot for young lovers. Peter was Bubbles' first love and it was one evening on the soft sands of the beach, sheltered by the rugged cliffs that they became lovers. There was a silent understanding between them both as they walked home up Cross Lane holding hands.

Invitations had been sent out to family and friends, inviting them to what would be classed on the Island as 'The Wedding of the Year'. Peter's first cousin, Winifred Farthing, was marrying Frederick H. Smith. Frederick was Bubbles' first cousin. The wedding was truly splendid and attracted considerable local attention. Winnie's Dad, Mannie Farthing - brother to Jim - was the local dairyman and Frederick's Dad was the local baker. Both families were extremely well known.

Family and friends arrived at the local church in posh cars and dressed in highly fashionable clothes. Winnie, the bride, had chosen to wear a very unusual pink, crepe-de-chine gown in Redingcote style with a head-dress of pearls and orange blossom and a long flowing veil. She was attended by five bridesmaids. All the Farthings and Smiths were at the wedding, including Peter and Bubbles. This was probably the last happy occasion where the loving teenagers were ever allowed to be together again.

Sitting together at the reception, they both secretly knew that Bubbles was carrying Peter's child. She was now about three months pregnant. No one could have possibly predicted the reaction of Bubbles' mother when she found out her daughter was pregnant. The pain and heartbreak endured by a lonely sixteen year-old, unable to have any contact with the father of her hidden child must have been almost too much to bear.

The baby as it grew in the mother's womb was being concealed by a very tight corset and later bandaged tightly to hide any give-away bulge. Even her closest friend was unaware that she was pregnant. Ada and Jim had very little contact with the Smith family after the truth came out about the couple's mistake, although they were allowed to pay for Bubbles to go into a private nursing home in Colchester to have the baby.

Bubbles was just seventeen years old when her baby was born. On the 2nd May, 1939 she gave birth to a baby girl, weighing approximately five and a half pounds. No one seemed to have any idea what was to become of the tiny little girl. Granny Smith was adamant that she didn't want the baby to return to the Island. So what would be the child's destiny?

It's uncertain how it finally came about, but Ada's sister, Lily and her husband, Harry Collins lived in Bishops Stortford, Hertfordshire. Lily was a trained nanny and nurse, and it was agreed that they would take the baby to live with them in Hertfordshire. At just a fortnight old the baby left the arms and familiar smells of its mother to be handed over to two kind and loving strangers. Her mother was to be left scarred for life by this horrendous experience of having to give away her baby and accept that she couldn't be with Peter again. Jim and Ada were happy knowing that their grand daughter was safe and would be well looked after.

War was inevitable but no one could have predicted that in the short period of only a few weeks Harry Collins would be called up into the forces. Bubbles' baby would have to be brought back onto the Island as Lily returned to the safety of Cross Farm with her own two children, Bill and Muriel, plus the baby, Ann, who was now known as 'Pixie' because of her pixie bonnets. Pixie was now going to be brought up in the idyllic surroundings of Cross Farm. Ada was soon to be known as 'Mummy' and Jim as 'Daddy'.

She was surrounded by love and an abundance of toys - everything a child could wish for. Then, one day, there was a *knock on the door. Bubbles had recently got married and her husband, Harry Conway, was standing there uneasily trying to explain the purpose of the call. Bubbles wanted her baby back and he was ready to help and support her. Ada stood there, the shock draining every bit of colour from her face. She started to shake and then she pleaded, the tears rolling down her face.*

"Please, please don't take her from us. She's become part of our lives and she only knows this as her home. She will feel lost anywhere else. We have had her for three years."

Bubbles was standing at the gate crying.

Harry was a kind and thoughtful man, six years older than Bubbles. He gazed into the kitchen and saw the large rocking horse and all the beautiful toys. At that moment he realised that they could never give the child the sort of life she had been used to. It was then that the couple left, leaving Ada shocked and frightened.

When Jim came in at one o'clock Ada was still feeling emotionally drained by the young couple's disturbing visit. Jim listened to Ada as she told him what had happened. He was also hurt and angry. They both agreed that it was time to go and see their solicitor. The advice they got from the solicitor wasn't exactly what they wanted to hear.

The baby was never legally adopted by Jim and Ada - its grandparents - therefore the child's mother still had certain rights. However, a court might consider it best for the child to stay with its grandparents, but this couldn't be guaranteed. The best advice they were given was to leave things as they were, but never to leave the child unguarded, or even out of their sight. If the mother did get hold of her, it would be very hard to get her back again.

So here was the best kept secret of a baby that had to be guarded twenty four hours a day in case she was kidnapped by her own mother. Pixie luckily had a normal, carefree childhood, oblivious of any emotional battles or worries that were going on around her.

CHAPTER 31

The company van,
Southend lights and a nice
surprise in Romford

OVERLEAF: *Geoffrey Hewes (left) and
Norman Priestly with their friend Faye Moles.*
ABOVE: *Auntie Tod and Uncle Fred Haywood.*

Alan had served his time as a Police Cadet and now had to decide if he wanted to make the police force his career. Our recent conversations suggested that he would probably leave. He'd covered all aspects of the job during the past three years and there had been many times when he seriously questioned whether it was what he really wanted to do.

When he finally decided on a career change everything seemed to open up to his advantage. Joy Buy, one of the married women who worked with Alan, told him that there was a job going at JP Neal's Corn and Seed Merchants. It was general office work with some van deliveries to farms. Joy's husband worked within the trade and got to hear of the vacancy.

Alan telephoned Mr Neal to enquire about the work and was told he could go for an interview on Thursday afternoon. The interview went well and he got the job. Jack Neal, his boss, taught Alan to drive and introduced him to many of the farmers on his books. After only a few weeks Alan had passed his driving test and as well as doing office work was now calling on farmers in the area. One evening as he was about to leave work to catch the bus home, Jack called him back.

"Alan, you might as well start using the van to go home in but if you want to use it for private use you'll have to put the petrol in yourself."

Being able to use the works van was as good as a pay rise - probably better! The first thing he did when he arrived home was to drive to our house. I heard the sound of a motor outside then the 'pip-pip' of a hooter. I went out to see what was going on.

Alan was sitting behind the wheel of a practically new Ford van using the accelerator to keep the engine gently ticking over. The smile on his face said everything. He wound down the car window and said,

"Whose luck's in, then? I've now got the use of the works van so I'll be able to come and pick you up later."

He drove off before I had the time to reply or even look at the vehicle. When I told Mum and Dad that Alan now had the use of the works van their comments were that they hoped he would drive sensibly. I assured them that he would and that he was a good driver. I don't think that they were altogether convinced.

It wasn't long before we heard the sound of the car back again. I was all ready and looking forward to going for a short drive. We drove round the Island and then ended up at 'Lynton'. Susan's boyfriend, John Benns, was there with Terry and John. The novelty and excitement of having a vehicle to go out in encouraged us all to consider where we could drive for the evening. It was eventually narrowed down to either Clacton or Southend. I said I would like to see Southend lights. Terry said,

"Yes, then we could go to the Kursaal."

Southend was agreed. The back of the van was made comfortable with cushions from the settee and pillows off the beds. There was plenty of room for four in the back. I was Queen Bee and sat in the front with the driver. There were no seat belts in those days. Pete and Dot were agreeable to us all going out for the evening but we knew we'd get some opposition from Mum and Dad. We couldn't just go off without letting them know where we were going, as we knew we'd be late home.

It was just as we thought. Dad wasn't happy about us driving to Southend.

"I don't know why the devil yer want to go off out at this time of the day."

"Dad, we're going to see the lights. There wouldn't be much to see during the day. We'll be fine so stop worrying."

Dad opened the back doors of the van to make sure everyone was safe and comfortable and had a word with John Benns who was the oldest of us all.

"Look here, mate. Don't let them young 'uns get up to anything daft, will yer?"

"I'll keep an eye on 'em," said John.

The door of the van was then shut securely leaving all of us in the mood for fun. None of us had seen the lights before so we didn't know what to expect. Arriving in Southend, we drove right along the esplanade enjoying the colourful and entertaining display of lights.

Everywhere was alive with people wandering about all over the road, not at all worried about vehicles trying to get past. Driving along with the windows open we could hear that most people had what we would call a proper London accent. With Southend being the nearest coastal resort to London's East End I suppose it would be a popular place for day trippers and workers' outings.

To get to the well known, domed Kursaal Amusement Park we had to go to the Eastern Esplanade. Our passengers in the back of the van were getting rather noisy. Terry and John were laughing loudly at the many silly hats people were wearing. Some even had 'Kiss Me Quick' written on them and others were wearing cowboy hats. Sue was trying to get the pair of them to calm down. John Benns, who was looking through the small rear windows of the van door, thankfully saw somewhere to park.

We had a wonderful time at the Kursaal spending money on all the amusements. Southend had been good fun but we were all ready to get back home again to the peaceful way of life on Mersea Island.

Auntie Lil and Uncle Harry were coming to stay for the weekend. Their photography business in Hornchurch was doing well but as there were no weddings booked for the weekend he took the opportunity to come and visit us. As usual, the house was open to any family or friends who wanted to pop in. They always liked to see Auntie and Uncle while they were visiting.

Friday evening was taken up playing cards round the dining table in the sitting room. There were so many playing Newmarket that the leaves at each end of the table had to be drawn out to make enough room for everyone to play. The stake was tuppence a game - one penny on the horse and one penny in the kitty. Halfway through the evening, Mum went out into the kitchen for some refreshments. She came back with some home made wheat wine as well as sherry and beers that were delivered to the door every fortnight by Cooke's Wine Merchants.

"If anyone prefers a cup of tea, I'll put the kettle on to boil and make a pot."

"I would love a piece of your home made cake, Ada, please," said Uncle Harry.

No one seemed to want a cup of tea so Mum returned with her special fruit cake and a stack of tea plates and serviettes. As the evening progressed the room was filled with laughter which got louder as tales of past and present were told.

"Well, just listen to this," said Auntie Tod. "When I went down to the Cresta Stores there was a queue of people waiting to be served. I joined the queue and noticed that Roly Green stood just in front of me. Now he usually lets me have some rhubarb out of his garden, so I said, "Hello, Roly. Is yer rhubarb up yet?"

"Mate, ass allus up."

Auntie Tod paused for effect.

"I felt myself going red as everyone turned to look. 'You dirty old man! I said. He roared with laughter and so did everyone else in the shop!'"

This little anecdote made for another round of laughter. It was at this point I decided to repeat the story of Dad putting on his black working trousers to find one of the legs had worn very thin at the knee, showing the white of his long johns. He solved the problem by blacking out the white of his underpants with shoe polish. He said that he didn't want to 'look a mug' wearing his Sunday best trousers for work. We all laughed at this story, especially Dad.

"You don't believe in dressing up then, Jim?" said Uncle Harry.

"No mate, not if I don't have to. My suit only comes out of the wardrobe for christenings, weddings and funerals. Well, I don't know about you lot, but I am getting tired and I want to be up early in the morning."

Dad excused himself and went up to bed. He had been getting chest pains recently and said it was indigestion but deep down he knew the recurring pains were the result of having rheumatic fever as a child. It had left him with a weak heart. There were times when he was digging the garden that he would have to lean on his spade for a moment and put a tiny tablet under his tongue to relieve the pain in his chest.

Sometimes the pain was very bad. He would sit down and ask me to massage his back between his shoulder blades until he felt better. He would say,

"Don't tell Ada - it will worry her."

Dad thought I was strong and could cope. I never told him how scared I was when he got the pain. I would pray so hard to God not to take him from us.

After Dad had gone to bed everyone seemed to slow down. The cards were packed away and Mum brought a pot of tea to the table. Everyone had a cup of tea and it wasn't long before they all went home and the rest of us retired to bed.

323

What a lovely evening we had all had and there was another day to go before Auntie Lil and Uncle Harry returned home.

Sunday evening came around all too quickly and it was time to wave goodbye to our visitors. I hated goodbyes but it was different this time because in just a fortnight's time Alan and I were going to visit them in Hornchurch and stay overnight. We could then go to Romford market. We stood at the gate and watched the car move up Victory Road. Mum said her usual thing,

"Don't watch them go out of sight. It's bad luck."

I always turned my head away just before they went out of sight and turned the corner. Dad would laugh and say,

"What a load of ol' Tommy rot!"

To this very day I find myself repeating her saying and turning my head away just as I did all those years ago.

Neither Mum or Dad were too happy about us going to Hornchurch and staying overnight. They kept coming up with various excuses for us not to go. In the end Peter was able to convince them that Alan was quite capable of driving there and back without any problems and they were both to stop worrying.

The next two weeks seemed to pass quickly and there was only one more day to go before we would be going to see Auntie Lil and Uncle Harry. We decided it would be better to travel on Friday evening after Alan got back from work.

Just before we started our journey Dad put two large cardboard boxes in the back of the van, each containing an assortment of fruit and vegetables from the garden, as well as two dozen chicken eggs. At last we were ready to go. I kissed Mum and Dad goodbye. They made Alan promise that he wouldn't drive too fast. He didn't - until we got out of sight. He then put his foot down. There wasn't a lot of traffic on the roads so we were able to make good time.

It didn't seem long before we all sat down to a tasty hot meal and chatted about what had been going on over the past fortnight. I had some exciting news. Colin Page from West Mersea Post Office came round to tell me that they needed a counter clerk at the Post Office and he was offering me the position. It was the same money that I was getting in Colchester with a rise of five shillings a week after three months. Also, I wouldn't have bus fares to pay out of my wages and I would be able to go home for a cooked dinner every day.

"Well it seems like a good deal to me to me Pix," said Uncle Harry, "even if Colin is a miserable ol' bugger at times," he laughed.

We were not too late getting to bed as we wanted to be up early in the morning to go to Romford Market. I lay in bed feeling lonely and unable to get to sleep, being in a strange room. I wondered if Alan was asleep in the room across the landing and decided that he probably would be as he was used to sleeping away from home. There had been times when he had played an away match for the police badminton team, missed the last bus home and slept overnight in the police cells.

The last time I remember looking at the clock standing on the bedside cabinet was three a.m. I wasn't used to the noise of the traffic passing by my window. At last I drifted off into a deep sleep and the next thing I knew was Auntie Lil knocking on the bedroom door and calling to me to get up as breakfast was ready. When I was fully awake I could smell the delicious aroma of bacon coming from the kitchen.

After a good old English breakfast of egg, bacon, fried bread, tomatoes and sausages we headed to Romford as planned. It was a lovely bright sunny morning with crowds of people wandering about gazing at the market stalls. I was surprised at the size of the market and the wide variety of goods on offer. There were bargains we just couldn't resist. I purchased some pretty cotton material to make myself a new dress, also sweets, cakes and tinned fruit without proper labels on.

I was happy to window shop, looking at the latest fashions elegantly displayed in the large shop windows. We were walking down one of the main streets holding hands when Alan hesitated and stopped to look in James Walker's, the well-known jewellers. The window was full of gorgeous jewellery arranged in sections that made it easy for the customer to select any item they might be interested in.

I was of course attracted to the diamond rings. Dare I even hope that Alan might have the same interest in stopping to gaze!

"What are you looking at?" I asked.

"I am just looking at the watches."

"There's some pretty little rings."

"They're all too expensive and there's no point in looking as your father would go mad."

With that thought in mind we began to walk off. When we got back to the car park we put the shopping in the back of the van then sat down talking quietly in the front seats. I steered the conversation back to engagement rings, wanting to know why Alan was so worried about facing Dad. If he was that nervous maybe it was best to get engaged first then tell Mum and Dad afterwards. He began to smile and leaning closer he gave me a big hug and then said,

"Let's do it shall we?"

He didn't wait for a reply as he knew what the answer would be. The moment was more exciting than romantic. I couldn't believe it was actually happening. For some time I had felt slightly envious of my two friends, Pauline French and Dorothy Carter. Pauline was engaged to Brian 'Spadgy' Jay and they planned to marry in September. Alan was to be best man. Dorothy was engaged to David 'Mowie' Mussett and they were to be married the following April.

CHAPTER 32

An angry reaction, the cunning punter and Dad's collapse

OVERLEAF: *Auntie Lil and Uncle Harry.*

Before going back to the jeweller we went to the main Post Office to withdraw some money from our National Savings Accounts. We both had our books. It was the easiest and most convenient way of saving. Money could be drawn out at any Post Office anywhere in the country during normal working hours, usually nine a.m. until five-thirty p.m. six days a week. Today there was still plenty of time before the shops closed.

Holding hands, we walked back down the street to the jeweller. I was having a job to keep up with Alan as I was wearing some smart but very high heeled shoes with stilettos clip-clopping on the hard paving stones. We were there at last, looking in the window at the beautiful array of rings. The shop assistant brought us a good selection to choose from in a varied range of prices.

The ones I chose to try were then displayed on a black velvet cloth which he unravelled with an expert flourish and laid on top of the counter. Even though I had reduced my choice down to just a few I was still stuck for my final decision between the rings displayed on the velvet. I then tried on a pretty little three-diamond gold ring which was a perfect fit. The shop lights caught the white diamonds, making them sparkle and glitter, turning them into the colours of the rainbow. I knew instantly that this was my choice.

"This one is beautiful and it's exactly my size."

"Would you like that one?" asked Alan, who wasn't a man of many words.

"Yes, I love it. It's perfect."

"Would you like me to put it in a box for you, sir?"

"Yes please."

The ring was placed in a red leather case lined with padded cream satin. The case was snapped shut and placed in a small bag. After paying at the till we left the shop with Alan carrying the special package. Returning to the car park and to the romantic interior of Jack Neal's works van, we got engaged. Alan undid the little bag, opened the box and then gently placed the ring on the third finger of my left hand. At that moment I knew we had so much love to give to each other and no one would ever part us. Our gentle kiss said everything. I couldn't have been more happy but for a fleeting moment I wondered if happiness came at a price.

When we arrived back at Park Lane, Hornchurch, I couldn't wait to tell Auntie Lil and Uncle Harry what we'd done. They were surprised to hear of our engagement but were genuinely very pleased for us, although Harry did say laughingly,

"Christ, boy. You'll be in trouble with Ada and Jim."

He left the room while he was still talking, returning seconds later with one of his best wines to celebrate the occasion. As he opened the bottle he said,

"Look mate, I think I ought to follow you back to Mersea tonight as you may need some support when you give them your news. Jim may not be too pleased."

I'd always had a liking for Uncle Harry. He always seemed to take my part but I thought that this time he had it all wrong. I was sure Dad would be happy for me. Mum may be a bit off hand but not Dad.

Uncle Harry telephoned Betty living next door to ask her to let Mum know that we would all arrive either late afternoon or early evening and they would be staying overnight, leaving on Sunday. We had a quick journey home. The roads were fairly clear and both Alan and Uncle Harry were fast drivers. In fact Uncle Harry was such a fast driver that he used to scare anyone else in the car.

Arriving back on the Island, I began to feel slightly apprehensive about breaking the news of our engagement. I wanted everyone to be as happy as I was. Mum was pleased to see Auntie and Uncle and said,

"I am surprised to see you so soon. I wasn't expecting you to come down for a few weeks, especially with Harry being so busy with his photography."

"Well mate, Pixie has got some news for you so we thought we would come and be part of the surprise."

The happiness I had experienced was suddenly ended when I announced that I was engaged. The look on Mum's face could only be described as a mixture of anger and horror.

"I suppose Harry is at the bottom of it all."

"No, Mum, not at all. It was nothing to do with Uncle Harry. He was just happy for us and so was Auntie Lil."

I looked at Dad for some of his usual support and hopefully for his approval but by the expression on his face I knew all was lost. All I could do was ask if he would like to see my ring. He looked at me in disgust and replied,

"No. I don't want to see it. Neither of you two have got any sense or money and never will have at the rate you are going."

I was crying inside, but strong enough to hold back my tears. How could my Dad, who I loved so much, be so unkind? I made for the door and said,

"I'm off out of here and don't worry if I am late back."

Alan followed me out saying,

"I thought this would happen."

He overtook me at the gate got into the car and started it up, revving the engine angrily. I got into the car and he took off up Victory Road like a bat out of hell. I sat in the passenger seat not daring to say a word as I could easily have said the wrong thing. It was a humiliating experience for me facing my family's attitude so I knew Alan must have felt embarrassed.

"Where are we going?"

"As far away as possible from your bloody family."

"Please... take me to see Peter and Dot."

"I don't know what good that will do."

"Please, Alan."

Eventually we turned into Fairhaven Avenue and stopped outside 'Lynton'. I got out of the car and began walking round to the back door. Then I realised that I hadn't heard the slam of the other door. Walking back to the van I could see Alan was still sitting in the driver's seat.

"Aren't you coming with me?"

"Not to be made to look stupid again."

"I promise everything will be different with Peter and Dot."

I walked away, praying to myself that he would eventually come indoors. I had just entered the kitchen when I heard the car door slam then Alan followed in behind me. We went into the lounge. Peter and Dot were watching the television. Dot looked at us and realised by our faces that there was something wrong.

"Neither of you look very happy. So what's wrong?"

I sat down on one of the large comfortable armchairs and Alan perched on the arm of the chair. I then told them everything. When I had finished talking Peter came over, gave me a hug and said,

"Well, my love, I am happy for both of you. This definitely calls for a celebration drink. Congratulations and good luck."

He then began to laugh.

"Good old Uncle Harry. He knew what you would have to contend with from Mum and Dad. Both him and Auntie Lil would have talked them round by the time you get home." He looked at me tenderly.

"Poor old Dad - he's just frightened of losing his little girl. He didn't get cross because he wanted to hurt you. That's the last thing he would do."

Everything Peter said made sense and it made me feel a lot happier. Alan was more relaxed as he sat back in the other big armchair drinking a glass of port.

When we eventually got home Alan dropped me off outside the house, kissed me goodnight and then drove off home. I was actually relieved when he didn't suggest coming indoors. I wanted time to make things right with Mum and Dad and I felt I could probably manage it better on my own.

When I got in, Uncle Harry looked up from the supper table and gave me a wink. I took this to mean that things had improved since early evening. They all sat around the table eating a late supper of cold beef, new potatoes, cheese, pickled onions and home made chutney. In the middle of the table stood a decanter of home made wine.

After apologising for being late I went to the pantry and got out a bottle of Tizer. Mum asked if I would like anything to eat. I declined at first but was later persuaded by Dad to have a beef and mustard sandwich. Uncle Harry was telling what Mum would refer to as one of his smutty jokes. It was a nice light-hearted atmosphere to return to.

Our engagement wasn't mentioned again and we just left well alone. It is strange how it was simply ignored from then on as if the whole issue would go away if it were not talked about - although Mum did suggest one day that I should start to collect for my bottom drawer instead of buying more clothes.

Working on the Island was strange to begin with. I missed being part of the town life in Colchester, meeting up with friends for lunch or sitting in Castle Park at lunchtime to have my sandwiches. But it was nice to go home at one o'clock every day to a cooked dinner. I could be home in less than five minutes on my bike so I always had a good lunch break.

Daphne Hewes, who was one of my friends when we attended Mersea School, also worked at the Post Office. Daphne served at the shop counter which sold stationery, tobacco, cigarettes, sweets from jars and fancy gifts among other things. She also helped out on the Post Office side by emptying the outside letter box and sorting the mail so anything local could be kept in the Mersea office and the rest could go to Colchester in the mail van.

Collection times for the letter box outside the Post Office were ten a.m., three p.m. and six p.m. The date stamp for the letters had the times changed for every collection. Mr Page was very particular about the box being emptied at exactly the right time. One day I was to find out exactly why it was so important and witness my boss getting angry with me. A gentleman who lived within close vicinity of the Post Office opened the front door and hurried to the counter leaving the door open. He slid the envelope he was holding under the protective brass grid and said,

"Just stamp that letter for me dear with the three o'clock stamp."

Wanting to oblige the old boy, I took the letter and did as he asked. He hastened out and quickly disappeared - but not soon enough to avoid Mr Page catching sight of him.

"What was that crafty old bugger up to?"

"He just wanted to make sure he had the three p.m. date stamp on the letter."

Mr Page went into the sorting office and picked out the last letter to have been date stamped. It was still lying on the stamping mat.

"Just as I thought. It's addressed to Hills the bookies." He threw down the letter and looked at me sternly.

"It's a postal bet and was probably for the three o'clock race which he would have listened to on the radio to get the result of the winner before running to catch the post."

This time, because of my lack of understanding of postal betting, he would no doubt be a successful winner. The betting company would scrutinise the time and the date the letter was posted for it to be valid. An old saying I'd heard at home came to mind. It went something like:

There's a little bit of bad in the best of us and a little bit of good in the worst of us.'

Dad had a home visit from Doctor Jones, our family doctor. I am not quite sure how it came about but I suspect Peter may have asked him to call in as Dad had been feeling unwell lately and his chest pains had become more severe. No one could persuade him to go to the doctor.

"I'm all right, mate," he would be quick to say, especially if the doctor was mentioned.

Doctor Jones had a wonderful manner with his patients and had no trouble in persuading Dad to have a quick medical examination. The outcome wasn't too bad. We all knew that he was suffering with a heart condition and his blood pressure was high but he was assured that it could soon be put right and he should then feel much better. This seemed to be good news.

Two days later Dad had been messing around in the garden and began to feel a bit dizzy. He started to walk down the garden path. Mum caught sight of him and realised he was having a problem walking.

"Pixie, come here quick. Your Dad's not well."

I ran from the sitting room to the back door, where I could see him clutching his chest as he struggled to walk. With only a few more steps to go he managed to get just inside the door before his legs crumbled under him and he collapsed in a heap on the floor.

"Jim… Jim, whatever's the matter? Pixie, help him… do something."

For a second I was rooted to the floor, absolutely terrified. Then I moved quickly to his side. Lying him flat on the floor, instinct told me to loosen his clothes. I knelt on the floor beside him and began to rub round the area of his heart. I looked up to see Mrs Fenn a nearby neighbour standing there. I don't know how or why but she just always seemed to turn up at the right time.

"What shall I do?" I asked.

"Don't panic and carry on with what you are doing."

"Please don't go."

"Of course I won't go, my dear."

My arms were beginning to ache but I thought if I stopped he could die. Under my breath I was repeating over and over again,

"Please, God, don't let him die."

Mrs Fenn was still there comforting Mum and at the same time encouraging me to keep massaging as he looked as though he was beginning to get a better colour. Suddenly he made a noise and then his head turned. Mrs Fenn's quiet gentle voice said,

"Don't stop now, Pixie, he's beginning to come round."

His eyes flickered, then opened. He looked straight at me, a surprised look on his face.

"Are you all right, Dad?"

He looked up and nodded.

CHAPTER 33

The Test Pilot, a Special Licence and the saucy poster

OVERLEAF: *Jim, Ada and Pixie Farthing*
just before the wedding.
ABOVE: *The saucy poster!*

We kept Dad comfortable until the doctor arrived and he was then helped upstairs to bed. Doctor Jones explained how difficult it was prescribing drugs for people with high blood pressure and to know exactly how each individual would react to a certain dosage. Dad's previous prescription had brought his blood pressure down too low too quickly which caused him to collapse. The dosage would be adjusted and would correct the problem.

It wasn't long before Dad was about again and working in the garden but he never did seem to get back to being his old self again. I often wondered if he would have been better off without the medication. Luckily it didn't affect his sense of humour and he was still able to play a mean strategic game of croquet. One day while I was at the doctor's I decided to ask him about Dad and if there was anything more that could be done about his condition. I felt he gave me a wonderful answer.

"Ann, for Jim it's like living the life of a test pilot. He could be gone in ten minutes or he could still be here in ten years time."

Being an optimistic person, I settled for ten years and left the surgery in a happier mood.

More than a year had passed since that awful day when we first announced our engagement. Now we were thinking about how long it would be before we could actually get married. Alan suggested we could put our names down on the list for a council house. I must have inherited some of my parents' snooty views because I answered without thinking,

"I would rather live in a caravan than put my name down for a council house."

"What's wrong with a council house?"

"Nothing really but once you start in a council house that's it - you never seem to move on to your own property. Alan, I would like to think that we could be a bit more ambitious."

I knew I'd said the wrong thing but I couldn't help the way that I felt. It was unfortunate that he happened to be living in a council house and maybe I could have been more tactful with my choice of words. That evening I told Mum and Dad about the discussion Alan and I had about council property. Dad said,

"He don't want ter do anything like that. I'll talk to him tomorrow night when he comes down."

When Alan arrived I told him to expect to have a talk with Dad.

"I don't want a bloody lecture on what I should do," said Alan.

"I don't know what it's about. He just said he wanted a word with you," I replied.

It wasn't long before Mum went across the road to see Mabel and Jim Clarke, leaving the three of us together. Dad got out his tin of Digger Honeydew, a Rizla paper and carefully rolled himself a cigarette. He lit it with his old brass petrol lighter which left a whiff of petrol in the air as he snapped the lid down.

"Do you want one, mate?" he asked as he passed Alan the tin.

"No thanks, they're a bit strong for me thank you. I smoke the ready mades."

Dad sat back in his chair drawing on his cigarette, and said,

"Look here now you two young 'uns. I know you eventually plan to get married and I didn't hold with it at first

340

but I know you've been committed for some time now so what I want to say to ya is this house would be plenty big enough for all of us. You can have the other large front bedroom and the sitting room directly below but you'll have ter share the kitchen."

We both sat very surprised at what he was offering us. His next words were hard for me to take in. They were words I didn't want to hear or accept.

"We all know it's just for the time being. I ain't gonna be here for ever. I've been living on borrowed time for a long while now and I hope it will continue but I want to know if anything happens to me that Ada and me little ol' gal will have some support. There won't be no rent to pay, only a share of the electricity and rates, so it'll give ya the opportunity to put some money on one side."

He hesitated at this point, then said,

"What do ya think then, boy?"

I was feeling emotionally full up and took hold of Alan's hand, hoping that he would be the one to respond. He looked at me, then at Dad. His words were just what I hoped for.

"That's a very kind offer, Jim. 'Course I will be there with my support and help, whenever it may be needed."

"Dad, you've heard the old saying about cracked pots always lasting the longest," I said, "well, I think you will be here for a long time yet."

"Well, let's hope so dear."

I was feeling sad about Dad's thoughts regarding his health but happy about us being able to live at 'High View' in our own two rooms, separate from the rest of the house. We could now start to think about our wedding day.

Every girl has a dream about how she would like her wedding to be. At first I began to think about the traditional white wedding at the church where I would walk up the aisle on my father's arm to the sound of the organ playing The Wedding March. Then my dream came to a stop as I began to consider who should give me away.

Would it be Dad or should it be Peter? Either way, someone could be hurt. With a church wedding the banns would be announced to the congregation and I would have to be announced as Ann Smith because my father's name wasn't put on the birth certificate when my birth was registered. No - I knew I couldn't have a church ceremony. It would be too complicated and uncomfortable for me and my family.

The alternative was a Registry Office. Alan wasn't at all worried about the Registry Office as he didn't want a 'big fuss' anyway so the two of us arranged a visit to book the date for our special day. There was nothing about the place that made it feel in any way romantic. The building was an old brick built house that had been converted into offices. It stood nearly at the top of North Hill, Colchester, with the entrance directly onto the pavement with three well-worn steps which headed to the open door. Heavy traffic was passing up and down the hill only a few feet away.

Outside the building stood a notice board protected by a slim, hinged glass door with announcements of forthcoming marriages. Standing there reading the names I knew only too well that our names would soon be posted on the board unless we were able to get a Special Licence which would allow a marriage to take place at short notice without all the legal formalities. At last we were able to arrange our wedding without having our names put up outside the Registry Office.

Our marriage was to be by Special Licence on Thursday, 16th March, 1961.

Dot helped me to choose my wedding outfit. The two of us went into Colchester and looked in all the dress shops that sold fashionable clothes with well-known labels. I wasn't the sort of person to dress conventionally. I liked clothes that were not run of the mill. However, Dot persuaded me to settle for a smartly tailored navy blue two-piece suit with a lacy white blouse topped off with navy and white accessories.

We then went to the florist and ordered the buttonholes. Mine probably cost nearly as much as a bouquet. It was a biscuit coloured orchid selected from a catalogue and had to be specially ordered from Covent Garden in London. It would arrive the day before the wedding and had to be kept cool. Dot said that she would pay for my buttonhole as she was the one responsible for convincing me to have an orchid.

My wedding was to be a small affair so it was agreed that the reception would be at 'Lynton'. Peter and Dot suggested that we stayed overnight on the eve of the wedding. Mum and Dad would then be there to help with the preparations.

I awoke to see the sun shining through the gap where the curtains met in the middle.

One of Mum's old sayings came into my head.

'Blessed is the bride that the sun shines on.'

I hoped that it would be true today as I was just beginning to feel nervous about the day ahead. After I had my bath I went downstairs in my dressing gown and looked into the lounge. Everything looked beautiful. Auntie Kath Clark was there putting the finishing touches to the floral arrangements. She did many weddings and other special functions for the people who'd heard of her artistic flair with flowers.

The four-tier wedding cake which Alan's Mum had made and decorated stood at the back of the long dining table. On top of the cake was an arrangement of fresh flowers in a silver vase I'd been given as a present for my twenty first birthday. Mrs Weaver's good name for cake making stretched as far as the United States of America and Canada. Her wedding cakes had been very carefully packed and posted there. Ours looked extra special. It was the first time she had made one with four tiers.

A red brick archway stretched across the room separating the two fireplaces. Only one had a fire burning as the day was warm. One of the French doors was open, letting the heat of the early spring sunshine stream through the east facing doorway. I could see the preparations were well under way. A large tea trolley stood next to the sideboard. The bottom shelf was packed with bottles offering a large choice of drinks and the top shelf held glasses and an enormous bottle of champagne.

I could hear Mum calling from the kitchen. I went through to the dining room. My fried breakfast was already on the table. I think this was the only time I would have dared to go to the breakfast table in my dressing gown. On any other occasion it would have been frowned upon as 'not the right thing to do'. Today was different though and besides, it was still too early to get dressed into my new outfit.

Once breakfast was finished I was aware that the time was going quickly so I rushed upstairs to the bedroom where all my clothes were laid out on the bed ready to put on. It didn't take me long to get ready. I looked at myself in the full length mirror and was satisfied with the image I saw standing there. I wasn't too sure about the hat but it was too late to do anything about it now.

Standing there gazing in the mirror I thought about a little conversation I had with Peter the night before, when he looked at me and said,

"Pixie, you do know who I am, don't you?"

At first I was puzzled, then realisation came to me regarding what he must be talking about. He quickly added,

"I am your father. Your real father."

"Yes, Pete. I know. I worked it out some time ago."

He gave me a huge cuddle and said,

"I love you so very much and all I want for you is to be very happy."

His words came from a loving father. I was so lucky to

have two lovely Dads.

What an unusual wedding it was to be. There was Dad all dressed up in his best suit down the garden doing some gardening. Peter, as usual, when the occasion called for it was well dressed in his dark suit drinking a quick whisky 'just to calm the nerves'. Dot, in her neatly fitted dress, was checking that nothing had been forgotten. Mum was nowhere to be seen.

All we were waiting for now was the groom and his Mum to arrive. Alan was to drive us to the Registry Office and if he didn't arrive soon we would be caught on the Strood by the high tide. At last they arrived. We could hear the car rattling over the bumps of the unmade road outside. My husband to be came in looking smart and handsome in his new suit. We all went outside to get in the car. Peter sat in front with Alan and I sat in the back with his Mum.

Mum, Dad and Dot came to the car to wish us good luck then we drove off on that beautiful sunny day to get married.

We arrived in Colchester with little time to spare so it was lucky that we were able to park just a short distance away from the Registry Office. The four of us arrived at the reception desk and Peter and Mrs Weaver were ushered away to one side. They had been mistaken as the ones to be married! After lots of laughter at the mistake we were escorted through to the Registrar who performed what to me seemed a short ceremony and declared us man and wife.

I was now Mrs Weaver.

Alan's sister, Jo and her husband, John Heggerty, were outside waiting to take some photographs just as we stepped through the door. Peter had agreed to drive us home and we arrived back at the car to find several people standing there laughing. They were unusually friendly and some called out,

"Good luck!"

I thought it must be our smart clothes and buttonholes that gave us away as being newlyweds. After getting into the back of the car with Alan and moving off we heard the terrible sound of tins clattering along the road. Peter stopped the car and found the tins had been concealed cleverly underneath the car and it was virtually impossible to remove them without getting messed up with grease and dirt.

On the front of the car was a large, cleverly hand-drawn poster, which of course said: 'Just Married'. The large drawing was of a bare female (Pixie) being chased by a male (Alan) in his night shirt. So that's what made the shoppers stop and smile! It made us smile too when we saw it. No one but John Heggerty could have been responsible for creating such a drawing. He was extremely good at drawing cartoons.

It was lovely to return home to be greeted by family and friends. Mr Botham, the local photographer, was already there waiting to take the photographs. He was very amused by the message on the front of the car and took a photograph of it.

I can honestly say that our wedding reception was just right.

CHAPTER 34

The apple pie bed, Auntie Lil's outburst and a little porker

OVERLEAF: *After the wedding, outside 'Lynton'. From Left: Margaret Weaver, Peter Farthing, Alan Weaver, Pixie Weaver, Ada Farthing, Jim Farthing, Dorothy Farthing.*
ABOVE: *Harold Cutts on Regatta day.*

Auntie Lil and Uncle Harry owned a guesthouse in Dover and that's where we were going for our honeymoon. The wedding party was going well with everyone enjoying themselves. There was plenty of food and drink left so it would probably go on for a long time yet but after the cake cutting we thought that it would be all right to get away as we hoped to get well on the journey before dark.

I went upstairs to the bedroom where I'd left my suitcase safely locked and carried it down to the front door. Alan's case was already in the boot of the car. Uncle Les Clark had let us have a car on loan for a week as the van was needed at work and I certainly didn't want to go to on my honeymoon in a van. I began moving around the guests to let them know that we would soon be leaving. I then realised that Dad wasn't about.

"Mum, where's Dad?"

"I don't know dear. I don't expect he's far away."

"Has anyone seen Dad?"

Dot said,

"The last time I saw him he was going into the back garden."

I went into the garden and there was Dad, still in his best suit, doing some digging.

"Dad, what are you doing out here digging in your best suit?"

"Well mate, I thought I'd jest turn this bit of soil over ready to plant some spuds, then Peter won't have to do it."

I think Dad was probably feeling a bit apprehensive about the changes coming into his life now that I was married and working in the garden was therapeutic for him. I wanted to tell him that nothing was really going to change. I would still be living at home and Alan would now be there to help him with any heavy work that he was now finding more difficult - but there wasn't time just now.

"I've come to let you know that it won't be long before we start on our journey."

"All right, dear. I'll be down to see you off."

It was sad saying goodbye to everyone but this was the beginning of a whole new challenge for us as a married couple. I was looking forward to our married life together and tonight we would be able to sleep in the same bed. (The last time we stayed in the guesthouse in Dover, Mum instructed Auntie Lil to put us in separate rooms and on different floors).

We'd just passed over the Strood onto the mainland when Alan pulled the car over and stopped the engine. I thought perhaps he had forgotten something but he took me in his arms and kissed me, saying,

"I love you, Mrs Weaver."

"I love you too."

The journey to Dover took about two and half hours travelling on the A2 with no motorways and having to pass through all the major towns. Our honeymoon could be described as unusual from the time we arrived at our destination - Clevelands Guest House, 2, Laureston Place, Dover.

Uncle Harry was at the front door waiting to greet us and help with our cases. He took us straight upstairs to a large and comfortable double room where we left our luggage ready to be unpacked later as dinner was being served in the dining room. After dinner we went to the lounge and got talking to some of the guests who were working in the docks. The men told us they booked in at the guesthouse from

Monday to Friday and then went home to their families at weekends.

It was while we were talking to them that they admitted to knowing we were on our honeymoon and wished us all the best for our future. I had hoped to be known as a paying guest and not as 'the honeymooners'. Before going up to bed, Auntie Lil and Uncle Harry gave us our wedding present, a 1920's granddaughter clock which had Westminster chimes. Uncle Harry said they chose it because they wanted us to have something to keep and also something that would remain in the family that could be handed down as an heirloom. It still stands against the wall where I live today, chiming away on the hour, and every quarter and half hour - a wonderful memory of the past.

As we got to our bedroom and began to unpack I started to feel rather shy about my nightdress. I thought it was exquisite when I first bought it but now I was wondering if the pale pink chiffon material was too revealing. It was a pretty design with delicate smocking at the waistline, giving it a little stretch, then falling into gathers down to the ground. I asked Alan if I could be first to use the bathroom. I got my dressing gown, toiletries and the nightdress and took them to the bathroom which was just along the corridor. After putting on my nightdress I looked at myself in the mirror and thought perhaps I should put on a pretty pair of knickers as well - then changed my mind, put my sensible dressing gown back on and returned to the bedroom.

While Alan was in the bathroom I stood in front of the fireplace enjoying the heat coming from the fitted gas fire. The night had turned very cold and frost was forecast. It wasn't long before I heard Alan's footsteps returning to the room. I took my dressing gown off and threw it over the chair before going to bed. As I tried to get into bed I realised something was wrong. The covers were not pulling up properly and I couldn't get my feet down the bed. I started to laugh.

"My feet won't go down the bed."

"What the hell do you mean, your feet won't go down the bed!"

I couldn't answer him - I was laughing too much. I got out of bed again, revealing the full extent of my nudity beneath the fine chiffon material. Between my fits of laughter I was able to say,

"The joke's on us. We've been given an apple pie bed."

"That's just the thing your Uncle Harry would get up to."

"I expect Auntie Lil had a hand in it as well."

Our married life together started with laughter. After remaking the bed, our night together was perfect.

The next day we spent revisiting some of the romantic spots we'd been to previously. There are some lovely walks along the cliffs and it was fascinating to watch the large ships coming into dock. The weather was getting worse and snow was forecast so we made the most of the fine weather while it lasted.

A day later we were getting the odd flurry of snow and Uncle Harry was taking us out for lunch. Once the breakfasts were over and the cleaning lady had been, Auntie Lil was free until the evening meal.

Uncle Harry drove us to a smart restaurant in Margate where the waitresses were dressed in black dresses and wore little white aprons with caps on their heads. The tables were covered with white damask tablecloths. A waitress wasn't long in coming to take our orders. It was as we sat there talking in general that Auntie Lil and Uncle Harry had a slight difference of opinion. This wasn't unusual for them so we didn't take much notice.

After the waitress brought our meals the arguing started up again - quietly at first, then gradually getting louder. I think Uncle Harry thought he was winning until Auntie Lil clenched her fists and banged them down on the table, making the cutlery rattle and jump. At the same time she shouted,

"Arseholes man!"

I was so ashamed as I gazed around at the other diners looking in our direction. Alan reached over and gently touched Auntie Lil's hand, saying,

"Calm down, Auntie Lil."

She looked at him angrily and said,

"You can shut your mouth as well."

The situation seemed to suddenly calm down and we were able to continue our meal with no more upsets. Uncle Harry left a very generous tip, probably to make up for any embarrassment they may have caused.

By the time we left the restaurant snow was falling heavily, making the journey back to the guesthouse both slow and hazardous. It was nice to get indoors in front of the fire. Our honeymoon would definitely be one to remember. We were now stranded in Dover waiting for the weather to lift and the roads to clear enough to make a safe journey home.

We had been away longer than expected due to the bad weather conditions but we were now nearly home and approaching the Strood. I wound down my window to take in the smell of the sea and the seaweed laying on the salt marshes. Our island is like a magnet to those who are born and bred here. The ones that do move away usually get pulled back again. For others just a day away is enough. I wouldn't live anywhere else.

I could feel a real sense of belonging as we drove through the village and along the coast road home. When we arrived, Alan pipped the hooter to let them know we were back. Mum and Dad were so pleased to have us home. They had real joy on their faces. It was the first time I had been away from home for that length of time.

Our new red carpet had been delivered as well as the fashionable studio couch which converted into a bed. I couldn't wait to get the carpet laid and the furniture in place. I had already made and hung the curtains before going away. Both our rooms had been decorated and were fresh, clean and ready for us to use. It would be strange for me not to be sleeping in my own bedroom that night but I was now sharing the front bedroom with my husband.

We all had to get used to living together. One of the first things I learned was that mornings were not a good time for Alan. I was soon to find out that he woke up bad tempered every morning and the only way to deal with it was to leave him alone for at least half an hour - it was best not to talk to him. I found this a little upsetting, especially as I was bright and cheery as soon as I was awake but on the whole everything was going well with no major upsets. I had thought that Alan might find it difficult moving into a household that was very different from what he had been used to but he certainly coped very well and most of all he liked and got on well with Dad.

Harold Cutts had asked me to go and work for him at Wyatt's the boat builders and yacht chandlers and the wages he offered me were very good. I would be required to do general office duties and work in the shop when they were busy or needed extra help. I felt it was time for me to move on from the Post Office and accepted his offer.

The premises were situated on the waterfront in Coast Road just a short cycle ride away. I enjoyed working for Harold despite his reputation for being rude and uncouth. I found him to be a kind and generous man, full of devilment and teasing, but capable of being blatantly honest, probably to the point of being rude. Many people went to Wyatt's just to see Harold at his worst or best - whichever way you wanted to interpret what he was saying.

There was an occasion when he called in to see a close

family friend. The lady sat down comfortably in the armchair opposite Harold, unaware that she was showing her underwear. He said,

"Gal, if you ain't careful, I'll see yer harbour light!"

I had been home from work for a long time and began to wonder where Alan had got to as he usually arrived home from work at about six o'clock. It was now after seven and he was still not home. I found myself checking the time and looking at the clock every few minutes then I heard the familiar sound of his van coming down Victory Road. It wasn't long before he came running in the back door. He looked at me excitedly and said,

"Come out to the van - I've got a present for you."

We hurried out to the van.

"It's in the back but be careful how you open the doors."

I opened one of the doors very gingerly and peered inside. There, looking back at me, stood a tiny pink piglet hardly old enough to leave its mother.

"Where did you get it from?"

"I called at a farm to see the farmer about some feeding stuffs and the poor little thing was about to be knocked on the head. I arrived just in time to save him. He was the runt of the litter, always being pushed to one side. As your Dad would say, 'always left with the hind tit' where there wasn't so much milk."

Alan looked proudly at his acquisition who blinked gratefully back at him with bright piggy eyes.

"The farmer knew he wouldn't be strong enough to survive. Now he's got a chance!"

Dad came out to look in the van.

"Well, I'll be dayed if you ain't got a little ol' cad. We'll soon get some weight on that little feller."

"Do you think it will be all right?"

"Yes, mate, of course it will. We'll soon see to that own't we yer little ol' chap?"

Dad picked up the piglet and tucked him under his arm, which made the poor little thing squeal in terror. Then he took him indoors where he let him loose to run around the kitchen. Off went the two men to find him a bed for the night.

Mum looked at me and said,

"I thought we'd finished with pigs and the like."

"I know, Mum, but he is a sweet little chap."

"He is at the moment but you won't think he's quite so sweet in a few weeks time when he's rooting up the garden. I must say, though, your father's as happy as a sand boy."

Mum put the kettle on and was breaking up some pieces of bread into a bowl as she had done many times before. When the kettle boiled she poured the hot water over the bread and once the water had soaked in, poured on some cold milk. The hot water on the bread mixed with the cold milk made the mixture the ideal heat for a piglet's food.

When Dad and Alan came back indoors they gave the pig his supper. It must have been just right - he devoured the lot. They had cornered off a section of the shed for the little fellar and put down a deep bed of straw to keep him warm. Alan got up early to give the pig his first feed and Dad sorted it during the day. He began to fatten up very quickly and we named him 'Wilfred' after my Uncle Wilfred who was very portly. It wasn't done to be unkind - more as a joke - and he would never know as he and his wife, Grace lived many miles away.

CHAPTER 35

The bed moves, on the buses and labour pains

OVERLEAF: *Uncle Wilfred and Auntie Grace.*

We had only been married a few months when gales and storm force winds were forecast for the night. By nine o'clock in the evening the wind had become fairly strong and the living room carpet was lifting where the wind blew up through the cracks between the floorboards. This wasn't anything unusual – it was something we'd become used to over the years. The house wasn't built on proper footings and underneath the floorboards was bare earth.

It was going to be a rough old night with the sou' westerly wind blowing directly off the water. Dad and Alan had already been outside to check all the sheds and outbuildings. One of the sheds needed its felt roof tacked down as one end was beginning to lift but other than that everything seemed alright.

After we'd gone to bed I said to Alan,

"I bet it won't be long before Dad gets up again. He hates the wind and he'll spend half the night drinking tea and pacing the floor."

"Why doesn't he like the wind?"

"I don't know and I don't think he knows either."

The gale force winds became stronger and suddenly the dustbin blew over, sending the lid crashing around the yard. I heard the sound of footsteps and knew it was Dad. Alan got out of bed to look out of the window and as he stood there a sudden gust seemed to move the whole room – it felt as if the bed was moving.

"Alan, the bed just moved."

"Don't be so bloody stupid. Of course it didn't move."

"I tell you it did. Come and lie down then the next time it blows you'll know what I mean."

He got back into bed and we both lay there waiting. Then it happened – a huge gust of wind seemed to make the whole room move. All the lights went out. The gale must have brought down an electricity cable as the street lamps had gone out as well.

"Now did you feel some movement in the room?"

"Yes I did."

It's strange but during all the time I'd slept in the small back bedroom – even during the worst gales – I'd never felt anything like I did this night in the front bedroom.

"I'm going down to have a cup of tea with Jim," said Alan.

"I'll get up as well."

I didn't want to stay upstairs on my own, especially with the house shifting about in the gale. Everywhere was in darkness. Dad had got the candles out and was just lighting the oil stove to boil a kettle as no one knew when the electricity would be back on again.

Mum came into the kitchen with a candlestick lighting the way – she always kept it in the bedroom in case of emergency.

Eventually the wind began to drop but then torrential rain rattled hard against the windows. What a terrible night.

Alan was beginning to get dissatisfied with his job. He knew that he couldn't earn any more where he was because the firm wasn't large enough to pay out big wages. His brother Fred was earning a lot more money doing less hours as a bus driver with The Eastern National Bus Company. Alan had the use of the van which was a big consideration, but he reckoned that if he was earning more we could probably afford our own car.

It's strange how things are 'meant to be'. Only a week had gone by since we were talking about another job and perhaps getting our own car when Freddie let Alan know that there

360

was a vacancy for a bus driver on the Colchester to Mersea Island run. Alan applied for the job and was luckily accepted. When it came to handing in his notice he felt rather uncomfortable about letting the firm down but knew he wanted to have a change. He left his job on good terms and within a fortnight he was employed by The Eastern National Bus Company. It wasn't long before he got his Public Service Vehicle (PSV) licence and was able to drive buses.

Another bit of good luck that came our way was to hear about an old Ford car that was being sold. Although it was old with spoked wheels and doors that opened the opposite way to modern cars, it had been well looked after by two elderly unmarried sisters who had only used it for shopping on the Island. Jack Cudmore, the next owner, had only used it on high days and holidays. It was immaculate, with a very low mileage.

On the back was a luggage rack which was probably designed to hold a picnic basket. We didn't care too much about it not being a modern car. It was our own vehicle with no hire purchase - we paid one hundred pounds cash. It would no doubt be a very reliable car. We were also able to take Mum and Dad out and about for drives in the countryside. Dad loved to go out at harvest time to see which farmers had the best crops and the earliest harvest. He never wanted to go far - the greatest distance would be ten miles from Mersea Island.

Having a car meant Alan could do extra shifts in Colchester if required. One morning he was on an early shift and should have been at the bus station in Mersea to take the first bus out to Colchester. Eastern National offered a good service covering most main roads on the Island including as far as the Yacht Club on Coast Road where the bus turned around and then picked up passengers on the way back.

On this particular morning we overslept. I awoke to a strange rattling sound outside and couldn't think what it could be. I got out of bed and peeped through the window. There stood a double-decker bus! The top deck was level with our bedroom and I could see the people sitting in their seats. Buses didn't come up Victory Road so what was happening?

"Alan! Wake up! There's a double-decker bus outside!"

Alan jumped out of bed and looked out of the window himself, not really believing what I had said.

"Christ, I've overslept and Crackers Wells is outside with the bus."

'Crackers' was the depot caretaker and was previously a bus driver so he still held his PSV Licence. Alan quickly grabbed his black uniform trousers and jacket, pulling them on over his pyjamas. I started to laugh, seeing the funny side of the situation.

"It's not bloody funny."

He ran downstairs and out of the front door. Then, I heard the bus drive off.

Apparently, Alan received a round of applause as he took the driver's seat. Alan was the youngest driver working with the Mersea crew with his brother Fred coming a close second. It was probably because of their ages that they were prone to livening up what sometimes seemed a boring occupation with a little bit of light hearted tomfoolery.

As a challenge, Fred would sometimes leave the bus park nearly fifteen minutes late but would still make it to Colchester on time. One night, Fred was driving the last bus home to Mersea Island. It was time to leave Colchester bus park and everywhere he looked there seemed to be courting couples trying to hide in the shadows. He quietly opened the driver's door and got behind the wheel, telling his conductor Jimmy Robinson to ring the bell. Fred started the engine and moved off. The courting couples came from all directions chasing the bus, which didn't stop until they all had a 'good run for their money'.

When I had to go to Colchester by bus I would try and

arrange to travel on the bus that Alan was driving. I sat there one afternoon waiting for the driver when a lady got on with her little boy and sat directly behind me. Alan walked along the side of the bus ready to get up in to the driver's seat. The little boy spoke to his mother and said,

"Oh dear, mummy, we've got a boy driving the bus today."

I sat and smiled to myself as usually the drivers were much older than twenty one.

When I got home from Colchester, Mum was reading the local paper. She was upset to read that Terry had been fined two pounds by Winstree & Lexden Magistrates' Court. He hadn't displayed 'L' plates on a motor car while being the holder of only a provisional licence as he drove along Victoria Esplanade. I had wondered how long it would take her to realise that the sun didn't shine out of his bottom and that all teenagers take silly risks. Some get caught and some do not.

On the whole the summer had been good. Wilfred the pig had matured into a fine big porker and it was sad to think that the arrangements would soon have to be made for him to be slaughtered. He had become a pet to us but as Dad said, we all knew that the time would come for him to go. Nothing lasts forever. Alan would take Wilfred for a walk up Rosebank Road in the evenings. He didn't require any sort of lead. He followed obediently by Alan's side, grateful to exercise his legs after being shut in his sty.

Mum received a letter from Auntie Grace to say that she and Uncle Wilfred would like to come and stay for a few days and could it be next week, for a long weekend? Mum read the letter out to us all, then she looked at Dad and said,

"Jim, whatever shall we do about the pig?"

"I dunno, mate. You'll hev ter think of something else to call it. Yer can't call it 'Wilfred' that's fer sure."

Both Alan and I started to laugh - a lot. When we had

363

stopped laughing we decided we just had to call him 'The Pig', which worked out very well until Tim came down with his dad and said,

"I want to see Wilfred."

"He's in the other room, dear," said Auntie Grace.

I quickly grabbed Tim by the arm and said,

"I've got something to show you in the garden."

When we got outside I had to explain that Uncle Wilfred was in the sitting room, and while he was staying with us the pig was just to be known as 'The Pig'. After the weekend they would be returning to Kettering in Northamtonshire and we could then call the pig Wilfred again.

We were now nearing the end of September and Doctor Jones confirmed that I was pregnant with the baby due the following July. Although we didn't expect it to happen so quickly we were both pleased that we should soon be parents. The early morning sickness was lasting all day and it got so bad that I eventually had to give up my job.

I had almost made up my mind that there would never be any more babies when gradually it began to get better. One morning I woke up and felt well and healthy again. The next time I went to see the doctor I asked if it would be all right for me to give birth to the baby at home as I had been told that anyone without a bathroom or hot running water would be refused. We had neither. His answer was,

"Of course you can have your baby at home. There are some people I would refuse, even if they had two bathrooms and hot running water!"

"Thank you, doctor. I was hoping you would say yes."

The district nurse came to visit me at home and looked at the bedroom where I would be having the baby. She was happy with what she saw and said that it was a nice big airy room. The large marble top washstand with a blue and white patterned jug and basin set was an acceptable alternative to a bathroom.

Nurse Lucy Hulbert suggested on one of her visits that I may like to attend 'Relaxation Classes' which were held in the clinic at the church hall in High Street North and run by the Health Visitor, Miss Wharton. The classes taught pregnant mums how to relax and breathe properly during the different stages of labour. I wanted to do whatever was best for me and the baby so I would definitely be going to enrol. I continued to stay fit and healthy all through my pregnancy with Auntie Tod keeping an eye on what I was doing - most of the time giving advice on what I should or shouldn't do.

Auntie Tod attended many of the births on the Island, helping the nurse in any way she could. Never making any charge, she just enjoyed being there and being able to help.

On Friday 27th July we went to bed wondering if we would get through the night. My time was getting very close and for the past week I had been wondering before going to sleep if it would be that night. I did ask the doctor one day why babies usually come at night time and his reply was,

"My dear, that's when they are got!"

I settled into that first deep sleep and awoke in pain just after three in the morning. I managed to wake Alan with difficulty, as he was a heavy sleeper.

"Alan, I've got pains in my tummy."

His reply was,

"Go back to sleep - it's probably wind."

I thought he may be right and didn't want to disturb anyone for no reason. I lay in bed quietly trying to get back to sleep, but the pain was very uncomfortable.

"Alan, wake up please. I think it is the baby."

"Are you sure?" he said, sleepily. He wasn't convinced.

"Yes. Please go and get the nurse."

He must have gone through to wake up Mum who came to see how I was feeling. She said it was best to go and get the nurse. It didn't take long for nurse to arrive and not long afterwards Auntie Tod turned up. With everyone around me I felt less nervous and the pains were now less severe, but coming at fifteen-minute intervals.

The nurse went home for a bit, leaving me in the capable hands of Auntie Tod. What a long day of discomfort! By five o'clock that evening I'd been in labour for thirteen hours and was now telling the nurse,

"I can't push any more."

Auntie Tod was rubbing my back saying,

"It won't be long, dear."

CHAPTER 36

James arrives, Jim departs and a family wedding

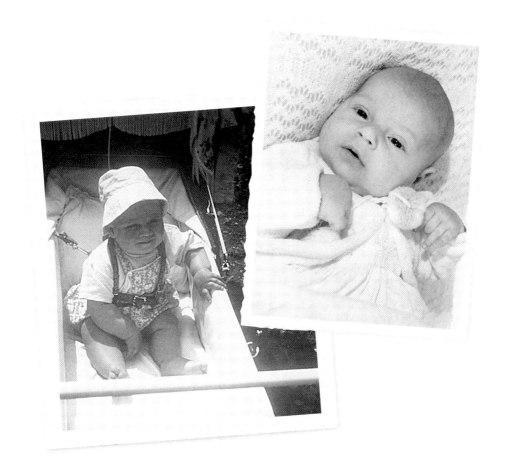

OVERLEAF: *James Weaver, six weeks old,*
and in his pram at 11 months.
ABOVE: *John's and Rene's wedding day.*
From left: Dorothy Farthing, Peter Farthing,
John Farthing, Rene Farthing, Mr and Mrs Hewes.

The nurse went to ask Alan if he would like to be present at the birth and he said he would rather not. He'd been very supportive all the way through the pregnancy so if he felt uncomfortable about the actual birth I didn't mind him not being there. I had a sudden urge to push but the nurse said that I must wait and use the breathing exercises. The baby was nearly here.

"I can just see its head!" cried Auntie Tod

"You can push now. Push hard!" said the nurse.

I pushed and pushed.

Almost immediately the pain went away and I heard the nurse say,

"Well done, you've got a baby boy."

As the baby cried for the first time, Alan came in to the room.

"You've got a baby son!"

The baby had a strong pair of lungs and was soon letting everyone know that he was here. The rest of the family was downstairs waiting to hear if it was a boy or a girl. Dad must have been at the bottom of the stairs. Alan shouted out,

"It's a boy!"

I heard Dad reply,

"What a shame, I wanted a little girl."

Then Alan said,

"He's got dark hair!"

Dad's reply was,

"I like 'em fair."

As I lay back on the bed exhausted I saw the funny side of Dad's disappointment and started to laugh. He was hoping for another 'Little Pixie'.

The baby's first bath was in the china wash basin from the washstand. Afterwards, he was dressed in a little cotton crossover vest tied with ribbon. On top was a long nightdress. His terry towel napkin was lined with a soft muslin liner for extra comfort and then a pair of thin rubber pants went over the top to stop the bed getting wet. Now it was time for his Daddy to hold and cuddle him. We had decided on the baby's name before he was born. If it was a boy, he would be James Alan Weaver.

The doctor came in to check that all was well with baby and myself then went downstairs to have tea with Mum and Dad. Peter and Dot were downstairs waiting to see the new arrival. The nurse told them that after they had seen baby James I should have a rest. She would call back later to check that everything was all right.

When Dad held the baby for the first time he looked at him and said,

"Hallo me little ol' fellar. You'll hev to be well taken care of."

From that moment, Dad was there for him whenever he was needed. The first time I bathed little James on my own I got everything ready with the enamel baby bath standing on the white enamel, metal-framed stand in the middle of our sitting room. Everything I needed was lying on the settee. Dad came in to the room, drew a chair up to the bath and sat down.

"Dad, what are you doing?"

He began to chuckle.

"I'm gonna make sure ya don't let me little ol' boy slip in the bath."

Despite his laughter he couldn't have been more serious even though I'd been shown how to bath the baby properly by the nurse. Every evening, Dad was there to help with the bath time routine and afterwards gave James his bottle. Mum would then have her time nursing and cuddling the baby before he was put to bed.

The carrycot then stood next to Dad by the settee until we all went to bed. James was a lovely little baby who enjoyed all the love and attention he got from everyone and in turn it made him a happy and contented child.

Dad still did the garden which produced most of our fresh fruit and vegetables but it was noticeable that he was tiring more easily so Alan would give him a hand.

The baby had certainly given my Dad a new interest. His main love now was the time he spent playing with him.

On the evening of 6th April, 1963, James had just been bathed and Dad said he was going to cover up the potatoes in the garden as a frost was forecast. He said he wouldn't be gone very long. We'd been laughing and talking for quite a while when I asked Alan if Dad had come in yet.

"No, I don't think so. I expect he's still in the garden."

I called through to Mum.

"Is Dad in yet?"

"No, dear. I haven't seen him lately."

A cold fear gripped me. I ran to the back door and shouted loudly.

"Dad! Dad!"

And then I ran, Alan following behind. I could see he wasn't in the greenhouse, neither was he in the garden. I ran to the door of the large work shed. I lifted up the latch and threw open the door. My worst fear was facing me. Dad was collapsed in a heap against the workbench. I heard Alan say,

"Oh my God, no," and then he disappeared.

I was there all on my own. What should I do? I moved towards Dad, absolutely terrified. I couldn't leave him there, crumpled and uncomfortable. I didn't know if he was dead or alive but I managed to drag his body across the floor. It was so heavy but I knew I must make him more comfortable.

By the dim light in the shed I could see that he wasn't a very good colour.

After I laid him flat on his back I felt for his pulse - but I couldn't find anything. I was so scared. I knew Dad was dead. I began to shake uncontrollably - then the shed was suddenly full of people.

I had to get away. I ran indoors looking for Mum. How would she cope without him? How would I manage without my Dad? What would our baby do without his Granddad? At least the nine short months James had with my Dad would have given him something very special in his life.

Peter had arrived and was sorting out the arrangements. I went in to the sitting room to see if Mum was all right. Auntie Tod had just arrived and was listening to Mum talking about Dad. The fire in the grate was giving off plenty of heat and my shaking was easing off. Someone came in and started talking to Mum. After a while, Mum said,

"Tod, I have to find something else for Jim to wear. The undertaker says I should get some pyjamas."

She went upstairs and came down with some brownish, red-striped pyjamas. Dad always slept in his long johns and a vest so the pyjamas had been lying in the drawer for some time. She went to the kitchen and returned with the wooden airing horse, putting it in front of the fire and hanging up the pyjamas.

"Mum, what are you doing?"

"I'm warming his pyjamas for him."

Auntie Tod looked at me and shook her head, indicating that I shouldn't say any more. Peter came in for the pyjamas and gave them to 'Hardy' Weaver the undertaker - no relation to Alan's family. Then Dad was gone from the house forever - but he wasn't gone from our hearts or our minds. There was a horrible emptiness in the house and Mum burst into tears saying,

"Tod - whatever will I do without him?"

"Would you like me to stay for the night?" she asked tenderly.

"Yes please, Tod."

Waking up to a house without Dad was painful for us all but the saddest thing for me that morning was to see his glasses still sitting on the television - the place he always left them when the programmes finished. I just stood there looking at them, unable to see properly for the tears that were blurring my vision.

I remember virtually nothing from the day of the funeral but the thing I will always remember that Dad left us all with a legacy of knowledge and family traditions that are alive today.

It was now summer and Mum was beginning to get on with her life. James seemed to be filling the empty space that Dad had left behind. He was learning to talk but he didn't start to walk until he was about fifteen months old. He preferred rolling on the floor.

The first words Peter painstakingly taught him were 'Pisson er rain', much to Mum's disgust. She would take him out for a walk in his beautiful coach-built pram, and he would look the perfect baby. Then, one of Peter's mates - particularly Harold Cutts – would come along and say,

"Hello boy, what's the weather doing today?"

James would then reply,

"Pisson er rain."

I was finding it increasingly difficult to get all the washing done by boiling kettles and saucepans for the hot water. Burco had just brought out a modern square design ten gallon wash boiler and I'd seen one locally in Wilfred Carter's Electrical Shop.

The boiler cost twelve pounds and ten shillings but Mrs Carter said I could pay a deposit of two pounds ten shillings and the balance by weekly instalments. I decided the boiler was a necessity and agreed to the purchase. Although I now had a wonderful white enamel boiler standing in the scullery I still had to walk outside to the massive, old fashioned mangle to wring out the wet clothes after they had been boiled and washed. It was hard work, especially with the thicker items.

Large cogs turned heavy wooden rollers over the thick linen, squeezing out the last drop of water. The rollers then closed with a 'clonk' - I always took care to keep my hands out of the way. I wondered how long it would take me to get a washing machine.

Just a few feet away from the mangle was the meat safe. We didn't have a refrigerator. The meat safe was a square cupboard made from fly-screen wire mesh with a wooden shelf. It was screwed to a shaded outer wall of the shed and fresh meat was kept in there - uncovered but safe from all the flies - on a china plate. Sometimes the meat was covered with greaseproof paper or the waxed bag from a cornflake packet. Cling film was unheard of and I can't remember ever having tin foil.

James was growing into a delightful and happy little boy, always laughing and being spoilt by everyone. He was never far from me or his Nan but soon he was to go on a family journey.

On 20th February, 1964, brother John and his girlfriend Irene 'Rene' Hewes got married at Colchester Registry Office. It had been a particularly worrying time for both families. Rene was only seventeen years old and John eighteen. With a new baby on the way they had a big responsibility in front of them.

The reception, which was held at 'Lynton', had been a small friendly family gathering with plenty of food and drink and, as usual, one of Mrs Weaver's wedding cakes. John and Rene were going to stay in Dover for their honeymoon with Auntie Lil and Uncle Harry.

It was to be even more bizarre than our honeymoon.

Alan was to drive them to North Station in Colchester where they would be able to get the train. Just before they were due to leave home Peter called Alan to one side and asked him if he would take the newlyweds all the way to Dover by car. He said to take his car, a big six-seater Ford Zephyr which was lovely to drive and very comfortable.

"Pixie could go with you if she wants to."

"She wouldn't leave James and Ada," replied Alan.

"I tell you what - take mother as well. It will do her the world of good to get away for a few days, especially to see Auntie Lil."

John and Rene were consulted on what they would prefer to do and agreed that they would like to travel by car. John wasn't at all perturbed at the idea of taking his Nan on honeymoon as well as his sister, brother-in-law and nephew. It did take a little time to persuade Mum to go but she agreed in the end. The luggage was loaded into the boot of the car. Mum sat in the front with James and Alan and I sat in the back with John and Rene. Occasionally James would clamber over the front seat into the back but eventually he got tired and dropped off to sleep. We had a fast comfortable journey to Dover. It was a very powerful car and I'm sure there were times when Alan exceeded the speed limit. At one point, Mum said,

"I hope you're going to slow down, otherwise you will have me to contend with."

When we arrived, Uncle Harry joked about having a family honeymoon but went on to say how pleased he was to see us all, especially Ada. We all enjoyed ourselves including the honeymooners and I hadn't seen Mum laugh so much for a long time. Every day we all went out. John and Rene were able to get about and do a lot more than if they had gone their own way by train as originally planned and I'm sure that John and Rene never forgot their honeymoon.

* * *

Six months after James was born, Lucy the District Nurse gave birth to her own little girl, Jackie. We had become close friends with Lucy and her husband Peter and now James and Jackie had become such close friends they were almost like brother and sister. After Lucy decided to return to work she asked me if I would like to look after Jackie for her in the mornings. She would usually be home in the afternoon and by the time she went off to work in the evening Peter was home from work and would be there to look after Jackie.

This proved to be a good arrangement all round. James and Jackie were never lonely and got on well together. I was getting paid which was very useful in those days, plus I did enjoy having the two children together. I suspect that the reason they got on so well was because James was so easy going and gave in to Jackie all the time.

CHAPTER 37

The new tricycle, nursery school and business problems

OVERLEAF: *James' first bicycle.*
ABOVE: *(Top) 'Whitegates', Mrs Ewens Nursery School.*
(Below) from left: Julie Benns, James Weaver and
Jackie Hulbert in wedding fancy dress, Sept. 1965.

Eventually Peter and Lucy bought a house in Rosebank Road and became our next door neighbours. It was then easy for the children to call for each other when they wanted to play. Rosebank Road was still unmade and a very safe place for children with few cars passing through. Jackie now had more bargaining power as she was living just up the road and if James wouldn't play the games she wanted to play she would simply say,

"Right. I will go home then."

"Please don't go home Jackie."

"Yes I am going," she would answer, repeatedly looking back to see what effect it was having before saying,

"I really am going, right now."

I whispered to James,

"Let her go - she will soon be back again."

But James wouldn't risk her going home.

"Alright Jackie. I will play what you want to play."

She would win every time. He was such an easy-going little fellow but at least there were never any arguments. The children had now reached an age when we felt they would benefit from going to Mrs Ewans' private Nursery School.

Mrs Ewans was a genteel lady who had a wonderful way with children, teaching and preparing them for full-time education, usually to attend the local school. The Nursery School was part of her beautiful old home called White Gates in Bower Hall Lane. It had been built in the sixteenth century. The large secluded lawns had swings, slides and seesaws to play on. Parents with cars took turns to transport the children as Bower Hall Lane was about two miles outside the village centre.

Doreen Fox had a green camper van which I think was the children's favourite as it was much more of an adventure to ride in the van. Some of the children I remember giving lifts to were Francis Fox, Roly Mann, one of the Cokertons and of course, Jackie Hulbert.

One winter's day Doreen was just leaving Willoughby House, where the Mann family lived. Willoughby Avenue was an unmade road and full of icy puddles. The camper van got stuck in the ice but the youngsters all got out and pushed the vehicle into action, ready to carry on their journey into the unknown.

I think that one of the most pleasurable toys we purchased for James must have been his brand new tricycle. I first saw it in Thorp's shop window. Vincent Thorp ran a taxi hire business in the High Street and his wife Claire managed the shop where they sold bicycles, toys and prams. The blue and red, shiny new three wheeler stood next to a large coach-built pram. I knew as soon as I saw it standing there that we had to get it for James' birthday in July. It had a large metal storage box on the back with a hinged lid - ideal for carrying toys or shopping. There was only one problem. It was very expensive. When Alan came home and I told him all about it, he said,

"We can't afford it."

"Yes we can," I countered, "Mrs Thorp said if I paid a deposit, she would keep it for us and by the time it's his birthday I will have saved the rest."

"Well it's up to you if you think you can manage it."

I knew I could. Once I had set my mind on something, my determination would certainly see it through. That evening we cycled round to Thorps as I wanted Alan to see the bike. He

agreed it was a great idea for James' birthday present.
The next day I paid the deposit and any time I had money to
spare I took it to the shop where Mrs Thorp wrote my
payments down in a little notebook. I managed to pay for
the three wheeler a whole week before James' actual birthday
and couldn't wait for the day to arrive when he would see
his present.

James was pleased with his birthday present but we noticed
he was having a struggle to reach the pedals properly. I was
beginning to think that maybe it was a mistake. Uncle Peter
saved the day when he arrived and found some 'whood' in the
shed and made blocks which he screwed neatly to the pedals,
making it safe and just the right height for the little chap to
ride. After forty years, this well-travelled bike is still in use.

During 1963 the family's fortunes seemed to take a downward
turn and there was much speculation and local gossip about
what was actually going wrong and why. Tradesmen were
talking about bills that were not being paid on time. Peter was
a busy self employed builder but all small businesses were
vulnerable to just one bad payer starting a chain of debt.

Peter had individual customers owing him money as well as
a much larger unpaid job. Every week payment was being
promised 'in a few days time'. The large job was for a
businessman who was thought to be honest and wealthy but it
turned out that he was rich only in unfulfilled promises.

However, the workmen needed to be paid each week so
another job was taken on in an attempt to solve the cash flow
problem. Lunchtimes would often see Peter treating his men
to drinks in one of the pubs to keep up morale. Evenings were
also a time for him and Dot to go out for a drink to relax. He
was always ready to buy rounds of drinks but Peter's
generosity at a time of hardship added to the problems of an
already struggling business. Drinking and socialising was a

solace they could ill afford.

The beach kiosk which Dot had been running since 1956 had often been able to subsidise some of the bills for the building materials but Dot owed money to ice cream suppliers and the kiosk subsequently closed down. Peter and Dot were now looking for a way to solve their immediate financial crisis. Susan was a fully qualified hairdresser and Dot was going to set up a hairdressing business with her - seen as a good move at that time as Mersea Island needed a good hairdresser. It wasn't long before Dot formed a company with Susan and another person to run a further hairdressing business on the outskirts of Colchester.

P. J. Farthing, Builder and Decorator was not succeeding financially. It was hard to believe that this could be happening to a man who was so well qualified and good at his profession but the truth was his business acumen was lacking when it came to the finances. They now decided to take a huge gamble by purchasing a grocery and general stores called Woodwards in High Street, West Mersea.

Susan bought out Dot's share of the hairdressing businesses freeing up money for reinvestment in the new project. Sadly, Woodwards Stores was not as successful as they had hoped and a series of circumstances changed their lives, and ours, forever.

Meanwhile, Peter was desperately trying to hang on to 'Lynton'. Woodwards had now been sold at a loss and the only asset left was five acres of agricultural land called Hubbard's Croft situated along the East Mersea Road. Peter and I had inherited it from Dad. One day Peter asked if he could use my half, together with his, as security for a loan from the bank. I, of course, agreed.

Peter and Dot were now about to lose everything. Dot was declared bankrupt that summer. Lynton was to go under the hammer and in less than two weeks they would be homeless. Tim was only seventeen years old and still living with his parents at the rear of the shop, and it was having a devastating effect on everyone. When Peter called in to see Mum, he broke down and cried. I couldn't bear to see him in such a state. Mum went to the cupboard and got out the whisky, mixing it with sugar and hot water from the kettle.

"You drink that down, dear. It'll make you feel better."

Going through to the sitting room he sat down in the armchair, drank the hot whisky, then dropped off to sleep exhausted. I asked Mum if she would look after James for a little while as I would like to go out on my bike.

"I don't mind, as long as you're not gone too long," she replied.

I was going to search for somewhere for them to live - it was no good crying. I pulled my bike from the shed and cycled through the village, searching up and down the avenues and along the roads. I eventually rode along the rough tracks through the fields leading to the unmade Willoughby Avenue and the small stretch called Howard Avenue. It was here that I noticed the small wooden bungalow standing in the grounds of a large house called 'Mandeville'.

The bungalow was overgrown with shrubs and bushes and the curtains were drawn together. They were faded and fraying at the edges. The place had obviously not been lived in for a long time. Leaning my bike up against the hedge, I walked up to the main house which had Georgian style windows and a front door with coloured glass. I knocked loudly, making sure I was heard. I had everything I was going to say already planned in my mind.

The door was opened by a grey haired elderly gentleman.

"Yes? Can I help you?"

"Hello," I said nervously, then went on to explain that I had noticed that there was nobody living in the bungalow that stood in his grounds and would he possibly consider renting it? He said that it was in need of repair. I replied that it didn't matter as my father was a builder and he would soon be able to put it right.

"Does he like gardening?" asked the old gentleman.

"Yes, he does," I replied, hardly able to contain my excitement. I sensed that he was interested.

He asked if Peter would be prepared to give him a hand in the garden at Mandeville to which I assured him that he would. He said that if Peter would put the bungalow right and help with the garden now and again he would rent it to them for twenty-five shillings (£1.25) a week which even then was a bargain.

Obviously he wanted to meet Peter and Dot and I said that this evening would probably be a good time for them. I cycled home full of excitement about the bungalow. I pedalled so quickly that I was out of breath when I arrived home.

"Where on earth have you been?" asked Mum. "You said you wouldn't be long."

I know," I panted, "I'm sorry but just listen to what I have got to tell you."

I told Mum and Peter everything from beginning to end.

"Come on gal, get in the car. Let's get back to the shop and tell Dot."

Dot was overwhelmed with relief when she heard the news. They had only a week left at Woodwards.

A family that once had so much was now left with so little. Nonetheless, one thing that couldn't be taken away was the great love and support of the family. That evening, Peter and Dot went to Mandeville to meet their potential landlord who introduced himself as Mr Wish and showed them over the bungalow. Right away they knew they would love it and Peter would be able to begin the repairs immediately.

After seeing Mr Wish, they returned to High View with the good news that they could move in whenever they wanted.

After they'd moved in and put their own furniture into place it began to look more like home. It had a cosy, friendly atmosphere and there were now new curtains up at the windows and a nice thick rug in front of the fireplace. With no passing traffic, birdsong could be heard all around.

Peter gradually got their own piece of garden the way they wanted it with plenty of fresh vegetables as well as occasionally helping Mr Wish with his beautiful grounds.

At last they were happy again with what seemed like a new start. Peter and Dot always had a very affectionate relationship and never felt uncomfortable about sharing a tender cuddle in front of the family. When they were living at the shop this aspect of their life was noticeably absent and everyone was pleased to see them return to normal.

About two years after Dad died we had taken out a mortgage and the house had been extended. We now had a bathroom and toilet upstairs and one very small extra bedroom. Downstairs, I had my own large modern kitchen and Mum had her own kitchen which had also been modernised.

On Friday 24th November 1967, the weather was extremely cold. We were running short of coal and were using wood to eke out the coal until the next delivery. I was nearly four months pregnant and feeling very fit and healthy. I had just used up the last of the wood on the fire and as Alan wasn't expected home until much later, I thought I would saw some wood.

I did just enough to last the evening. The night had got colder so I got the hot water bottles ready and put them in the bed. James was fast asleep in his bedroom. We were going to have an early night.

CHAPTER 38

The bacon slicer, Digby's illuminations and Spain

OVERLEAF: *'The Griffon Garage'* situated opposite Digby's.
ABOVE: *Dr John Llewellyn-Jones* BA, MBBS, LRCP, MRCS.
A caring family doctor with a good sense of humour.

I was the first one up on the next morning. I went to the bathroom and realised I had a small loss of blood. Feeling worried, I got straight back in to bed again and told Alan. He told me to lay quiet and relax and he would go and get Lucy. She came down before starting her rounds and suggested calling in Doctor Jones. When the doctor arrived, I said,

"It's my fault isn't it, doctor? I was sawing wood yesterday afternoon."

"No," he replied kindly, "it's certainly not your fault. If you do happen to lose the baby, it's nature's way of saying that something is not quite right."

He gave me an injection and said I was to rest in bed, promising that he would call back to see me later. I knew things were getting worse and when the doctor called back later that afternoon I had a miscarriage. It was late Saturday afternoon on the 25th November. I was very upset. Doctor Jones looked at me and said,

"Ann, I guarantee within about three months, you will be pregnant again."

"How do you know I will?" I asked.

"Because that's the way nature works."

Toward the end of the nineteen sixties I took a part-time job at Howards Stores, a high-class grocers and delicatessen in Church Road - only five minutes from where I lived. It was a unique business owned and run by the Dixon family and I enjoyed the time I spent working there. Greengrocery and fresh fruit were artistically displayed in the window. Red apples were polished with a soft clean cloth to make them especially attractive to customers and stacked in a perfect pyramid next to the oranges and seasonal fruits. A sweet aroma greeted customers as they walked through the door.

I got on well with Mark, the youngest member of the family. Mark hadn't left school very long and he looked after the wine shop - a new extension to the main business. It was separated from the rest of the store and accessed through an arched doorway which meant that he was usually on his own and away from family arguments. His sister, Carol, did most of the accounts and the eldest son, Repton, seemed to do a bit of everything, including some of the deliveries.

One day Repton did something to annoy his mother and an argument started. Bessie - a feisty lady - went to the shop window, picked up some oranges and began to throw them one by one at Repton who was ducking to avoid being hit. Bessie was shouting,

"You stupid boy!"

I walked through the archway to where Mark was standing and we both laughed - but from a safe distance.

Bessie Dixon worked very hard, not only in the shop but at other jobs such as laundering all the white overalls and aprons. She would boil, iron and starch them herself; proud of the finished traditional grocers' uniforms worn by the staff.

Percy Bacon was another valued member of staff. He kept a sharp eye on what I was getting up to when I served the customers. On one occasion a well spoken lady came into the shop and asked for a half pound of very lean bacon. Wanting to please the customer I took the large joint off the cutting machine, turned it sideways and cut off some nice thin slices. I weighed them on the scales, wrapped them neatly in the greaseproof paper and told the lady the price. She left the shop happy with her extra lean bacon. Percy waited until the lady left the shop then said to me,

"What on earth have you been doing with the bacon?"

"The lady wanted it very lean so I turned it round."

"Good gracious me gal! It'll be as tough as Ol' Harry. You're goin' against the grain. You can't do that sort of thing."

I burst out laughing. I really should have known better. Dad always carved joints the correct way to get tender meat.

"You'd better not let the boss know - she'll go crazy."

Another one of the Island's unique shopping experiences could be had at Digby's, the local ironmonger who must have been used regularly by every household on Mersea. Their motto was 'If you can't eat it, get it at Digby's'. One of their early advertisements even declared they could supply anything from a sewing needle to a traction engine. I could never understand how they were able to find anything at all in the shop.

Behind the counter were shelves stacked with little wooden boxes full of nuts, bolts, nails, screws and spare parts for virtually anything anybody might use. And whoever was serving always knew exactly where to look for whatever was required.

One day I went in to Digby's to purchase a pretty glass fruit bowl I'd seen displayed in the window. The shop was dark inside as the large assorted displays of stock kept out any light that may have come through the window. A length of dark brown electric flex hung over the counter with the light bulb dangling down loosely - giving out just enough light to serve at the till. A torch had to be used to locate anything needed elsewhere in the shop. I stood waiting to be served, when the shop door opened and Mr 'Snowball' Hewes came in. He looked at me and said,

"Hello there, mate."

"Hello Mister Hewes," I replied.

He looked all around the shop and spoke to me again in his broad Mersea Island accent.

"Good gracious, me gal. The luu-minations in 'ere are somethin' bloomin' tree-mendous, ain't they?"

I nodded and laughed in agreement. I think that something must have gone wrong with their lighting that day as it wasn't usually that bad.

When I worked at the Post Office, Mr Banham who worked at Digby's would bring in their bundle of mail, all in pre-used envelopes. Letters would even be put into window envelopes. I don't know if this frugality stemmed from the war when everything was scarce but it pre-dated our current teaching on re-cycling by quite a few years. Digby's was the only firm that re-used envelopes and Mr Banham may have been the only man on the Island who used a length of string to tie round his long coat.

Auntie Lil and Uncle Harry had sold the guesthouse in Dover and moved to Vinaroz in Spain where they intended to retire and enjoy the sunshine. We heard from them regularly. Each time they wrote they asked when we would visit them in their new home - which had been built to their specifications. We were always kept up to date with how the garden was progressing and now the swimming pool was also nearing completion. Alan and I started to think that a holiday in Spain wouldn't be much more expensive than staying in England. We knew Lil and Harry would make us welcome and wouldn't charge anything for our keep.

Just after New Year, my cousin Dorothy, her husband Michael and their little boy, Mark came to visit us from their home in Cambridge. They had the same idea as us about going to Spain although they were talking about travelling by train and we were thinking about motoring. If we all went by car and shared expenses it would be much cheaper. None of us had much money and shouldn't really have been considering a holiday that year at all.

We were soon caught up with the excitement and decided to get together as soon as we'd been in touch with Lil and Harry to make sure it was all right for us all to go and visit at the same time. Lil and Harry were pleased that we all wanted to visit them at Villa Clair Lois and they would certainly be able to accommodate us all at the same time.

Dorothy and Michael came to see us again in February to finalise the travel arrangements. Alan had made enquiries with the R.A.C. and everything could be arranged through them including the Cross Channel tickets, all the necessary insurance and a detailed route by road from the time we got off the boat to our final destination in Vinaroz. Everyone decided it would save a lot of bother by going through the R.A.C. even if it was slightly more expensive. The bookings were made and deposits paid for our departure in June.

Neither Alan nor I had been abroad before so we were excited but also a little apprehensive about the journey. It was going to be quite an undertaking to get four adults, two children and all the luggage into our little black Volkswagen Beetle.

When we decided to take in the scenic views of Andorra by motoring through the mountains, the families became a bit worried. They thought that the journey would be too much for the children.

By the end of April the lovely spring weather should have been making me feel on top of the world. I loved the spring. It was one of my favourite times of year but I was feeling slightly off colour and began to suspect that I could be pregnant again. I was feeling rather uneasy about our holiday arrangements. We both wanted another child, but were not expecting it to happen so soon. The doctor confirmed that I was expecting a baby. When I explained about the planned holiday in Spain and how we hoped to travel, he said that by June I would be four months pregnant and by then it should be safe to travel. We should go off on holiday and enjoy ourselves.

With just over two weeks to go before we were due to leave for our holiday there were still major problems in France. It all began on 6th May with a student demonstration when over four hundred arrests were made and three hundred and forty five policemen were injured. They called it 'Bloody Monday'. On 13th May, thousands of people demonstrated on the streets of Paris. By the 19th May, two million French workers were on strike. After a further two weeks the number had swelled to nine million.

We were listening to the news and reading the newspapers every day and beginning to get worried that it would affect us with our travelling or even prevent us from going on holiday - especially as road blocks were being set up to stop petrol tankers getting through to the cities. Three days before we were due to set off, the R.A.C. said that the petrol supply situation in France was practically non-existent and many of the Cross Channel boats were out of operation. However, our particular ferry was still crossing to Calais.

The next morning we heard on the news that although the petrol situation was still bad, there was a slight improvement. After talking over the telephone each day with Michael, we decided between us to go and make the best of things. We couldn't drive right through France without refuelling. Alan had given some thought to the predicament we could find ourselves in and he worked out how many miles we could go on a full tank of petrol. Once we had used up half the tank, if we couldn't get any fuel at that point, he knew we would still have enough in the tank to return to Calais.

James was getting very excited about the journey that was going to begin the next day. Dorothy, Michael and Mark would be arriving in the evening. They were staying overnight as we had to make an early morning start. The men would be able to get the car loaded up with all our luggage first thing, including food supplies for the first part of the journey through France. Our supplies consisted of tinned new potatoes, fruit, tinned ham, cheese, bread, butter and salad which we'd prepared ourselves as well as plates, cutlery and drinks. Luckily we were all able to squeeze into the car. Mum and Auntie Tod were at the gate to see us off. Auntie Tod had stayed the night as Mum had got herself into a state worrying about us. We were glad she was there to support Mum especially when it was time for us to actually leave. At last we said our goodbyes.

The early morning weather on 6th June was terrible but it didn't stop the children's excitement. Hopefully, Mum's old saying 'Rain before seven - fine before eleven' would prove to be true today. It was six-thirty a.m. and we were ready to go. The boat was due to leave Dover at ten thirty. Hidden well beneath all the luggage and towels, child's potty and a toilet roll, was one gallon of petrol. This was considered essential in the circumstances.

The car looked so loaded with its six passengers and luggage it's a wonder we ever got to Dover let alone made the rest of the journey but as Alan was later to say, "... it motored like a good 'un." It would be a wonderful experience for the two boys and something they would never forget. Standing on the boat watching the White Cliffs of Dover fade into the distance made me feel slightly homesick. I didn't say anything to the others as I thought they would think that I was a right softie, and Alan would say,

"The trouble with you is you've been mollycoddled."

CHAPTER 39

French hotels, the donkey cart and paella

OVERLEAF: *Pixie, Alan and James in Vinaroz, Spain.*
ABOVE: *Pictured in Andora with cousin Dorothy and Mark.*

We left Calais to motor through central France, by-passing Paris. The children were both getting tired which wasn't surprising considering the number of miles we'd already covered. It was time for a break and our first picnic in France. We chose a lovely spot just off the main road, well away from the traffic and surrounded by woods and meadows. We all enjoyed the break from driving.

Dorothy had brought a goody bag with toys and treats for the boys which they were given at various stages of the journey, especially when they were being good. Our next stop would be a hotel for an evening meal and a bed for the night. I was absolutely exhausted and ready for a rest. I didn't want to overdo things.

At last we were at the Hotel Routiér close to Chartres and were pleased to find that the restaurant was still serving meals. We booked in for the night and were told we could order breakfast in the morning. Having taken our luggage up to the rooms we went to the restaurant.

The children had been so good considering the long day they had to contend with. Unfortunately, they now had to see one of the adults have an embarrassing mishap. Michael was sitting with his back to the window and as he leant back to stretch out his arms after being cramped in the car for so many miles, he unfortunately dragged on the curtains, bringing the lot down on top of him, including the curtain rail.

Poor little Mark looked horrified to see what his dad had done. James - taking after his mother - burst out laughing.

Alan was trying to rescue Michael from beneath the curtains while Dorothy reassured Mark that all would be well and I carried on laughing. Soon the restaurant was returned to normality. We were then able to order and enjoy our very tasty French meals, afterwards all retiring to our beds.

After a good night's rest we enjoyed breakfast and were then ready for the next stage of the journey - three hundred and fifty miles to Toulouse. The weather was hot and the journey seemed unending. We made numerous stops that helped to break the monotony of travelling, especially for the children, and we were running out of ideas to keep them amused. James was two years older than Mark so it was easier to keep his attention.

There were times when the journey became tedious for me. I would feel the slight movement of the baby and my thoughts would turn to the comforts of home. The roads were good with fast moving traffic but it seemed very strange driving on the wrong side of the road. We were now passing road signs that said 'Toulouse'. Thank goodness - we were nearly there.

The hotel said there were two family rooms available so we asked to view the rooms. The first room was acceptable to Dorothy and Michael. However, in the next room we viewed I noticed a crack right across the wash basin.

"Is this the only room you have available?"

"Yes, Madame," said the woman showing us round.

I pointed out the crack in the basin and explained that it wasn't good enough. We left the hotel feeling rather fed up and got back into the car ready to resume our search for rooms for the night. Fortunately, we didn't have to travel far before we found what we thought was a nice place to stay. As soon as I walked through the door I knew this was more the sort of hotel we wanted. It was in a different class to the other place.

Our luck was in. There were rooms available and this time everyone was impressed with the bedrooms. Alan signed us in and we were lucky enough to find a spare table in the large dining room. The tables were beautifully laid and well presented with a candelabra in the centre of each table and white table napkins at each place setting. We ordered from the menu beginning with a starter of thick pea soup. The soup came in a silver plated tureen with a large serving ladle by the side. Dorothy served the two boys their soup then we helped ourselves. Michael reached across to help himself to some bread and caught the ladle which was still standing in the soup. It bounced out, splashing soup everywhere. How embarrassing! The worst was still to come. Michael called the waitress across and tried out his French by saying,

"Madame - splish splosh accidonte!"

He had been bragging that his French was good enough to get him by, but this really took the biscuit. Alan looked at him in disbelief and said,

"Whatever sort of French is that Michael?" as all of us burst into laughter, including Michael.

The next day would be the last leg of our journey, taking us to Andorra through the mountains then on to Barcelona and down the coast to Vinaroz, a small fishing port. Andorra was a place of great beauty with snow still lying on top of the mountains. The children were overwhelmed by the expanse of the enormous hills which in places caused the sound of their voices to echo eerily.

We stayed in Andorra for about two hours enjoying the fresh green of the land lying at the foot of the mountains. Further up, the children took their buckets and spades that had been packed for the Mediterranean and made 'snow castles'. With no fuel problems here, we were able to fill up with tax-free petrol ready for the last stage of the journey. Travelling was becoming wearisome and the heat of the sun overbearing in our small, overcrowded car. We drove for mile after mile on dusty roads bordered by scorched grass. The monotony was only broken when just ahead of us a huge snake slithered across the road. Snakes don't bother me but it shook Alan after he swerved to avoid it.

An hour had passed since we'd driven through the outskirts of Barcelona so we knew we didn't have far to go. Aunt Lil and Uncle Harry lived in a very rural setting with just a few English people as neighbours. Most of the Spanish people living in the area were still very poor and used donkeys and carts to travel in to town.

We arrived and suddenly the long journey seemed to have been worth it. The weather was hot and the boys were overjoyed at the sight of a swimming pool in the garden - especially as Uncle Harry had bought inflatable boats for them to use in the pool, along with rubber rings and other toys.

I was relieved to be there at last as I felt tired after all the travelling. We hadn't finished yet as we still had to unload the luggage. It was a job to know where to start. Once everything was unpacked, including the seven pounds of pre packed bacon for Uncle Harry - the bacon in Spain wasn't quite what he had been used to - we were able to have a hearty evening meal on the traditional Spanish style patio as we watched the sun set over the unfamiliar countryside. We laughed and chatted with Lil and Harry in the warm evening air, catching up on all the news. Uncle Harry was the same as ever, full of jokes and funny tales.

The next morning the boys were up early and had their breakfast outside. They were eager to get into the pool. The adults also had their share of fun in the pool, especially with the inflatable dinghies.

Night time was party time. Often, some of the local police would pop in for a drink and a chat and three Spanish fishermen, Miguel, Jose and Juan were also regular visitors. The English people living nearby would turn up to join in the dancing and fun and during the day, when we went in to the small town, the Spanish shopkeepers made us so welcome, treating us like celebrities and giving the children lollipops and sweets.

One evening, Miguel the fisherman suggested that we might like to visit the port to see them bring in their fishing boat and land their catch ready for auction in the fish market. We agreed to see them the next day. The port was busy with various sized fishing boats coming in and landing their catches. James and Mark enjoyed watching all that was going on and we returned to the villa with a feed of fish from Miguel for our supper.

That evening, Dorothy and I wanted to go shopping in Vinaroz. Alan was suffering with toothache and he said Michael could take us in the car as he preferred to walk. We put the fish in the fridge and Dorothy made us a quick tea of poached eggs on toast followed by Auntie Lil's home made cake. Alan set off without having anything to eat as he didn't want to aggravate his tooth.

He'd been gone for a little while but we were expecting to catch him up on the unmade road which ran about two miles into town. Ahead of us we could see a donkey and cart plodding along the sandy track stirring the dust. When we got closer we could see that the passenger sitting on the back of the cart with his legs dangling was Alan. It made James' day.

"Look! There's Daddy sitting in the back of the donkey cart."

One day, Louise, an English friend of Auntie Lil, invited us to her villa to have real paella. She employed a Spanish lady to cook it the Spanish way. I had never tasted anything quite like it. It was all cooked and prepared in the open with octopus as well - although we didn't find this out until we had all eaten and enjoyed it.

Eventually, Alan had to go to the dentist. The building had a dingy, scruffy-looking exterior which nearly made him change his mind but the pain was so bad he was glad to do nearly anything to get rid of it. Inside, the building was immaculate and so was all the equipment. The Spanish dentist explained in the best way he could that there was an infection that needed treating first. He recommended antibiotic suppositories to clear the infection. We all laughed when Alan said,

"I can't believe I've got to put something up my arse to make my mouth better."

We had a wonderful holiday in Spain but for me the outstanding memories had to be the undeveloped way of life that still existed for many of the poor people who lived happily in the countryside, working to earn a living the best way they could.

Coming home, our little car was even more loaded than when we started. We were returning with presents, souvenirs, two large garden parasols and cheap wine, plus the luggage we'd brought out with us. The heat was beginning to wear me down. We chose an alternative route home through the Zaragoza Plain.

It was sad saying goodbye to Auntie Lil and Uncle Harry. We'd enjoyed a wonderful time but I was ready to return to England and dear old Mersea Island with its salt marshes, sea breezes and early morning birdsong.

On the return journey Alan took a wrong turning and we ended up on an unknown road. It didn't seem to be shown on the map. We'd stopped the car to take stock of our exact location when suddenly we seemed to be surrounded by what looked like Spanish peasants crowding round the car. They looked strange - as though they were caught up in a different time warp. The women were in long dark dresses and shawls. Their skin looked tough and wrinkled. The men also looked old with their skin sun-baked - but their movements were nimble which indicated that they weren't as old as they appeared.

For a while I felt scared with my heart beating quickly. I put my arm protectively around James. The men stood in front of the car, waving their arms and shouting in a language that we couldn't understand. It would be impossible to drive off without causing offence or injury. It was difficult to see what their mood was. Were they cross, or were they happy to see us?

Eventually, Alan and Michael got out of the car and were able to communicate with sign language and establish some sort of understanding between them. It was so rare for a car to pass this way that it caused a huge amount of interest. I was relieved when Alan and Michael got back into the car and we were able to get back on to the right road again.

"Phew, that was scary," said Dorothy, laughing.

I realised she had been feeling the same way as I did. There had actually been reports of tourists being robbed in secluded mountain areas. The rest of the travelling was less eventful and the worry of petrol was no longer an issue in France.

Back on the road again we were able to find a hotel for the night, still in Spain but close to the French border. It was on Harry's recommendation that we stayed here overnight. The accommodation and food were excellent and the cost so reasonable we thought they'd made a mistake with the bill. The hotel had a grandiose look. Normally we would have considered it to be too expensive but Uncle Harry had told us it was a place we could afford.

Our next overnight stay would be in France before boarding the ferry home. Arriving at customs we had no problem whatsoever. They took one look at the overloaded car and six dishevelled passengers and waved us through, laughing and joking, at the same time wishing us good luck on the journey. The sun was just breaking through the light mist as we boarded the ferry that was to take us across the Channel to Dover. It was wonderful to see the White Cliffs of Dover getting closer and closer. We were nearly home. All I could think about was one of Mum's steak and kidney puddings.

Peter dies, I lose Hubbards Croft and we look to the future

OVERLEAF & ABOVE: *A spring tide covers the road and Mersea becomes a true island.*

Peter was spending quality time with James, showing him how to use a hammer, knock nails in wood and make floating boats. He was soon to learn to say 'a piece of whood' instead of wood. James still has loving memories of his 'Uncle Peter' which is what he called him because he never knew him as 'Granddad'.

When we returned from holiday I had time to enjoy being pregnant and the beautiful summer weather we had that year. Peter, Dot and Tim had been living at Howard Avenue for over a year and they were used to the different way of life without all the 'mod-cons' in the small bungalow. However, they all appeared to be happy and that was all we could hope for. On the evening of 16th September, Peter, Dot and Tim called in to see Susan and John. While they were there, Peter began rubbing his chest saying,

"I've got a bit of indigestion." He took a couple of Rennies out of his pocket to chew.

"It will ease up in a minute. Come on you two, it's time to go home."

They all went out to the little green Morris Minor pick-up truck that was parked in the road outside. Tim climbed behind the two front seats, where there was just enough room for him to squeeze in. Peter got in the driver's seat and drove off. They only got as far as Broomhills Road and the corner of Victoria Esplanade, near the beach huts, when Peter suddenly collapsed over the steering wheel. Dot screamed out,

"Peter! What's wrong?"

The vehicle was still moving but Dot had the presence of mind to pull on the handbrake. Tim was trapped behind the seats, unable to get out, with his Dad laying across the wheel. Neither of them knew if Peter was dead or alive. It must have seemed an eternity to Dot sitting in the passenger seat with Tim panic-stricken and unable to move, although it probably all happened over a period of less than a minute. Following behind was Peter Green who hurriedly pulled to the side of the road and tried to help. Someone telephoned for a doctor (although there were no mobile phones in those days).

By the time the doctor arrived Peter Green had been able to lay Peter more comfortably in the back of his car, folding the seats down flat. Sadly, it was too late for anything to be done. Peter was dead.

That evening, we were all at home, when Terry's friend Peter Guy came round and asked to talk to Alan. They went out into the garden for a while and when he came back in again, he looked seriously worried.

"What's going on, Alan?" I asked.

"I need to talk to you and your Mum."

Alan asked me to go into Mum's sitting room and he said to me,

"Sit down for a minute. I want to talk to you both."

"Tell me now, Alan. There's no need to sit down."

"Please do what I say and sit down."

I looked at his face and knew he was going to say something serious. I sat down on the chair.

"I am so sorry. The news is bad." He paused. "Peter collapsed and died over the wheel of his car earlier this evening."

I looked at Mum, who said,

"No, no. Not my Peter," before bursting into tears.

I was glad that I was sitting down as I felt sick, then shaky. My heart was pounding and the baby was suddenly kicking hard inside me. This was almost too much to bear but I had to take care because of my unborn child. I couldn't remember much after that. I was worried for Mum - first she had lost her husband and now her son. I had lost another Dad and he was only forty nine years old.

Later on we all went up to Susan's where everyone was in a state of shock. The mood of sorrow was all round the room. I knew that only time would help to heal the hurting. Terry was the eldest son and he bravely took on the responsibility of all the funeral arrangements. The doctor said that there would have to be a post mortem to establish the cause of death. We were so close to this man and loved him so much. It was hard to imagine what life would be like without him.

We all returned to our homes. For me the next few weeks are too hard to remember.

The land that Peter had used to secure a loan at the bank now had to be auctioned off to repay the amount still outstanding. I went to the bank to ask if I could repay the loan in full as I didn't want to lose my half share of the land. It was the last piece of the Farthing estate. Alan and I had already made arrangements with our bank in Colchester for a loan large enough to secure what was classed as agricultural land. I sat opposite the bank manager at Barclays Bank, West Mersea branch, silently willing him to agree to my request, but it wasn't to be my lucky day.

"I'm sorry Mrs Weaver but the land is going to be put up for auction."

"But if I clear the debt why can't I have what is half mine already?"

"I am sorry but you will have to attend the sale if you wish to purchase the land."

I was devastated by his final decision but resolved that I would go to the auction to bid for my own land.

The sale day arrived but Alan had to work and wasn't able

to come with me. The auction took place in the old Quaker's Meeting Hall in Colchester and I travelled to town by bus. My mind was in turmoil - one minute I was hopeful that I would return home with the deeds of Hubbard's Croft; the next wondering what I would do if I had to return empty handed. I made sure I was in plenty of time.

However, when I entered the hall I could see the rows of wooden chairs were nearly full and the occupants were virtually all men. I took a seat on the end of a row halfway up the hall. I sat there feeling daunted by the presence of what appeared to me to be a lot of wealthy people. My tummy turned over as the next lot was mentioned. It was the lot I was going to bid for. The auctioneer went on to describe the plot and where it was situated. I clutched at the catalogue ready to hold it in the air when the bidding started. Sadly, I only raised my hand three times. A higher bidder had snatched my land from me. The hammer came down with a bang,

"Sold to the gentleman in the third row."

The man in the third row was a Mersea Island farmer. It was all over. I left the hall feeling utterly lost. There was nothing left from the Farthing empire. A week later, as I was coming out of the Post Office, that same farmer passed me and mocked,

"Good morning. There's the little lady who ran out of money."

I found his arrogant comment cruel and hurtful but decided to hold my head high and rise above it all without saying a word. Returning home to High View, I sat alone in my familiar kitchen and began to reflect on recent events. The sale of the land at Hubbard's Croft signified an end of the sort of life we had once lived. Cross Farm had gone and I had lost so many people who were dear to me but no one could ever take away my memories and what I had now was very special. I had a loving husband and family, an adorable son and another baby on the way. I could not change what had

412

passed, but I could hope for a happy future.

During my childhood years I experienced a way of life on Mersea Island that had not changed for hundreds of years. Communications and the opportunities for travel were strictly limited for most of the population. The community was governed by unwritten values and life measured with the passing of the seasons when geese migrated and herring returned, apples ripened and meadows were mown.

In my lifetime I have seen the population increase. I have seen many of the old landmarks disappear and new ones rise in their place - but my island home retains its timeless natural beauty and unique atmosphere.

As long as there is a Mersea Island, there will be Mersea people and I dedicate this book to them.

GLOSSARY

bevvy *drink (usually alcoholic)*
bou *boy*
cad *something or someone that is 'not quite right'*
coco matting *mat made from coconut fibre*
coopies *chickens*
celerette *drawer in a sideboard with holes*
  to keep bottles cool
dayed *damned*
didicoi *a gypsy*
flack *flap*
folley *an alley or footpath*
frimmicky *fussy*
fried snowball and a glass of wind *nothing –*
  a nonsense expression
Kursaal *large amusement park in Southend*
own't *won't*
shaled *split open*
whood *wood*

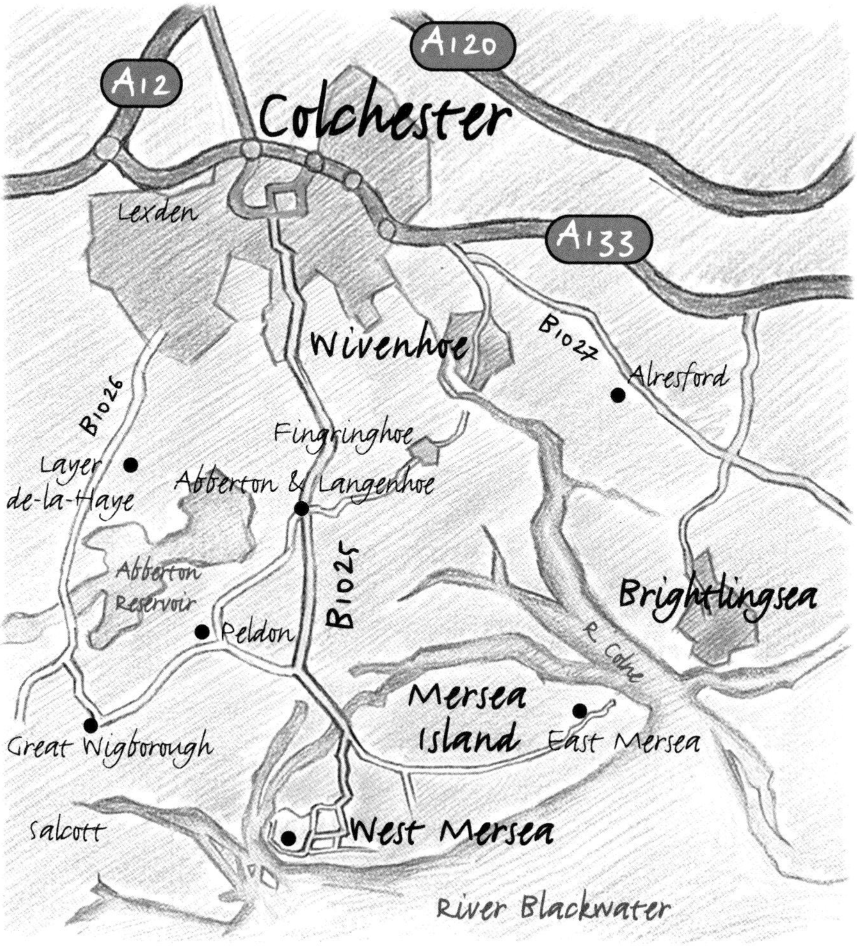
A12
A120
Colchester
Lexden
A133
Wivenhoe
B1027
Alresford
B1026
Fingringhoe
Layer
de-la-Haye
Abberton & Langenhoe
Abberton
Reservoir
B1025
Brightlingsea
Peldon
R. Colne
Mersea
Island
East Mersea
Great Wigborough
Salcott
West Mersea
River Blackwater